# Colloquial French Grammar

# Blackwell Reference Grammars
## General Editor: Glanville Price

**Published**

*A Comprehensive French Grammar*
*Fourth Edition*
L.S.R. Byrne and E.L. Churchill
Completely revised and rewritten by Glanville Price

*A Comprehensive Russian Grammar*
Terence Wade
Advisory Editor: Michael J. de K. Holman

*A Comprehensive Spanish Grammar*
Jacques de Bruyne
Adapted, with additional material, by Christopher J. Pountain

*A Comprehensive Welsh Grammar*
David A. Thorne

*Colloquial French Grammar: A Practical Guide*
Rodney Ball

**In preparation**

*A Comprehensive German Grammar*
Jonathan West

*A Comprehensive Italian Grammar*
Shirley Vinall

*A Comprehensive Portuguese Grammar*
Steven Parkinson

*A Comprehensive Ancient Greek Grammar*
David Langslow

*A Comprehensive Latin Grammar*
Jonathan Powell

**Grammar Workbooks**

*A Russian Grammar Workbook*
Terence Wade

*A French Grammar Workbook*
Dulcie Engel, George Evans and Valerie Howells

# Colloquial French Grammar:
## *A Practical Guide*

*Rodney Ball*

Copyright © R.V. Ball 2000

The right of R.V. Ball to be identified as author of this work has been asserted in accordance with the Copyright, Designs and Patents Act 1988.

First published 2000

Transferred to digital print 2006

2 4 6 8 10 9 7 5 3 1

Blackwell Publishers Ltd
108 Cowley Road
Oxford OX4 1JF
UK

Blackwell Publishers Inc.
350 Main Street
Malden, Massachusetts 02148
USA

*British Library Cataloguing in Publication Data*

A CIP catalogue record for this book is available from the British Library.

*Library of Congress Cataloging-in-Publication Data*

Ball, Rodney, 1940–
    Colloquial French grammar: a practical guide / Rodney Ball.
        p. cm. — (Blackwell reference grammars)
    Includes bibliographical references and index.
    ISBN 0–631–21882–3 (alk. paper) — ISBN 0–631–21883–1 (alk. paper)
        1. French language—Grammar. 2. French language—Textbooks for foreign speakers—English. 3. French language—Spoken French. I. Title. II. Series.

PC2112.B25 2000
448.2′421—dc21

00–028914

Typeset in 10 on 12pt Times
by Graphicraft Limited, Hong Kong
Printed and bound in Great Britain by Marston Book Services Limited, Oxford

This book is printed on acid-free paper

# Contents

# Acknowledgements

My indebtedness to others who have written about the French language will be obvious throughout this book. On a more personal level, I would particularly like to thank the following for much-valued help, advice or information: Françoise Carré, Anthony Grant, Fabrice Hauchecorne, Jim McGivney, Florence Myles. Also the series editor, Glanville Price, for his encouragement and support. And last but not least, Donald Whitton, who introduced me to this subject many years ago. The responsibility for any inaccuracies, omissions or other shortcomings is, of course, entirely my own.

ALSO AVAILABLE...

L.S.R. Byrne and E.L. Churchill's *A Comprehensive French Grammar*
*Fourth Edition*
Completely revised and rewritten by Glanville Price

This book has been the standard textbook of French grammar since its first publication in 1950, and is still unrivalled. This fourth edition has been completely revised and rewritten by one of Britain's most distinguished French-language scholars. This comprehensive textbook is furnished with full, clear explanations and numerous examples, and is now completely up-to-date.

*Contents*:
Preface.
Technical Terms and Abbreviations.
Introduction.
The Noun.
Phrase.
Verbs.
The Structure of the Sentence.
Adverbs, Prepositions and Conjunctions.
Appendix.
Index.

600 pages
0-631-18165-2 Paperback
1993

*A French Grammar Workbook*
by Dulcie Engel, George Evans and Valerie Howells

Developing on the success of *Byrne and Churchill's Comprehensive French Grammar* revised and rewritten by Glanville Price, this book is designed to be used either as a companion volume to the reference grammar or independently. It includes a range of exercises, from simple substitution drills and multiple choice to grammatical quizzes and translation exercises, with every important grammar point illustrated and explored. The workbook also features a key for students working on their own and suggestions for following up particularly difficult areas in more detail.

*A French Grammar Workbook* covers all aspects of French grammar and incorporates the range of contemporary vocabulary, making it an ideal text for all English-speaking students.

232 pages
0-631-20746-5 Paperback
1998

This book can be bought through your local bookshop or you can order a copy by calling Marston Book Services on (0)1235 465500 for orders outside the Americas, or by calling (800) 216-2522 (toll-free in North America) if ordering from North or South America.

Or visit our website at http://www.blackwellpublishers.co.uk

# 1 Introduction

## 1.1 Dimensions of grammatical variation

The grammatical patterns of languages often vary according to such factors as the formality of the situation in which a discourse or conversation is taking place, the social background of the speakers, or the medium being used (speech or writing). For example in English *we weren't there*, with *not* contracted to *n't*, is characteristic of spoken language, where it is appropriate in all but the most formal situations. *We wasn't there* is also 'colloquial', but has strong associations with working-class or uneducated usage. *We were not there* is more characteristic of written texts, and usually creates a 'stilted' effect in conversation (unless *not* is emphasized).

Similar differences exist in French, and they are the subject of this book. **Je ne comprends pas** (with **ne** and **pas**) is normal in writing and occurs in some spoken usage too. But in much everyday conversation, negatives are formed with **pas** only ( **je comprends pas**). Other colloquial forms are stigmatized as 'uneducated' or 'lower-class': **j'ai rentré** (as opposed to **je suis rentré**), for example, is socially marked, just like *we wasn't*.

These three dimensions of variation (speech versus writing, formality/informality of situation, social level of speaker) need to be carefully distinguished, even though they do overlap to a considerable extent.

Spoken language is not inevitably more informal than written language. Someone speaking in public, for example, might well feel it appropriate to use features which would otherwise give a 'bookish' effect. Conversely, there are many novelists and journalists whose writing is characterized by its deliberately colloquial flavour (a number of examples will be given later, especially in 8.2).

The formality/informality dimension is also in principle independent of the social background dimension. Large numbers of speakers never use forms like **j'ai rentré** or *you wasn't*, no matter how relaxed and intimate the conversational setting might be. On the other hand, those who do have such patterns as a regular part of their linguistic repertoire may well be capable of switching to a more 'middle-class' style when the need arises (if drafting a job application, for instance, or answering questions at an interview).

Grammatical structures can also vary from one geographical region to another. For example: some southern French speakers use **être** as its own auxiliary (**je suis été**); the past historic occurs in everyday conversation in southwestern France; speakers in the north-east use structures like **j'ai acheté un sandwich pour moi manger**; in Belgium **au plus . . . au plus** is encountered alongside **plus . . . plus** ('the more . . . the more'); in Switzerland demonstratives may be placed before infinitives (**on peut ça faire**). See Sanders (1993), Tuaillon (1988) and Walter (1988) for more details.

Striking though such uses may be, they are nevertheless rather exceptional, and should not obscure the very considerable extent of the 'core' colloquial French shared by all speakers, irrespective of their region of origin. Regional distinctiveness is in fact more apparent in pronunciation, and even in vocabulary, than in grammar. This dimension will therefore not be explored further here. Instead, this book concentrates on features which, though typical of everyday usage in the Paris area, are widely encountered elsewhere in European and for that matter North American French.

## 1.2   Sub-categories of standard and colloquial French

In what follows, a basic distinction will be drawn between 'standard' and 'colloquial' French grammar. Within the colloquial division, grammatical forms like **j'ai rentré**, which have social class connotations, are sub-categorized as 'popular'. (*Popular/populaire* in this context does not mean 'widely appreciated or enjoyed', of course, but relates to the 'usage of the (common) people'.) 'Popular' forms should be distinguished from 'familiar' ones (**je comprends pas**, for example), which are usable by all speakers, irrespective of their background. So *familiar/familier*, unlike *popular/populaire*, is a formality-related not a class-related term: it need not imply 'used exclusively by upper- and middle-class speakers'. Note the term *(français) relâché*, which is sometimes used as a general expression covering both these categories, and is equivalent to 'colloquial'.

Words, phrases and idiomatic expressions are also often categorized (e.g. in dictionaries) as *familier* or *populaire*, though rather haphazardly and inconsistently. The distinction between the two is probably easier to draw in relation to grammar: lexical (vocabulary) items pass through social class barriers with much less difficulty than grammatical features. However, even when grammar is being analysed, *familiar* and *popular* are not altogether watertight compartments: it is sometimes a moot point whether a feature should be regarded as 'popular' or not, and within each of these two categories there are peripheral as well as more central items. Hence the need for qualifications: some familiar forms may be 'very' familiar, others only 'slightly' so.

One further difference between the sociology of grammar and that of vocabulary is that the so-called *langage des jeunes* (alternatively *langage des cités* or *langage des banlieues*), which is currently the object of so much interest and discussion, lacks distinctive grammatical features: the celebrated differences between the French of adolescents and that of their elders are almost entirely lexical. Reports of the non-use of verb endings by teenagers on high-rise estates are misleading. Only newly coined slang verbs are sometimes affected: **je pachave**, **j'ai pachave**, **je vais pachave** (**pachave**: 'sleep'). And even these usually contain an erstwhile ending which has been displaced by the syllable inversion characteristic of *verlan* ('backslang'): **j'ai pécho** (for **j'ai chopé**: 'I stole'). One or two minor innovations located on the borderline between grammar and vocabulary are none the less mentioned in 3.3.4 and 5.1.3.

Standard forms like **je ne comprends pas** (with **ne** as well as **pas**) are characteristic of writing and speech which adheres to the rules of approved usage – the *norm* – drawn up by grammarians over the last three centuries (see below). But some standard features have particularly formal or literary connotations (the imperfect subjunctive is an example), whereas others are usable in a much wider variety of situations.

Consequently, just as the colloquial range needs to be sub-divided, so too it is customary to set up sub-categories within the norm: the term *soigné* is applied to features which are strongly marked for formality or 'literariness'; *courant* to those which are more neutral (the **ne . . . pas** negative would fall into the latter category). Again, there is a gradient rather than a sharp transition from one division to the other. Taken together, *français courant* and *français soigné* constitute *le bon usage* ('correct usage') – *la norme*, or 'standard French' as the term is understood in this book.

There is a profusion of alternative French terminology in this area. *(Français) soigné* is also known as *français soutenu, français cultivé, français châtié* or (particularly when a hint of archaism is present) *français littéraire*. Instead of *français courant*, some writers refer to *français commun*, or (somewhat confusingly) *français standard*.

There are of course many areas of French grammar in which no variation is present and where informal and formal discourse follow the same patterns. To take one example: despite the many distinctive characteristics of colloquial relative clauses (see 2.3), the **que** in a phrase like **la voiture qu'il conduit** can never be omitted in French – of whatever variety (unlike *which* or *that* in English: 'the car he drives'). If a point of grammar is not discussed in this book, it is likely to be one where standard and colloquial usage coincide.

## 1.3   Levels of language

The various sub-categories are often aligned in a continuum and referred to as *registers* or *levels of language*:

*français soigné* ↔ *fr courant* ↔ *fr familier* ↔ *fr populaire*

This is convenient enough for the purposes of description and classification, as long as it is remembered that the formal/informal and the social class dimensions are partly conflated here: 'popular', as was explained in 1.2, is not simply a 'more colloquial' or 'more informal' extension of 'familiar'.

The following table shows how the various dimensions combine. The arrows in the section labelled 'medium' indicate that any register can in principle be either written or spoken, but that most examples of *français soigné* are written, whereas familiar and popular features are predominantly spoken.

|  | STANDARD ↔ COLLOQUIAL |
|---|---|
| degree of formality: | *formal* ↔ *neutral* ↔ *informal* |
| register/social variety: | *soigné* ↔ *courant* ↔ *fam* ↔ *pop* |
| medium: | *writing* —————————————→ |
|  | ←————————————— *speech* |

N.B. Because of the co-existence of several parameters, and the lack of clear-cut transitions between categories, there has been much debate about these classifications, and various other schemes have been proposed. For example, a number of accounts of French published in the UK (Ager 1990, Batchelor and Offord 1982, Offord 1990) make use of a three-way register division centring on the 'degree of formality' dimension, with R(egister)3 corresponding to 'formal', R2 to 'neutral', and R1 to 'informal'.

It is important always to bear in mind that, despite the use of terms like *la langue populaire* or *la langue littéraire*, it is not the case that 'popular French grammar', 'colloquial French grammar' or 'literary French' are complete, well-defined and self-sufficient systems. For one thing, the number of specifically popular features is actually fairly small. Moreover, as has already been pointed out, many grammatical features are common to all levels, and it will emerge in the following chapters that there can be fluctuation between alternatives within one and the same level.

The relationship between the various 'grammars' might be represented by three concentric circles. The innermost circle contains specifically popular forms; the next largest is for the more extensive set of familiar forms (used also by *français populaire* speakers when no popular equivalents are available); the outermost circle contains the standard features, some of which also occur in colloquial usage, again in the absence of alternatives. Of course, as there are no sharp transitions, all the circles have fairly permeable or 'fuzzy' boundaries.

## 1.4   Origins of the standard/non-standard divergence

As the Table of Contents suggests, the points on which standard and colloquial French grammar diverge are many and varied. Undoubtedly, there are more of them than in the case of standard and colloquial English. And some very central areas of grammar are affected. The reasons for this need to be outlined, as the divergence has come to have important consequences for users of the language.

The rift began to appear in the seventeenth century, under the centralizing monarchies of Louis XIII and XIV. Much progress was made at that time in standardizing language use at the royal court: the French Academy (the 'guardian of the language') was founded in 1634; uniformity was imposed in large numbers of cases where usage had previously fluctuated (for example, the obligatory use of both **ne** and **pas** in negatives dates from this period); treatises on grammar began to appear in which the various rulings were presented and explained. Gradually the conviction emerged that a perfect language was being created: by the end of the eighteenth century it was widely believed in cultured circles that French possessed a logic and clarity that other languages lacked. Later generations of grammarians saw their task essentially as one of preserving the language in this pristine state; accordingly, the grammar of modern standard French has remained essentially unchanged over the last two to three hundred years.

Now although the users of the aristocratic French of Versailles were politically and economically dominant, their numbers were small: perhaps a few thousand out of a population of twenty million. Even so, before the 1789 Revolution, there was no attempt to spread the use of standard French more widely: attention was very much focused on the standardization process itself. So millions of people in the south, in Brittany, in Alsace and elsewhere knew little or no French, and continued to speak various regional languages. More to the point, even in the Paris region and other 'French'-speaking areas of northern France, the illiterate mass of the population were largely unaffected by the activities of the grammarians: everyday usage continued to evolve independently of their rulings.

This rift between standard and non-standard grammar began to be bridged only very much later – not until the latter half of the nineteenth century, in fact. Particularly important was the introduction in the 1880s of a national system of compulsory primary education, a central aim of which was to spread the use of standard French throughout the territory of the Republic.

This was certainly effective in marginalizing regional languages. However, as far as French itself is concerned, most of the non-standard features that had developed were too firmly established by this time for it to be possible to eradicate them entirely. Depending on their level of education, speakers approximate to the norm to a greater or lesser extent when monitoring themselves (especially when writing). But in unguarded moments, non-standard features 'creep in'. The extent to which this is the case depends very much on the individual: a schoolteacher's usage – even when 'unmonitored' – will contain far more *bon usage* features than a manual worker's. But there are a number of non-standard patterns (like the omission of **ne**) which are extremely prevalent in informal usage, whoever the speaker may be.

## 1.5 Normative and descriptivist approaches

There are essentially two kinds of attitude today towards this state of affairs. At one extreme is the *normative* view that divergences from standard usage are regrettable *fautes de français* – that the only 'correct' French is the aristocratic dialect perfected over the centuries by the grammarians and enshrined in the classic works of French literature. The term *purist* is often applied to those who believe that change in language can only be for the worse and is therefore always to be resisted. Their unflattering descriptions of grammatical mistakes (*solécismes*) give some insight into their feelings: 'abominable faute', 'monstre authentique', 'solécisme ignoble', 'outrage à notre langue', to quote but a few examples.

To be contrasted with this is the *descriptivist* view that non-standard features represent the 'natural evolution' of the language, unimpeded by the interventions of grammarians. Colloquial French, from this standpoint, has its own system and its own logic. It is not to be rejected out of hand, but should be analysed and described objectively – on its own terms, not as though it were some kind of degenerate version of the norm. It is characteristic of this approach that the positively oriented term *français avancé*, with its hint of the 'French language of the future', is sometimes used (notably in Frei 1929) as an alternative to the rather disparaging *français familier/ populaire*.

The consequence is that purists regard descriptivists as dangerous libertarians who are destroying a precious linguistic heritage. Descriptivists, on the other hand, regard purists as blinkered, unscientific pedants who are unable or unwilling to recognize that languages inevitably change from generation to generation.

Many commentators of course take one of various intermediate positions, accepting certain particularly widespread non-standard forms, or at least acknowledging that the more *soigné* areas of the standard language are not appropriate for all situations. A relatively liberal line of this type has been taken by authors of major works of reference like Maurice Grevisse (*Le Bon Usage*) or Joseph Hanse (*Dictionnaire des difficultés de la langue française*). Even so, such works set out to make recommendations about usage, rather than simply to describe and analyse, and popular French in particular is not something with which they are concerned. Because such commentators seem still to be 'steering' or 'directing' usage in a particular direction (however discreetly), this intermediate approach is often referred to as *dirigiste*.

Among the more overtly normative commentators are the authors of numerous books offering guidance to native speakers of French who feel that their proficiency in the language leaves something to be desired. Typical titles are *Je connais mieux le français*, or *Le Guide du français correct*. The school classroom also continues to be a place where *bon usage* is propagated, and examination syllabuses have an important part to play in this process. Educationalists are influenced by the periodic pronouncements on questions of grammar (*mises en garde*) made by the French Academy, and the views expressed in specialized journals like the highly conservative *Défense de la langue française* (sponsored by the Academy). A further platform is provided by the *chroniques de langage* – regular columns in national and provincial newspapers where matters of pronunciation, grammar and vocabulary are discussed – though these days the approach of most *chroniqueurs* is less strongly normative than was the case thirty or forty years ago.

Descriptivists form a much smaller and more homogeneous group. Typically, they are university specialists who see it as their business to apply the methods and principles of linguistic theory not just to standard French, but to other varieties of the language. A number of comments by academic linguists on particular issues are quoted in this book, and some of the results of their research are also presented. By way of contrast, various normative pronouncements of the more outspoken sort are also included, in order to demonstrate the kind of reasoning used by 'defenders of the language' and the extent of their concern about developments.

## 1.6   Insecurity and hypercorrection

The divergence between standard and non-standard French, and the veneration with which the *bon usage* heritage is regarded, have made the normative language tradition a central component of francophone culture ('francophone', not just 'French': some of the best-known commentators are from outside metropolitan France, the Belgians Maurice Grevisse and Joseph Hanse being cases in point).

The ordinary speaker of French, however, is in the unenviable position of making daily use of a range of forms which are officially proscribed or 'blacklisted'. Moreover, such prominent components of the standard language as the past historic, the imperfect subjunctive, the agreement of the past participle, or even certain features of relative clauses, have little or no currency in contemporary colloquial usage, and are therefore to a greater or lesser extent unknown territory to a surprisingly large number of francophones.

The result, even among middle-class speakers, is a widespread sense of failure to measure up to the norm, a distinct uneasiness about grammar and grammarians, and a belief that French is a difficult language which they do not 'speak properly' – an odd belief on the face of it, given that those holding it are native francophones. Such preoccupations account, among other things, for the continued viability of the *chroniques de langage* in the press, for the proliferation on bookstalls of 'guides to correct usage', and for the fascination with the intricacies of spelling revealed each year in the annual international dictation contest 'Les Dicos d'Or', with its televised final.

Another consequence of this sense of insecurity is that, in their struggle to speak and write 'correctly', language users sometimes overshoot the mark, as it were, and produce forms which are actually distortions of the norm at which they are aiming. Examples of *hypercorrection* exist in English: the legendary Cockneys who pronounce the *h* in *honest*, or the large number of speakers who say 'between you and I' instead of 'between you and me' (on the assumption that, because 'you and me' is sometimes incorrect, it must always be incorrect). An example of a hypercorrect form in French is **je n'ai pas rien vu**, where eagerness to include **ne**, as required by the norm, leads to the insertion of **pas** as well – though this is not of course 'correct' when **rien** is present.

From time to time in the chapters that follow, examples will be given illustrating various hypercorrections and other classic *fautes de français* of which linguistically insecure francophones are sometimes 'guilty', as the purists would put it. Meanwhile, here are two representative comments in which speakers give expression to the feeling that the language they habitually use is 'not proper French', or 'not good French':

(a)  l'imparfait du subjonctif ... le passé simple ... ce sont des temps qui sont d'une autre époque peut-être ... mais qui sont ... le vrai français ... le bon français emploie ces temps-là. (59-year-old secretary)

(b) – Qu'est-ce que vous pensez de votre façon de parler le français?
– Oh, elle est sûrement très mauvaise [rires].
– Pourquoi?
– Ché pas . . . tous les Français parlent mal [rires], eh, c'est comme tout le monde . . . on parle toujours un français qui n'est pas très pur, hein.
– Vous croyez?
– Y a des fautes de français, oui, on fait des fautes. (33-year-old doctor) (Fischer 1987: 101, 167)

The position was aptly summed up by the linguist André Martinet, when he likened standard French grammar to a minefield through which speakers have to pick their way:

Les Français n'osent plus parler leur langue parce que des générations de grammairiens, professionnels et amateurs, en ont fait un domaine parsemé d'embûches et d'interdits. (Martinet 1969: 29)

## 1.7 Grammatical variation and the foreign learner

Although brief reminders of standard usage are provided at various points in this book, it is in no way intended as a guide to *bon usage*, and in the event of uncertainty readers should consult one of the grammars listed in the References (Hawkins and Towell 1996, Judge and Healey 1983, Mansion 1952, Nott 1998, Price 1993).

Some general guidance can, however, be provided here for the foreign learner of French who is unsure which, if any, of the many non-standard forms presented he or she should actually use – as distinct from simply being able to recognize (though this in itself is an important part of competence in the language).

It should be clear from the preceding discussion that the use or non-use of a particular form depends on the situational circumstances or setting: the fact that one may have 'heard French people say *x*' does not automatically make *x* appropriate at all times.

In writing, it is advisable always to keep to the norm, unless a deliberately colloquial, probably journalistic, effect is being sought. (This can be a risky undertaking for a non-native speaker, unless his/her proficiency in French is extremely high.) For example, **ne** should not be omitted: francophones may well not use it in conversation, but they are unlikely to leave it out in writing.

In spoken usage, foreign students of French should avoid forms classified as 'popular'. In English, the effect produced by non-anglophones saying *you wasn't* is generally just one of incompetence in English: they are unlikely to be taken for native Londoners, Brummies or Scousers, unless the rest of their grammar (and pronunciation and vocabulary) is also impeccably 'popular'. The same applies to *français populaire* forms.

But 'familiar' features can certainly be used if the circumstances are relaxed enough and the relationships between the speakers are appropriate: Do they belong to the same age group? Are they social equals or not? Are they friends, acquaintances or strangers? Do they use the **tu** form or the **vous** form to one another? 'Ché pas' for 'je ne sais pas' would probably not be helpful in a job interview: it might well give an unwanted impression of flippancy or even insolence. But it would be perfectly acceptable in a café conversation with friends. There is of course an unlimited range of possible situations. What if the non-francophone is not relaxing in a café, but is a guest at a rather formal dinner given by a hierarchical superior? In this case, familiar features would probably be more acceptable later in the proceedings than earlier: but basically the best practice is to adapt to the usage of other people who are present.

To be in a position to do this, it is important to have a clear idea of the level of 'colloquialness' of the forms in question and of the way in which the various grammatical areas are organized at that level. Judgements relating to particular situations should then follow without too much difficulty. But it is also important to be consistent: for example, omitting **ne** while at the same time forming questions by using inversion (see 2.2) would result in some extremely unnatural effects.

## 1.8   Further reading

The above is only a brief outline of the sociological aspects of grammatical variation. Several books are listed in the References which provide more information. Lodge (1993) gives a full account of the emergence of standard French. Chapter 2 of Sanders (1993) is a useful discussion of the advantages and disadvantages of various approaches to register and language levels. Ager (1990), Ball (1997), Muller (1985), Offord (1990), Spence (1996) and Walter (1988) contain further information about the interaction between discourse situations and language structure.

In recent years, several excellent books specifically about the grammatical structure of spoken French have been published in France, though none is fully comprehensive. Gadet (1992), a handy paperback in the *Que sais-je?* series and written with the general public in mind, focuses on *français populaire* specifically: pronunciation and vocabulary are analysed as well as grammar, and there is some useful historical and social background. It replaces an earlier and in many ways less satisfactory *Que sais-je?* book with the same title (Guiraud 1965). Blanche-Benveniste (1997) and Gadet (1997) are more advanced treatments of conversational usage: various theoretical issues are raised relating to norm and variation, and a number of areas of grammar and pronunciation are explored. Blanche-Benveniste (1990) contains quite technical, in-depth discussion of several grammatical issues. Both this and her 1997 book are informative about the findings of the group at the University of Provence (GARS: Groupe aixois de recherches en syntaxe) which, over the last two or three decades, has carried out valuable research into spontaneous spoken French.

To return for a moment to publications intended for the non-specialist reader, two books by Marina Yaguello (1991 and 1998) contain a series of astute and entertaining observations about trends in contemporary usage, including some that affect grammar. Leeman-Bouix (1994) is a lucid and spirited attack on the purist tradition by a convinced descriptivist.

Not to be neglected either are the two classic pioneering contributions to the study of colloquial French. Both appeared in the 1920s, though they are very different in nature. *Le Langage populaire*, by Henri Bauche (a writer of boulevard plays, not an academic) is straightforwardly but entertainingly descriptive. Some of the features he mentions may no longer be current (particularly as regards vocabulary), but they are always picturesque. Bauche operated within a framework of traditional assumptions. On the other hand, *La Grammaire des fautes*, by the Swiss linguist Henri Frei is, as its title implies, a scientifically oriented attempt to present popular French as a coherent linguistic system in its own right. (Frei's account is based on a detailed analysis of letters written by soldiers during the First World War).

## 1.9   Points about this book

Whether or not you choose actually to work through the exercises, they will provide you with a large number of additional examples of usage. Exercises marked with a dagger (†) have well-defined solutions, which are given in Appendix 1. Those not so marked are more open-ended and are mainly intended as tasks or projects, or as material for commentary.

Appendix 2 contains concise explanations of all the grammatical terms used (*antecedent*, *indirect object*, etc.). See Appendix 3 for a guided introduction to the International Phonetic Alphabet, as used for transcribing French.

Quoted examples come from a number of different sources, notably collections of unscripted conversations: port employees in Le Havre (coded FH), working-class and lower-middle-class residents of the Paris suburbs of Argenteuil (DF) and Ivry (IVR), youngsters contributing to a phone-in programme (LFM), or simply chatting (CR), interviews with Paris Metro workers (PB), conversational utterances noted by the author (RB), or used on radio or television (FI, FR3, TF1). Some colloquial written sources have also been utilized: novels, comic books, newspaper and magazine articles.

Other examples are from various published descriptions of spoken French. A key to all the codes will be found on pp. 234–6.

Normally, colloquial vocabulary items in examples are translated only if not listed in the Collins-Robert French–English dictionary. Unacceptable (ungrammatical) phrases or sentences are preceded by an asterisk (*). It is important to remember that sentences can be unacceptable in terms of the grammar of colloquial French, just as they can be unacceptable in terms of standard usage.

# 2 Three Grammatical Processes

## 2.1 Forming negatives

One of the best-known indicators of formality difference in French is the presence or absence of **ne** in negative sentences, already referred to in the Introduction. But the situation is more complex than this bare characterization might suggest. This section explores the various intricacies of standard and non-standard negatives.

### 2.1.1 Negatives with and without ne

**Ne** is an integral part of almost all negative expressions in standard French (**ne . . . pas, ne . . . jamais, ne . . . rien, ne . . . plus, ne . . . guère**, etc.). However, it is conspicuous by its frequent absence in colloquial usage. Sentences like **tu comprends pas?, il vient jamais, elle a rien mangé, on te voit plus** ('we've not seen you for ages') are of frequent occurrence, with **pas, jamais, rien** performing – 'unaided' – the same negating function as the **ne + pas/ jamais/rien** combinations of more formal levels of the language.

At one time, by contrast, negation used to be expressed by means of an unaided **ne**. Literary French preserves a few relics of this in certain limited uses of the verbs **savoir, pouvoir, cesser** and **oser: il n'a cessé de pleuvoir; ne sachant où aller . . .** , and in occasional idioms like **si je ne me trompe**. Needless to say, such uses are impossible in colloquial French (and almost always optional even in formal discourse).

**Ne** is also omitted from negative commands: **pleure pas!, ferme pas la porte!**. In cases where the verb has one or more pronoun objects, the standard language places the pronouns after the verb in the affirmative, but before it in the negative:

| Affirmative<br>(standard and colloquial) | Negative<br>(standard) |
|---|---|
| **vas-y** | **n'y va pas** |
| **mange-le** | **ne le mange pas** |
| **regarde-moi** | **ne me regarde pas** |

In informal negatives, **ne** can be deleted (as in statements and questions) and the same word-order used as in standard negatives:

Negative (familiar)
**y va pas**      **le mange pas**      **me regarde pas**

But in popular French, the affirmative word-order ('verb + pronoun') is retained, with **pas** simply 'tacked on' afterwards:

Negative (popular)
**vas-y pas**      **mange-le pas**      **regarde-moi pas**

A few distinctive, and recent, idiomatic commands should be mentioned (the first two are entertainingly analysed in Yaguello 1998):

**pas touche!**      **t'occupe!**      **t'inquiète!**

These correspond respectively to 'hands off!', 'don't interfere!' and 'don't worry!'. In each case, the word-order is unusual (either by formal or informal standards). And it is interesting that the 'pronoun + verb' word-order in **t'occupe!** and **t'inquiète!** causes the phrases to have negative meaning, even in the absence of any negative particle. (The order is the same as in **ne t'occupe pas**, whereas the affirmative order is **occupe-toi!**) However, the parallel **la ferme!** ('shut up!') is always to be interpreted as an affirmative. Here too the word-order is anomalous (compare the normal order in **ferme-la!** or **boucle-la!**).

The 'expletive' **ne** used in standard **avant qu'il ne soit trop tard**, or **j'ai peur qu'un accident ne soit arrivé** is also very liable to be omitted. This is not surprising: expletive **ne** is probably even more redundant than the **ne** which occurs with **pas**, given that it does not in fact make its clause negative, and would simply remain untranslated in the English equivalents of the above examples: 'before it's too late', 'I'm afraid there may have been an accident'. This lack of meaningful content is confirmed by the hesitations that sometimes occur in formal usage: **sans qu'il ait dit au revoir** (favoured by normative grammarians) alternates with **sans qu'il n'ait dit au revoir** (felt to be more 'correct' by some): both variants mean 'without saying goodbye'.

The hallmark of popular English is the 'double negative' found in *I ain't done nothing*, where *not + nothing* still equals *nothing*. Double negatives are occasionally encountered in French (**ayant pas encore rien reçu**), but they appear to result from hypercorrection (see 1.6). They are not a regular feature even of *français populaire*: normally, whatever the register, **pas + rien** equals **quelque chose**.

---

## EXERCISES

1†  Add **ne** to the following colloquial structures (all used in a children's phone-in programme):

   (a)  ça fait quand même plusieurs années que personne l'a vu. (LFM66)

   (b)  Il paraît que ça fait longtemps que Patrick Sébastien il soutient Jacques Chirac, avant qu'il soit candidat. (LFM60)

   (c)  ils voudront plus jamais aller sur un bateau [ . . . ] (LFM25)

   (d)  parrainer un enfant qui a pas de quoi vivre [ . . . ] (LFM57)

   (e)  Ouais, mais ce type, il était vieux, il tuait plus personne ces derniers temps. (LFM11)

   (f)  le vrai danger de l'alcool, c'est que ça peut être un plaisir et c'est dur de pas se faire plaisir. (LFM154)

2†  Say what is non-standard about the following remark (made by the film star Catherine Deneuve in a televised chat-show):

   Mais comme on va pas citer ni les films ni les gens, je trouve que c'est pas [ . . . ] la peine d'en parler . . . (CB125)

3† Arrange the sentences in each of the following groups in descending order of formality:

(a) Je n'ose pas le croire.
Je n'ose le croire.
J'ose pas le croire.

(b) Je ne peux pas vous aider.
Je ne peux vous aider.
Je peux pas vous aider.

4† Give (i) familiar and (ii) standard equivalents of these popular commands:

(a) Casse-moi pas les pieds!
(b) Enerve-toi pas!
(c) Pas touche!

5† Which of the following are standard, which are colloquial, and which are unacceptable whatever the level of language?

(a) Je l'ai vu juste avant qu'il n'est arrivé.
(b) M'attends!
(c) M'attends pas!
(d) Laisse-moi!
(e) Laisse-moi pas!
(f) Ne laisse-moi pas!
(g) Jamais il ne m'a parlé.
(h) Il a pas rien payé.
(i) Nous en avons plus du tout, Madame.
(j) On m'a aidé plus que je n'ai demandé.

6† Distinguish between:

(a) Gagner un million de francs au Loto, c'est rien.
(b) Gagner un million de francs au Loto, c'est pas rien.

### 2.1.2 *Factors governing the (non-)use of* ne

The omission of **ne** has long been taken by many commentators to be specifically a feature of <u>uneducated</u> usage, and consequently greatly disapproved of. Even a descriptive linguist like Aurélien Sauvageot once commented:

*Si tu veux pas* est franchement vulgaire [ . . . ] Dans tous les cas, l'absence de *ne* confère au parler une tonalité de mauvais aloi. (Sauvageot 1972: 140–1)

'Vulgar' or not, the fact of the matter is that speakers from all walks of life are liable to omit **ne** (including, without the slightest doubt, the author of this quotation!). However, it may well be the case that educated speakers monitor themselves more carefully and therefore show more 'restraint' in this respect.

Françoise Gadet's analysis of recordings of her own speech shows very strikingly how the usage of an individual can vary according to the situation he/she is in. An hour's breakfast-time conversation at home yielded only one occurrence of **ne** in her speech. But later the same day, in a lecture to her students at the university, the proportion of negatives with **ne** came close to 100 per cent. Only when answering questions after the lecture did she occasionally omit it (Gadet 1997: 102–3).

In conversation, the omission of **ne** is in fact so widespread that speakers are hardly aware of it – hence perhaps the tenacity of the myth that it is a feature of working-class speech only. Its omission in written texts, however, has much more impact. The famous 1980s anti-racist slogan 'Touche pas à mon pote' owed not a little of its effectiveness to its grammatical structure. Advertisers, too, have taken advantage of the possibilities of non-standard grammar. Thus the slogan 'Mais pourquoi j'ai pas acheté une Mitsubishi?' was to be seen on hoardings a few years ago (for the no less colloquial interrogative used here, see 2.2.2).

Social and stylistic considerations apart, the use or non-use of **ne** can also be determined by phonetic and grammatical factors.

In the case of **il n'a pas écrit**, for instance, the speaker has the choice of two equally plausible options: to omit **ne** or to omit the **l** of **il** (this very common elision is discussed further in 7.4.2 and 8.1.1). Omitting both would result in an unwelcome hiatus between **i** and **a**: **i' a pas écrit**. So sometimes one option is taken (**il a pas écrit**), and sometimes the other (**i' n'a pas écrit**). Here a speaker hesitates between the two possibilities (and then opts for a different formulation altogether):

(1)  i' n'ont pas, i'z ont pas, i'sont encore verts. (DF778)

Another speaker chooses to insert **n(e)** (**je n'veux pas**) rather than reduce **je** to **j'** before a consonant (**j'veux pas**):

(2)  et bah moi je n'veux pas, je n'veux pas acheter dans les [ . . . ] des
     choses comme ça, dans les, dans les surfaces [*grandes surfaces*] comme
     ça [ . . . ] (FH)

Among the grammatical factors favouring the retention of **ne** is the presence of **rien** or **personne** as subject (**rien ne va changer** rather than **rien va changer**). It must be said that the phonetic difference between, say, **rien n'est** . . . and **rien est** . . . verges on the imperceptible (similarly with **personne**). So it is sometimes hard to say whether **ne** is actually present or not. This is one of the likely reasons for its demise in the first place.

**Ne**, furthermore, has a higher probability of being retained in commands or when the verb is immediately preceded by a noun subject (**mon frère ne l'aime pas** rather than **mon frère l'aime pas**). Conversely, omission is particularly frequent with **avoir, être** or **pouvoir**: **j'ai pas** not **je n'ai pas**, **c'est pas** not **ce n'est pas**, **i(l) peut pas** not **i(l) n(e) peut pas**, etc. In general, **ne** is more likely to be omitted from negatives with **pas** than from those with **rien, personne, jamais** or **guère**.

More details can be found in Gadet (1997) and Moreau (1986). The important point is that, like many differences between formal and less formal usage, the retention or omission of **ne** is not a clear-cut, 'either-or' matter: rather, it takes the form of a continuum and results from the interaction of various separate factors.

## EXERCISES

7†   In the light of the phonetic and grammatical factors referred to above, what are the chances of **ne** being omitted from the following (very likely, fairly likely, less likely)?

   (a)   Il n'est pas venu.
   (b)   Jean ne va pas participer.
   (c)   Rien ne va plus.
   (d)   Personne ne croit que c'est vrai.
   (e)   Marie, elle ne va pas partir.
   (f)   Tu ne peux pas refuser.
   (g)   Pierre n'est pas là.
   (h)   Je ne ferais jamais une chose pareille.
   (i)   Ce n'est pas moi qui le dis.
   (j)   Il n'est pas là, Pierre.

8†   In the chat-show excerpt from which the quotation in Exercise 2 was taken, there were five negatives with **ne** (Bauer 1984: 136–40):

   (a)   Non coupable, je n'ai pas pris l'argent.

   (b)   le vouvoiement n'est pas du tout un signe de [ . . . ]

> (c)   Elle avait accepté de faire un portrait de Malraux mais elle savait pas à l'avance si ce sera deux heures ou deux jours, alors Malraux n'a pas accepté.
>
> (d)   Vous savez l'amour que je vous porte – malheureusement vous n'répondez pas à mes efforts.
>
> (e)   y a longtemps que l'émission n'existerait plus.
>
> And there were twenty-two negatives without **ne**, typical examples being:
>
> (f)   ça m'étonne pas la surenchère
>
> (g)   i'faut pas le dire
>
> (h)   c'est pas vrai
>
> (i)   y a pas beaucoup de films que [ . . . ]
>
> (j)   on va pas faire l'historique complète
>
> Taking social/situational factors into account as well as phonetic/grammatical ones, explain the retention or omission of **ne** in these examples.

### 2.1.3   Aucun *and* nul; (ne . . . ) que *and* (ne . . . ) pas . . . que

**Nul . . . ne**, even in standard French, tends to be restricted to quite literary set phrases (**nul ne le sait, nul n'est censé ignorer la loi**) rather than to be used in spontaneous utterances. In view of this, it is not surprising that it is absent from the colloquial language, being replaced by **personne** or **pas**. But **nul** continues to be used in **nulle part** ('nowhere'):

(3)   Ça m'a menée nulle part, de pas en poser, des questions. (IZ23)

And it has wide currency as a colloquial adjective meaning 'sans valeur': **il est nul ce type**.

**Aucun**, too, is infrequent in colloquial usage. The ubiquitous **pas** tends to replace it, sometimes in conjunction with an intensifying expression: **j'ai pas la moindre idée** for **je n'ai/j'ai aucune idée**, or **j'ai pas du tout envie** for **je n'ai/ j'ai aucune envie**. When **aucun** is part of a subject noun phrase, the omission of **ne** is unlikely: **\*aucun bus a circulé ce matin**. But again, the preference would be for alternative expressions like **pas un seul bus**, or **pas le moindre bus (n') a circulé**, or simply **(il) y a pas eu de bus**.

**Ne . . . que** ('only') is reduced to a solitary **que** in familiar and popular French:

(4)   Le président il vient qu'une fois par an [ . . . ] (LFM147)

(5)   S'ils veulent s'exprimer sur la politique, ils ont qu'à devenir politiciens [*they have only to become; all they need do is become*]. (LFM60)

Whether **ne** is present or not, **que** in the sense of 'only' must occur immediately before the word or phrase which it restricts: **j'ai payé que mille francs**, **il a dit que trois mots**. This is different from *only* in colloquial English, where intonation and stress patterns are relied on to identify the relevant item: *I only paid a thousand francs* (stress on *francs*).

The negative expression **que dalle** should be noted in this connection. It is a colloquial equivalent of **rien**, found for example in **je comprends que dalle** ('I don't understand anything') or **on a gagné que dalle** ('we won nothing', 'we won damn all'). **Dalle** is believed to derive from the name of a medieval Flemish coin of small value – the *thaler*: 'we won only a thaler'. As it is restricted to colloquial use, **que dalle** is never preceded by **ne**. An abbreviation favoured by teenagers occurs in:

(6)   J'comprends keud. (TJ30)

Grammarians used to frown on **ne . . . pas que** ('not only': the negative of **ne . . . que**). But its use has become more and more acceptable even in quite formal written usage. Examples are: **il n'y a pas que Jean qui boit** ('John isn't the only one who drinks'); **il ne boit pas que de l'eau** ('water isn't the only thing he drinks' or 'he doesn't just drink water').

**Ne** can of course be omitted from these expressions too: **il boit pas que de l'eau; (il) y a pas que Jean qui boit**. (See 3.3.1 for the omission of **il**.) And note the phrase **j'ai pas que ça à faire** ('that's not the only thing I've got to do', i.e. 'I'm too busy to bother about that').

---

### EXERCISES

9†   Rephrase these negatives in a more colloquial style:

(a)   Cela ne présente aucune difficulté.
(b)   Aucun élève n'a répondu.
(c)   Aucun d'entre eux n'a voulu passer aux aveux.

(d)   Je l'ai dit sans aucune intention de l'offenser.
(e)   Je n'en ai nul besoin.
(f)   Il n'y a nul doute quant à sa culpabilité.

10†   Distinguish between the sentences in each of the
following pairs:

(a)   (i)   Ils mangent du poisson que le vendredi.
      (ii)  Ils mangent que du poisson le vendredi.

(b)   (i)   Je travaille la nuit que depuis une semaine.
      (ii)  Je travaille que la nuit depuis une semaine.

11†   Give standard equivalents, and English translations, of:

(a)   le maire d'une petite commune qui s'occupe que des
      vieux, des maisons de retraite [ . . . ] (LFM147)

(b)   Ça montre des jeunes obsédés par l'amour, mais il y
      a pas que ça dans notre vie. (LFM70)

(c)   T'avais qu'à pas signer. (PB69)

(d)   si le président i' n'est pas content quand on dévoile sa
      vie privée, il a qu'à se cacher (LFM48)

(e)   On comprend que ce qu'on veut. (IZ20)

(f)   Y a vraiment que ces cons de bourges [*bourgeois*] pour
      croire que les artistes peuvent créer que dans le
      dénuement. (EHA97)

12†   Can you interpret the following?

(a)   une vraie ruche avec quasiment que des filles (ACT)

(b)   on a le droit d'avoir des amis pas que français (LFM18)

(c)   – Qu'est-ce que t'en dis, toi [ . . . ] des coquillages?
      [ . . . ]
      – Il y a des perles dedans. Pas que dans les huîtres,
      dans tous. (RFC90)

> (d)  Heureusement qu'on en a pas que des comme ça!
> [*remark made by a schoolteacher about his least
> favourite pupils*] (FI)
>
> 13†  Distinguish between:
>
> (a)  Aujourd'hui Air-France assure que 75 pour cent de ses
> vols. (FI)
>
> (b)  Aujourd'hui Air-France assure que 75 pour cent de ses
> vols partiront.

### 2.1.4  Potential ambiguities

Although no 'threat' seems to be posed to communication by this most recent addition to the already numerous uses of **que**, there are one or two cases where a risk of ambiguity caused by the disappearance of **ne** has led the language to resort to other devices in order to preserve clarity.

One concerns pairs of sentences like:

(7)  Il ne peut pas gagner ('He cannot win')
(8)  Il peut ne pas gagner ('He can not-win', i.e. 'he may lose')

which fall together colloquially as:

(9)  Il peut pas gagner.

But the rhythmic and intonational patterns of the spoken language are sufficient for the two acceptances to be distinguished:

(9a)  Il peut-pas/gagner (with an intonation peak on **gagner**);
(9b)  Il peut/pas-gagner (with a peak on **peut** and a very short break after it).

A second case concerns the phrase **pas mal**, which, when used without **ne**, has become a slightly understated equivalent of **très** or **beaucoup**. **Pas mal** can modify verbs (**j'ai pas mal dormi**: 'I slept a fair bit'), be combined with **de** to modify a noun (**j'ai pas mal de travail**: 'I've got quite a lot of work'), or modify an adjective (**il est pas mal mouillé** (JE64): 'it's pretty wet'). Note, by the way, that in colloquial usage **beaucoup de** (+ NP) is very often replaced by **plein de** (+ NP) when understatement is not being sought: **j'ai plein de choses à te dire**.

The extension of the meaning of **pas mal** is restricted to those registers which omit **ne**. Reinstating **ne** has the effect of either restoring the original meaning: **je n'ai pas mal dormi** ('I've not slept badly'), or of producing an ungrammatical sentence: **\*je n'ai pas mal de travail**. So there is potential for genuine ambiguity in a (colloquial) utterance like:

(10)   On parle pas mal le français en Roumanie. (RB)

This can be interpreted either as 'they don't speak French badly there', or as 'they speak a lot of French there', which obviously do not amount to the same thing. Rather as in the case of **(ne) peut pas/peut (ne) pas**, the two interpretations are conveyed by different intonation patterns, depending on whether **mal** or **français** has the highest pitch. (Or, of course, alternative formulations could be used: **on parle assez bien le français . . .**, etc.)

Another, perhaps more significant case involves **ne . . . plus**. A colloquial sentence like **il y a plus de travail pour les ouvriers** can either mean 'there's no more work . . .' (corresponding to **il n'y a plus de travail**), or else 'there's more work . . .' (this, of course, being the meaning of **il y a plus de travail** in standard French).

However, there is no ambiguity in spoken usage: **plus** would be pronounced [ply] in the first situation ('no more work') and [plys] in the second ('more work'). As a consequence no doubt, **plus** meaning 'more' tends increasingly in informal speech to be pronounced with [s], even in clear cases:

(11)   On n'a pas plus [plys] vu le président de la République que le roi Hassan II. (FI)

However, this does not apply to the comparative of adjectives: **plus clair** is always [ply klɛʀ], never \*[plys klɛʀ].

---

## EXERCISES

14†   Which intonation pattern corresponds to which meaning?

(a)   Il peut/pas-être d'accord.
(b)   Il peut-pas/être d'accord.

(c)   J'ai pas/mal-travaillé.
(d)   J'ai pas-mal/travaillé.

15†   Which sentences should be given asterisks? In which of the acceptable ones could **pas mal** be replaced by **beaucoup** or **plein**, and in which is it equivalent to 'not badly'?

(a)  J'ai mangé pas mal.
(b)  J'ai pas mal mangé.
(c)  Je n'ai pas mangé mal.
(d)  Je n'ai pas mal mangé.
(e)  Pas mal de gens ne sont venus.
(f)  Pas mal de gens sont venus.
(g)  J'ai parlé à pas mal de gens.
(h)  J'ai pas parlé à mal de gens.
(i)  Je n'ai parlé à pas mal de gens.

16†  Indicate the likely pronunciation of **plus** in the following ([ply] or [plys]):

(a)  Les voeux de Nouvel An du Président: Plus de justice sociale. (FI)

(b)  Plus de chances de gagner plus! [*lottery advertisement*]

(c)  Plus d'espoir malheureusement, après 48 heures de recherches, de trouver des survivants. (FI)

(d)  Plus que quatre kilomètres de bouchons sur l'autoroute de Normandie. (FI)

(e)  Ouf! je commençais à plus y croire. (PA155)

17†  In the following account by a mother of an argument with her teenage son, **plus** would be pronounced [ply] on each occasion. When is it comparative, and when does it mean 'no longer'?

Une fois il a pris son sac d'école, il m'a regardée en fronçant les sourcils et il a dit: J'm'en vais, j'vais me chercher une autre mère, une plus jeune, j'en ai marre, t'es plus belle, t'es plus jeune. (DB127)

### 2.1.5 Reactions to developments

Here are some contrasting points of view about the omission of **ne**.

In his well-known book on how to speak and write better French, Jacques Capelovici states:

Oubliant la valeur négative du petit adverbe *ne*, de plus en plus nombreux sont les ministres, les parlementaires, les écrivains, les hommes d'affaires qui, négligemment, diront tant à la radio qu'à la télévision: «On sait pas», «Personne leur avait dit», «Vous croirez jamais», «Il est pas du tout certain». Le désir de «faire peuple» et de s'affranchir de toute contrainte s'exerce ici aux dépens du petit adverbe *ne*.

Certes, la présence du mot *pas* [...] indique clairement que les quatre phrases ci-dessus sont négatives. Mais étant donné qu'il ne tient qu'en une syllabe, l'emploi du petit adverbe *ne* n'exige pas un effort surhumain. C'est pourquoi, se référant aux quatre exemples susmentionnés, on dira de préférence: «On ne sait pas», «Personne ne leur avait dit», «Vous ne croirez jamais», «Il n'est pas du tout certain». (Capelovici 1990: 246)

The linguist Pierre Guiraud, on the other hand, recalls that **pas** (un pas: 'a step') was originally simply an intensifying expression, like 'an inch' in 'I didn't move an inch', but has become a negative particle in its own right. In the process the link with the original meaning 'step' has disappeared.

Etymologiquement, la négation est *ne*; *pas* est une marque emphatique [...]: *je n'avance* [...] et en insistant [...], *je n'avance pas* (pas même d'un pas).

Mais en se généralisant cet emploi a conféré à *pas* une fonction et une valeur négative. On dit très bien: *pas une seule geste, pas un nuage à l'horizon*, etc.

Ceci a entraîné la déchéance de *ne* dans la langue populaire où il paraît faire double emploi; et on dit *je crois pas*; forme cohérente et conforme aux tendances de l'idiome dans la mesure où elle transfère la négation sur un [suffixe]. (Guiraud 1965: 66)

[*étymologiquement*: from a historical (etymological) point of view]

This is echoed in Bodo Muller's textbook on the French language:

Il est [...] étonnant de constater avec quelle ampleur [...] le français populaire a fait du *pas* renforçateur d'autrefois une particule négative à part entière: cette simplification qu'il convient évidemment de mettre en rapport avec la faiblesse du ə [nə > n] et la place de *pas* qui porte l'accent à la fin d'un groupe rythmique, s'étend irrésistiblement dans le français courant; *pas* l'a déjà emporté dans la langue parlée. (Muller 1985: 246)

## 2.2  Forming questions

Even in standard French there is more than one way of phrasing questions, and many others are encountered in colloquial usage. Taken together, French interrogatives are an excellent example of the way in which different grammatical structures correlate with different levels of formality.

### 2.2.1  *Inversion,* est-ce que *and intonation*

A characteristic (though not exclusive) feature of *français soigné* is the inversion of subject pronoun and verb in order to signal a question: **vous fumez/fumez-vous?**. In the rather unlikely event of **fumez-vous?** actually being used in a conversation, it would be pronounced with a rising intonation.

If the subject is a noun, a pronoun is inserted for the purpose of inversion: **Pierre arrive-t-il demain?**. This is known as 'complex inversion'. In yes/no questions, the 'simple' kind of inversion in which nouns and verbs are switched directly (**\*arrive Pierre demain?**) is unacceptable in any variety of French. But it does occur in some WH-questions: **où habite Pierre?**.

There are perceptible differences of formality between one 'inversion-type interrogative' and another. As has just been suggested, **fumez-vous?** is quite 'stilted'. But third-person **fume-t-il?** is appreciably less so, especially when followed by further material: **fume-t-il toujours autant qu'avant?** Conversely, most inversions involving first-person **je** are distinctly *more* stilted: **fumé-je?**, **cours-je?** and the like are nowadays felt to verge on the grotesque, and are restricted to jocular, 'mock-literary' use, in written as well as spoken French.

Inversions (even a few involving **je**) are still current in conversation whenever polite and rather formal connotations are appropriate. They are most commonly encountered in set formulae like **désirez-vous...?**, **pourriez-vous...?**, **puis-je...?**, **que dis-je?**, or else in more spontaneous questions beginning with a WH-word: **où allez-vous?**, **combien veulent-ils?**, **que dois-je répondre?**. WH-questions generally have remained more accommodating towards inversion than the yes/no type.

But in most conversational use, other ways of signalling a question are preferred.

The formula **est-ce que** (literally 'is it that?') is one device: not **écris-je?**, but **est-ce que j'écris?**. **Est-ce que** contains an inversion within itself (**c'est** → **est-ce**), which makes further inversion unnecessary, and allows the question to retain the word-order of the corresponding statement, however long this may be: **les bombardements effectués par les forces alliées ont cessé** → **est-ce que les bombardements effectués par les forces alliées ont cessé?**.

Even in *français soigné* the use of **est-ce que** is usually obligatory nowadays for first-person interrogatives. In *français courant* and *français familier*, **est-ce que** has become a widely used device for other questions, both of the yes/no and the WH- kind (**est-ce que vous partez?**, **quand est-ce que vous partez?**). Questions with **est-ce que** bridge the division between standard and colloquial French and are appropriate in a variety of contexts and situations.

In many ways, **est-ce que** has come to resemble the interrogative markers which in a number of languages are placed before (or after) statements in order to turn them into questions: *czy* in Polish, for example. If French lacked a writing system and was being analysed for the first time, **est-ce que** might well be treated as an indivisible unit: [ɛskə].

The other favoured way of signalling the interrogative is simply to superimpose on to a statement the rising intonation typical of questions: **vous fumez?**. (In standard spelling, a question mark is the best that can be achieved by way of representing the pitch pattern.) Nowadays, even in *français courant*, the 'intonation interrogative' is as widespread in conversational yes/no questions as the **est-ce que** type. In familiar and popular French, it has become altogether dominant. Note that it is not possible to omit the pronoun, as happens in colloquial English (*smoke?*): there is no register of French in which *****fumes?**, without **tu**, would be acceptable.

The growing tendency to favour the intonation type of interrogative over the inversion and **est-ce que** types is in part due to linguistic factors (a general movement away from inversion: see 8.1 for further discussion). But there are also sociological reasons, notably the current preference for using informal language in situations where it would have been considered inappropriate a generation or two ago. This is captured in the following observation by the author of a critical account of the contemporary language, significantly entitled *Hé! la France, ton français fout le camp!*:

Jadis dans un café je demandais: «Combien vous dois-je?». Maintenant: «Qu'est-ce que je vous dois?». Et à côté de moi j'entends: «Je vous dois combien?» ou «J'vous dois quoi?». (Thévenot 1976: 164)

## EXERCISES

1† Convert the following inversion questions into **est-ce que** questions:

    (a)   Avez-vous bien dormi?
    (b)   Reprends-tu un peu de gâteau?
    (c)   Marie est-elle venue dire bonjour?
    (d)   Pierre travaille-t-il toujours aussi assidûment?
    (e)   Georges va-t-il bientôt arriver?
    (f)   Quand part-il?
    (g)   Pourquoi suis-je fâché?

2† Say whether the following questions are (a) *courant*,
(b) *soigné*, (c) grotesquely archaic or (d) ungrammatical in
any register:

    (a)   Combien est-ce que tu as payé?
    (b)   Où vais-je?
    (c)   Prenez-vous encore du café?
    (d)   Puis-je vous déranger?
    (e)   Est-ce que Marie est au courant?
    (f)   Où va Pierre?
    (g)   Rentre Jean bientôt?
    (h)   Vous gêné-je?

3† Arrange the questions in the following groups in descending
order of formality:

    (a)   Tu sors?
           Sors-tu?
           Est-ce que tu sors?

    (b)   Est-ce que Pierre arrive?
           Pierre arrive-t-il?
           Pierre arrive?

    (c)   Marie connaît Christiane?
           Marie connaît-elle Christiane?
           Est-ce que Marie connaît Christiane?

4† Following the pattern in the previous exercise, make groups of three questions corresponding to:

(a)  Il ment.
(b)  Vous le connaissez.
(c)  Le président a démissionné.
(d)  L'Otan va déclarer la guerre.

5 Here is an excerpt from a novel (teenage son addressing father). Can you translate this series of angry questions into idiomatic English?

> Où tu l'as pêché ce mec? Et pourquoi il a un accent aussi con? C'est un arborigène ou quoi? Et pourquoi sa femme elle est pas là? Il est veuf ou bien est-ce que c'est un divorcé comme toi? (PA68)

6 Comment on the use of **est-ce bien?** and **c'était bien?** in the following excerpt. It comes from the beginning of a conversation which the participants know is being recorded:

– Ouais. Alors t'as allé en Espagne?
– Comment?
– Tu es-z-allé en Espagne?
– Oui.
– Heu. Est-ce bien?
– Non, François, parle comme tu parles naturellement.
– C'était bien?
– Oh oui mais, i'faisait pas très beau temps hein. (CR80)

## 2.2.2  Informal WH-questions

As was pointed out in 2.2.1, questions introduced by WH-words follow a somewhat more conservative pattern than the yes/no type and are more amenable to inversion. Even so, the following, from radio interviews or from advertising, are very typical of everyday usage:

(1)  Quelle température il fait chez vous? (FI)

(2)  Comment vous allez faire? (FI)

(3)  Où va le pognon et à quoi il sert? (FI)

(4)  Et si on ne veut plus payer notre abonnement à l'Internet, tu dis quoi? [*advertisement*] (RB)

The basic tripartite pattern of variation that occurs with yes/no questions (inversion/**est-ce que**/intonation only) also characterizes the WH- type:

(5)  Où vas-tu? (formal)

(6)  Où est-ce que tu vas? (neutral)

(7)  Où tu vas? (colloquial)

But there are a number of further possibilities, depending on the form and position of the **est-ce que** and WH- elements. They all have one feature in common: there is no switching of verb and pronoun.

Taking **est-ce que** first, a rather more colloquial version of (6) would have **c'est** instead of **est-ce**:

(8)  Où c'est que tu vas?

And the following rearrangement enables more emphasis to be placed on the WH- word:

(9)  C'est où que tu vas?

Occasionally both **c'est** and **est-ce** are combined (just as they are in the standard **qu'est-ce que c'est que ...** ):

(10)  Où est-ce que c'est que tu vas?

If **est-ce que** is not used and the WH-word comes immediately before the subject, the colloquial effect is greatly increased:

(11)  Où tu vas?

The effect can, however, be reduced if the WH-word is placed at the end (giving more prominence to **où**):

(12)  Tu vas où?

The most colloquial form of all has **que** after the (initial) WH-word:

(13)  Où que tu vas?

This too has a somewhat less colloquial variant (see also 3.3.3):

(14)  Où ça que tu vas?

**Où que tu vas?** is unlikely to be used by middle-class speakers, and accordingly can be classified as *français populaire*. Not surprisingly, normative grammarians dismiss interrogatives like (13) as irredeemably 'vulgar'.

Here are the basic nine sentences again, arranged in descending order of formality (five of them are bracketed together, as they are differentiated more by the degree of emphasis placed on the WH-word than by subtleties of register):

Où vas-tu?
Où est-ce que tu vas?
⎧ Où c'est que tu vas?
⎪ C'est où que tu vas?
⎨ Où est-ce que c'est que tu vas?
⎪ Où ça que tu vas?
⎩ Tu vas où?
Où tu vas?
Où que tu vas?

**Où que tu vas?** is not to be confused with **où que tu ailles . . .** (with the subjunctive). This means 'wherever you go . . .', not 'where are you going?', and is a standard structure, with a different intonation pattern.

A number of other permutations of the above patterns are possible – in theory at least, as native speakers' intuitions as to what is and what is not acceptable tend to become unreliable when confronted with **où que c'est que tu vas?, où c'est que c'est que tu vas?,** and so forth.

The variations just illustrated by reference to **où** recur with other WH-words of course, though the possibilities vary from one to another. **Lequel** and **quel**, for example, do not allow the alternative with **ça** (**\*quel train ça que tu prends?**). One statistical survey (Behnstedt 1973) suggests that **combien, quand** and **quel** are more likely to be placed at the end of the sentence than **où** or **qui**. In particular, questions like **quand tu pars?,** with **quand** at the beginning and no inversion, are rather unusual. On the other hand, **pourquoi** is very resistant to final position: **pourquoi elle rit?** and **pourquoi qu'elle rit?** are common enough, but **elle rit pourquoi?** is very unlikely, unless there is an intonation break (**elle rit – pourquoi?**). **Que** ('what?') follows a rather idiosyncratic pattern, being replaced by **quoi** in stressed position:

Que veux-tu?
Qu'est-ce que tu veux?
C'est quoi que tu veux?
Qu'est-ce que c'est que tu veux?
Tu veux quoi?

**Quoi tu veux?** and **quoi que tu veux?**, with **quoi** in unstressed position, are unlikely (though **quoi tu dis?** is occasionally encountered). **Qu'est-ce que** can be reduced to **qu'est-ce** before **tu**. Note the attempt to spell this 'phonetically' in the following example of strip-cartoon dialogue:

(15)   Kes tu glandes [*fais*]? (TJ21)

Finally, in the case of WH- questions with noun subjects, a pronoun is usually present as well as a noun in colloquial usage (see 7.1 for discussion of 'topicalized' structures like these). Thus **où est-ce qu'il va, Jean?, Jean, il va où?** or **où il va, Jean?** rather than **où est-ce que Jean va?, Jean va où?** or (extremely unlikely) **où Jean va?**.

---

## EXERCISES

7† Give as many variations as possible on each of the following, in approximate descending order of formality.

   (a)   Quand part-il?
   (b)   Comment t'appelles-tu?
   (c)   Qui connais-tu?
   (d)   Lequel veux-tu?
   (e)   Quelle heure est-il?

8† The following are typical excerpts from dialogues in novels which aim to reproduce *français familier* or *populaire*. Rephrase them as inversion-type interrogatives.

   (a)   Où qu'est le malade? (RFC183)

   (b)   Qui tu aimes le mieux? (PA37)

   (c)   Où que c'est qu'elle danse? (RS112)

   (d)   Comment que tu vois l'an 2000, toi? (RFB23)

   (e)   Pourquoi qu't'as fait ça, Catherine? (RS88)

(f)   Qui t'es? (PS40)

(g)   C'est quand qu'on va au cirque? (DB119)

9†   Arrange the questions in each group in descending order
     of formality. One question (in just one of the groups) is
     unacceptable in any register: mark it with an asterisk.

(a)   comment que tu vas? comment vas-tu? comment tu
      vas?

(b)   qui vous êtes? qui êtes-vous? qui que vous êtes? vous
      êtes qui?

(c)   comment va ça? comment ça va? comment que ça va?

10†   Give (i) familiar and (ii) popular variants of the following
      questions:

(a)   Quand part le train de Paris?
(b)   Comment étaient déguisés les voleurs?
(c)   Combien ce repas a-t-il coûté?
(d)   Pourquoi prends-tu ta voiture?

11    The following dialogue was written for language learners.
      Make it more natural by altering the structure of the
      questions, in ways which are appropriate to the situation.

      −  Bonjour, mes élèves.
      −  Bonjour, monsieur.
      −  Duclos, vous bâillez! Etes-vous fatigué? Qu'avez-vous
         fait hier soir?
      −  J'ai fait mes devoirs, Monsieur.
      −  Et cela vous a-t-il rendu fatigué? A quelle heure vous
         êtes-vous couché?
      −  A dix heures et demie, Monsieur.
      −  Et à quelle heure vous êtes-vous levé aujourd'hui?
      −  A sept heures, Monsieur.
      −  A quelle heure avez-vous quitté la maison pour venir à
         l'école?
      −  A huit heures moins le quart, Monsieur.
      −  Combien de temps mettez-vous pour venir à l'école?
      −  Dix minutes, Monsieur.
      −  Et par quel moyen de transport venez-vous?
      −  A bicyclette, Monsieur. (Arnold 1968: 14)

### 2.2.3 Indirect questions

In standard French, direct and indirect questions are clearly distinct in structure. Inversion, as we have seen, is a characteristic feature of the direct type: **pourquoi ris-tu?**. But it never occurs in an indirect question: ***je te demande pourquoi ris-tu**. In colloquial French, on the other hand, inversion does not occur in either type. This means that direct and indirect questions can have the same form: **pourquoi tu ris?**; **je te demande pourquoi tu ris**.

This is no doubt why a number of other colloquial direct question variants also turn up in indirect questions, reinforcing the contrast between formal and informal structures in this area of grammar. Here are three examples. Note how the variations of the WH-word (in this case **pourquoi**) reflect those presented in 2.2.2 (**où est-ce que**, **où que**, etc.).

(16)  Je te demande pourquoi c'est que tu ris.
(17)  Je te demande pourquoi est-ce que tu ris.
(18)  Je te demande pourquoi que tu ris.

Like the corresponding direct questions, (16) is familiar, whereas (18) is distinctly popular. (17) comes somewhere between the two: it is certainly not acceptable in *français courant*, even though its direct counterpart (**pourquoi est-ce que tu ris?**) would be: **est-ce que**, like inversion, is not possible in standard indirect questions.

Very widespread too in familiar usage is the replacement of standard **ce que** by **qu'est-ce que**. 'I asked her what she thought', for example, is often **je lui ai demandé qu'est-ce qu'elle pensait** ('I asked her what did she think'), instead of **je lui ai demandé ce qu'elle pensait**. Once again, the indirect question follows the pattern of its direct counterpart, which in this case would of course be: **qu'est-ce que vous pensez?**.

---

### EXERCISES

12†  The following sentences are arranged in approximately increasing order of colloquialness. Give the standard equivalent of each (making any other grammar or vocabulary adaptations that may be necessary).

(a)  Nicolas Poincaré, vous pouvez peut-être nous dire où est-ce que vous vous trouvez? (FI)

(b)  On sait pas qu'est-ce qui se passe là-haut. (CR100)

(c)   Tu sais pas quand est-ce qu'elle me l'a avoué? (DF540)

(d)   mais je comprends pas pourquoi que tu . . . que tu sortirais [ . . . ] (RL20)

(e)   on savait plus où qu'on était, on était perdus (IVR)

(f)   fais bien attention où que tu mets les pieds, je viens de cirer (FCR56)

(g)   Y sait pas pourquoi qu'y bouffe, c'qu'y sont cons les jeunes de maint'nant! (RS48)

(h)   Je sais pas c'est qui. (GFO108)

13   The untypical inversions in the following may be attributed to 'hypercorrection' (see 1.6). Can you explain what has gone wrong?

(a)   Je me demande quand part-il. (GF0108)

(b)   Explique-moi où est-il. (GFP100)

(c)   Monsieur le président, pourriez-vous nous dire comment concevez-vous les relations entre la France et l'Irak? (TF1)

### 2.2.4   Questions with *ti*

One further question-type occurs in French, but, in urban speech at any rate, it is nowhere near as widespread as the **est-ce que**, intonation and even inversion types. The considerable attention it has attracted is out of proportion to its frequency, but its evolution is of some interest nevertheless. Sentences like the following show how this type is used:

(19)   Je peux-ti voir? [*est-ce que je peux voir?*]
(20)   Tu viens-ti? [*est-ce que tu viens?*]

The structure is a simple one: the only difference between the declarative and the interrogative is the presence of **ti** in the latter (together with rising intonation). **Ti**, like that other French interrogative marker, **est-ce que**, has the function of signalling the presence of a question. But unlike **est-ce que**, it is placed after the main verb, not at the beginning of the sentence. (In this respect, it has a close resemblance to the Russian interrogative marker *li*.)

The properties of **ti** can be readily understood if its origin is kept in mind. Only a few generations ago, the usual conversational interrogative of **il vient** would have been **vient-il?**, and in the plural **viennent-ils?**. Now the *l* of **il** was (and still is) frequently omitted in everyday speech: **i' vient** for **il vient**, **i'viennent** for **ils viennent**, and so on. Consistently enough, *l* was also omitted in the interrogative form: **vient-i'?** for **vient-il?**. This led to the **t-i'** sequence (the liaison *t* plus the vestigial vowel of **il**) being reinterpreted as a separate unit marking the question: **vien(t) + ti**, **veu(t) + ti**. So **t-i'** came to be added directly to declaratives like **il vient**, giving the interrogative **il vient-ti?** (or more likely **i'vient-ti?**). What is more, the pattern was extended to first- and second-person forms, where of course no liaison *t* or contracted **il** had ever been present: **je peux** → **je peux-ti?**, **tu viens** → **tu viens-ti?**. In this way a new interrogative marker came into being.

In the 1920s and 1930s the view was quite often expressed that the interrogative with **ti** could well become the most common form in conversation, perhaps even passing into the standard language. Commentators were struck, in particular, by the neat parallelisms that seemed to be developing:

| AFF/DECL: | je viens | tu viens | il vient |
|---|---|---|---|
| NEG: | je viens pas | tu viens pas | il vient pas |
| INTERROG: | je viens ti? | tu viens ti? | il vient ti? |

In the event, however, usage came to prefer the even more straightforward intonation type. The forms with **ti** became increasingly associated with rural speech, and today they are rarely used by urban dwellers. If indeed they ever were: there is a quite pervasive 'mythology' according to which **ti** is an archetypal feature of popular Parisian French (see some of the quotations below). **Ti** does survive in jocular contexts, however: mock surprise can be signalled by **voilà-ti pas** (**voilà-ti pas que le facteur arrive**), and a hearty, back-slapping **ça va-ti?** is a quite commonly encountered greeting.

**Ti** interrogatives are also used from time to time in dialogues in novels in order to create a rural or proletarian effect. Note that, since **ti** is a non-standard form, there is no agreed way of spelling it (*t'y*, *ty*, *ti*, *t-i*, *t-y* . . . ?) and it is not included in dictionaries. An incomprehensible *y* in a colloquial text may have nothing to do with the pronoun **y** meaning 'to it', but be part of the author's way of representing **ti**. Or of course it may represent **il** with *l* deleted – or even be a contraction of **lui** (see 8.1.1)! In (21) the first *y* is the pronoun ('will you be coming to it [i.e. the funeral]?'), the second *y* is part of the **ti** interrogative:

(21)   Et vous, Monsieur, vous y viendrez-t-y aussi? [ . . . ] Moi j'ai peur
       des enterrements, Madame [ . . . ] qu'il a répondu [ . . . ] (LFCV373)

## EXERCISES

14† Convert the following **ti** interrogatives into **est-ce que** interrogatives:

(a) te voilà parti sur les routes: je sais t'y seulement où? (FCR56)

(b) Et où c'est-y que vous allez, comme ça? (FCR27)

(c) mais les écoles chez vous, elles sont-i gratuites? (BT26)

(d) Alors, Honoré, c'est-y que tu me connaîtrais plus? (CE27)

(e) Qu'est-ce qu'il en sait celui-là si je suis folle? Il est-y dans ma tête? Il y est-y dans la vôtre? Faudrait qu'il y soye pour savoir . . . Foutez donc le camp tous les deux! (LFCV326)

15 Comment on the conflicting views expressed in the following quotations collected by Behnstedt (1973):

(a) Dans les tournures interrogatives ou exclamatives, la langue populaire se sert surtout de la particule ti. (Grevisse)

(b) mais ce qu'il faut reconnaître, c'est que ce 'ti' est le moyen auquel le peuple recourt le plus volontiers pour interroger quand la question ne contient pas de mot interrogatif. (Le Bidois)

(c) De nos jours l'aire d'extension de l'interrogation particulaire est considérable et le 'ti' s'insinue dans de nombreux recoins de la langue. (Renchon)

(d) Cette particule, pourtant, n'a jamais dépassé les limites du parler campagnard ou d'une littérature faussement populaire. Elle a eu plus de succès comme élément de renforcement d'un 'voilà' nié; elle n'est pas rare en ce cas dans la langue familière. (*Grammaire Larousse*)

### 2.2.5 Statistical studies

Various rather impressionistic indications were given above about the relative frequency of different types of interrogative. Several statistical investigations have been conducted, some of the results of which are summarized below.

1 Pohl (1965).    Middle-class Belgian francophones.

| Yes/no questions | Intonation type: | 698 |
|---|---|---|
| | **est-ce que** type: | 114 |
| | Inversion type: | 4 |

Various written sources.

| Yes/no questions | Inversion type: | 94 |
|---|---|---|
| | Other types: | 1 |

2 Coveney (1990).   Interviews with workers at holiday camp.

| Yes/no questions | Intonation type: | 77.4% |
|---|---|---|
| | **est-ce que** type: | 29.6% |
| | With inversion: | 0.0% |
| WH-questions | WH-word at start: | 47.3% |
| | **est-ce que** type: | 51.1% |
| | WH-word at end: | 29.8% |
| | With inversion: | 4.9% |

3 Gadet (1997).    Telephone conversations.

| Yes/no questions | Intonation type: | 136 |
|---|---|---|
| | **est-ce que** type: | 16 |
| | Inversion type: | 2 |
| WH-questions | WH-word at start: | 16 |
| | **est-ce que** type: | 11 |
| | WH-word at end: | 9 |
| | With inversion: | 5 |

**EXERCISE**

16  What conclusions can be drawn from these figures? How
    consistent with one another are the three investigations?

### 2.2.6  *Comments and reactions*

Before the Second World War, a regular *chronique de langage* was contrib-
uted to *Le Temps* (the leading Paris newspaper of the day) by a particularly
conservative though entertainingly outspoken commentator who wrote
under the pseudonym 'Lancelot'. Here he answers a reader's enquiry by
telling a somewhat implausible anecdote:

«Pourquoi, me demande un correspondant, certaines personnes affectées
interrogent-elles de la même façon qu'elles affirmeraient ou qu'elles
répondraient, comme si la langue française ne possédait pas de forme
interrogative?» Je suis bien aise que l'on me donne une fois l'occasion
de dire ce que je pense de cette mode. Elle est [ . . . ] ridicule et irritante.
[ . . . ]
Je me souviens que l'autre été, dans un hôtel de la côte basque, je
faillis me faire une affaire avec une famille bourgeoise de trois personnes,
le père, la mère et le fils unique – naturellement – qui déjeunaient à une
table voisine de la mienne, parce que la dame dit aux deux mâles:
«Pourquoi vous êtes descendus sans m'attendre? Et puis pourquoi vous
êtes pas venus à la plage ce matin?» Je ne pus m'empêcher de dire très
haut, en m'adressant au maître d'hôtel, mais en jetant à ces gens de
rien un regard de furieux mépris: «Pourquoi vous m'apportez pas la
suite? J'attends. Et puis, pourquoi vous m'avez pas donné le moulin à
poivre et la moutarde?»
Ce qui est à peine croyable et qui passa mon espérance, c'est qu'ils
eurent positivement l'air de comprendre que je me moquais d'eux. Je
pensai un moment qu'ils allaient le prendre très mal; mais après un
bref conciliabule à voix basse au cours duquel je dus être vilipendé,
Dieu sait en quel français, ils se contentèrent d'encaisser. [ . . . ]
*Pourquoi vous êtes pas venus?* au lieu de *Pourquoi n'êtes-vous pas
venus?* ne traduit rien du tout qu'un besoin pervers, étrange passé un
certain âge, de faire l'enfant. Je ne comprendrai jamais cette manie de
simuler la faiblesse d'esprit, quand la plus élémentaire prudence
conseillerait plutôt de la dissimuler. (Hermant 1936: 405–6)

A year or two earlier, the author of one of the first systematic studies of popular French had had this to say:

> Dans la langue parlée, la phrase interrogative semble aujourd'hui, de par le pullulement des formes concurrentes, extraordinairement compliquée: *Qui est-ce qui est venu? Qui c'est qui est venu? Qui c'est-i qui est venu? Qui que c'est qui est venu?*, etc. Si la phrase interrogative traverse une crise, tout ce désarroi s'explique cependant par les essais multiples que tente le langage avancé pour supprimer l'inversion, c'est-à-dire pour obtenir la même séquence que dans l'affirmative. [ . . . ]
>
> Dans la phrase interrogative traditionnelle, la place [des] pronoms et adverbes [interrogatives] ne concorde pas avec celle qu'ils occupent dans la phrase affirmative:
>
> *Où* est-ce qu'il habite?/Il habite *là*, à tel endroit.
>
> Or le français avancé a cherché, et à peu près réussi, à créer un type d'interrogatives où la séquence est interchangeable avec celle de l'affirmative:
>
> Il habite où? (= Il habite *là*). (Frei 1929: 158)

---

### EXERCISE

17  Compare and contrast the viewpoints of these two commentators.

---

## 2.3  Forming relative clauses

The organization of relative clauses in standard French is quite complex – and, in the view of many commentators, fairly incoherent, given the proliferation of relative pronouns that it involves. The more colloquial the register, on the other hand, the more straightforward, even logical, the system becomes.

### 2.3.1  Relative clauses in standard French

Here is a brief recapitulation of the standard system.

In a sentence like **les soldats <u>qui patrouillaient</u> étaient américains**, the noun phrase **les soldats** is modified by the relative clause **qui patrouillaient**. Other examples of noun phrases modified in this way are: **les soldats <u>que nous avons attaqués</u>** . . . , **le train <u>que j'ai pris</u>** . . . , **la dame <u>dont le chien aboyait</u>** . . . , **l'ami <u>à qui j'ai envoyé le message</u>** . . . , **le bureau <u>où je travaille</u>**.

Relative pronouns like **qui, que** or **dont** cannot be omitted in French – standard or non-standard. This contrasts with the situation in English, where *the train that I caught was delayed* and *the train I caught was delayed* are both possible.

Standard French has a further set of relative pronouns, which are not normally used for reference to humans, occur typically after prepositions, and are variants of the basic form **lequel**. Thus: **les raisons <u>pour lesquelles il a démissionné</u>**, **le problème <u>auquel je réfléchis</u>**, (**à qui** or **pour qui** would not be possible in such cases, as they are restricted to nouns denoting people: **l'ami à qui** . . . , etc.).

Taken together, the standard French relative pronouns make quite a varied array: **qui, que, dont, où, lequel, laquelle, lesquels, lesquelles,** plus various combinations of the last four with **à** and **de** (in most cases written as single words: **duquel, auxquelles,** etc.).

The characteristic feature of this system is that each relative pronoun has a dual function, providing two crucial kinds of information (the **lequel** series specifies number and gender as well). Firstly, the start of a relative clause is signalled: 'some information about the antecedent is about to follow'. Secondly, the relative pronoun specifies the relationship between the antecedent and the verb or other elements in the relative clause. In **les soldats qui patrouillaient étaient américains**, it is the soldiers who are doing the patrolling (subject relationship – **les soldats patrouillaient** – therefore **qui**); in **les soldats que nous avons attaqués étaient américains** it is the soldiers who get attacked (object relationship – **nous avons attaqué les soldats** – therefore **que**); in **les soldats dont les uniformes ont été volés**, the uniforms belong to the soldiers (possession, therefore **dont**); in **les soldats à qui le colonel a parlé**, it is the soldiers who are spoken to, so **qui** is the object of the preposition **à**.

This proliferation of different forms is a good example of the influence of the seventeenth- and eighteenth-century grammarians (see 1.4), with their fondness for the complexities of Latin grammar and their insistence on clarity and explicitness. In popular usage, ever since the Middle Ages, the tendency has been to use fewer relative pronouns – the **lequel** series in particular has long been of restricted occurrence.

However, the standard system has had a considerable effect on the usage of norm-conscious middle-class speakers in particular, with the result that relative-clause formation is an area where differences of social background come into play alongside criteria of formality or informality. The term *français populaire* can therefore be used with some justification here: many aspects of the system to be described are associated with 'uneducated' usage – so much so that they have become stereotypical features of the parodies of *français populaire* beloved of many journalists and novelists. Nevertheless, even middle-class speakers use non-standard relatives in their more unguarded moments. Conversely, standard forms can occur in working-class speech.

---

### EXERCISE

1† To check your familiarity with the standard system, insert suitable relative pronouns into the sentences below. Identify the antecedent in each case and say what grammatical relationship (subject, object, etc.) is indicated by the relative pronoun.

(a) Les soldats _____ nous avons vus étaient britanniques.

(b) Les soldats _____ nous ont vus étaient britanniques.

(c) Le train _____ était sur le point de partir était le dernier de la journée.

(d) Le train _____ j'ai raté était le dernier de la journée.

(e) La situation dans _____ il se trouve est très grave.

(f) Les étudiants avec _____ elle a discuté étaient étrangers.

(g) Les enfants _____ le professeur était tombé malade sont rentrés à la maison.

---

### 2.3.2  *Popular developments:* le décumul du relatif

The reduction of the number of relative pronouns in the 'fully fledged' popular system is illustrated by the following examples; **dont**, **qui** and **que** alternate in the standard language, whereas the most colloquial varieties of French use **que** in all cases.

STANDARD
(1) l'homme dont je connais le frère
(2) l'homme à qui j'envoie un message
(3) l'homme que j'ai frappé

POPULAR

(4)  l'homme que je connais son frère
(5)  l'homme que je lui envoie un message
(6)  l'homme que je l'ai frappé

The sole function of **que** in the 'popular' system is to indicate that further information about the antecedent is about to be provided ('relative clause coming up'). Relationships like subject, object, possession, etc. are specified by means of personal pronouns (**lui**, **le**) or possessive adjectives (**son**) located within the relative clause and referring back to the antecedent.

So in (4), **son** indicates whose brother is being talked about; in (5), **lui** indicates that it is to the man that a message is being sent; in (6), **le** indicates that the man 'undergoes' the hitting, i.e. is to be understood as the object of **j'ai frappé**. Some colloquial or regional varieties of English proceed in a similar way ('the bloke what I hit 'im').

Because the dual function of standard **qui**, **que**, **dont** etc. is divided between invariable **que** on the one hand, and **le**, **lui**, **son** etc. on the other, French grammarians refer to this type of relative-clause formation as *le décumul du relatif*. (*Cumul* refers to any combination of two or more functions: in politics a *cumul des mandats* occurs when one and the same person is both the mayor of a town and its MP. *Décumul* refers to the opposite process – the separation of the functions.) As **que** is 'relayed', 'taken up again' or 'resumed' by the pronoun, this kind of relative clause is known as a *resumptive relative*.

In fact, 'relative pronoun' is probably not the best term to apply to **que** when it is simply announcing an imminent relative clause: pronouns stand for nouns, and this is precisely what **que** is not doing in these cases: **il**, **elle**, **lui**, **son**, **en** and the rest are there for that purpose. Various alternative terms exist: *relative marker* will be used in the rest of this section.

Resumptive relatives are in no way unique to popular French (or English): the same kinds of structure are found in Arabic, Hebrew, Irish and Welsh, for instance. The difference is that, in these languages, there is nothing colloquial about resumptives: they are perfectly standard and have been so for centuries.

## EXERCISES

2†  Here are some further examples of resumptive relative clauses. Give standard French equivalents.

   (a)  l'homme que je lui ai écrit une lettre
   (b)  l'ami qu'on est sans nouvelles de lui

(c)  le collègue que j'ai aperçu sa voiture
(d)  la fille que je vous en parlais
(e)  le copain que je suis sorti avec lui
(f)  la dame que son chien aboyait
(g)  la dame que son chien va mordre Marie

3†  Convert the following standard relative clauses into colloquial
    relatives of the resumptive type (and make other appropriate
    adjustments – omission of **ne**, etc.):

(a)  la personne à qui j'ai montré votre lettre
(b)  l'homme dont je vous ai parlé
(c)  l'agent à qui il a demandé le chemin
(d)  la dame que nous visitons
(e)  un garçon que nous ne connaissons pas
(f)  les bêtes auxquelles elle a donné à manger
(g)  un ami sans lequel je ne partirais pas
(h)  la femme dont le mari vient de mourir

### 2.3.3  *Qui, que* **and** *où*

Rather more variation is found when there is a subject relationship between
the antecedent and the verb of the relative clause – that is, in cases where
standard usage has **qui** (**l'homme qui est là**, etc.). **Qui** is used in colloquial
French too, though before a vowel it is often reduced to **qu'**. Note that,
unlike (4), (5) and (6), the following sentences contain no resumptive
pronoun:

(7)  un p'tit vieux qu'a une bonne retraite (IVR)

(8)  tous ceux qui pouvaient pas rentrer, qu'étaient dehors [ . . . ] (RL36)

(9)  Méfie-toi des clébards qu'aboient pas. (SAO74)

(10)  C'est ça qu'a lâché [*that's what gave way*]. (JE68)

The *i* of **qui** can be elided only when **qui** is being used as a relative pronoun,
as in (7)–(10). **Qui est là?** and **A qui est cette voiture?**, for example, could
never, in any register, take the form **\*Qu'est là?** or **\*A qu'est cette voiture?**.
By contrast, **que** is reduced to **qu'** in all kinds of situations, so what we have
here looks almost like a replacement of **qui** by **que** – and as such, helps to
reinforce the dominance of **que** in the colloquial relative-clause system.

A popular-style resumptive pronoun *can* be used in sentences like (7), though its inclusion is especially likely to be stigmatized as 'uneducated'. **Qu'** in the following examples represents **que** not **qui**, of course: sentences like (11)–(13) are parallel to (4)–(6).

(11)  Les bateaux qu'ils arrivent [ . . . ] (RB)

(12)  un truc qu'ça va vous intéresser (IZ178)

(13)  il a été éjecté de la voiture par le choc qu'y a eu, qu'ça a ouvert la portière [ . . . ] (DF820)

(14)  tes piles que c'est des vieilles (IZ59)

Before a vowel, as in (11), **qu'ils** would be pronounced [kiz], with the usual colloquial elision of the *l*, and with liaison of the *-s*. Before a consonant, the elision of *l* means that **qui** and **qu'il(s)** are both pronounced [ki], with a consequent obscuring of the difference between standard and popular forms.

(15)  l'homme qui [ki] travaille (standard)
(16)  l'homme qu'il [ki] travaille (popular)
(17)  les hommes qui [ki] travaillent (standard)
(18)  les hommes qu'ils [ki] travaillent (popular)

Only with a feminine noun does **qui** retain its distinct identity:

(19)  les femmes qui travaillent (standard)
(20)  les femmes qu'elles travaillent (popular)

The **qui/qu'il(s)** ambiguity no doubt reinforces the tendency for **qui** to be assimilated to **que** in relative clauses, and for **que** to become the sole relative marker. Further evidence of the 'attractive force' of **que** lies in its use in the familiar equivalents of **c'est moi qui conduis** and **c'est nous qui le mangeons**. **J(e)** and **on** serve as resumptive pronouns:

(21)  C'est moi que j'conduis. (KL30)

(22)  Les paysans qui [qu'ils?] fabriquent le blé, et nous qu'on le mange [ . . . ] (LFM44)

(There is further discussion of **j(e)** in 7.4 and 8.1, and of **on** in 3.3.)
**Où** has resisted the encroachment of **que** better than the other standard relative pronouns – partly because of its frequent occurrence as an

interrogative adverb (**où tu vas?**), and partly because (unlike **qui**) it is phonetically distinct from **que**. Even so, **que** often replaces **où** in phrases referring to time:

(23)   le jour que ça va pas [ . . . ] (IVR)

(24)   on était à la maison la fois que tu faisais les choux (BBE74)

And some speakers extend this to phrases referring to places:

(25)   ces pays-là que les gens se soumettent et acceptent des situations inacceptables (RL38)

(26)   Le fameux cinéma qu'on s'était donné rendez-vous vient de fermer. (GFO118)

It is more usual for **où** to be used in cases like (25) and (26), even in familiar and popular French. But it is likely to be followed by **que, c'est que, est-ce que**, or other such extensions – just as in colloquial WH-questions with **où** (see 2.2.3). For instance:

(27)   les pays étrangers où qu'y a les Noirs (IVR)

Some further examples are given in 2.3.5.

---

## EXERCISES

4†   Complete the following in such a way as to make three different colloquial (resumptive) relative clauses in each case, abbreviating **qui** to **qu'** when appropriate. Incorporate the vocabulary items indicated in brackets. Then give the standard equivalents.

    (a)   le petit garçon que . . . (sa maman, un cadeau, a donné)
    (b)   le grand méchant loup que . . . (le petit garçon, bonjour, a dit)

5†   Arrange the sentences in each group from least to most colloquial. Indicate any which might be regarded as popular or uneducated:

    (a)   le train qu'est parti
         le bus qui arrive

l'avion qu'il est tombé en panne
un taxi lequel m'a acheminé à ma destination

(b)  l'hôtel où qu'on s'est installés pour un mois
le petit bistrot où c'est qu'on s'est bien amusés
le casino où on a fait banco
le café auquel il se rendait tous les jours

6†  Say which occurrences of **qui** could be replaced colloquially
by **qu'**:

(a)  Qui habite là?
(b)  Je sais qui habite là.
(c)  C'est Jean qui habite là.
(d)  Qui a appelé?
(e)  Qui est la personne qui a appelé?
(f)  C'est la personne qui est là qui a appelé.

7†  Which of the following are standard, and which colloquial?

(a)  C'est Jean qu'a dit merci.
(b)  Qu'a dit Jean?
(c)  Le journal qu'achète le passager . . .
(d)  Le passager qu'achète le journal . . .
(e)  Les enfants qu'écoutent la radio . . .
(f)  La radio qu'écoutent les enfants . . .

8†  The following have opposite meanings according to whether
they are taken to be colloquial or standard. Specify and
explain.

(a)  Le rat qu'a chassé le chat.
(b)  Le Paris-Saint-Germain [*football team*] qu'a battu
l'Olympique de Marseille.
(c)  Les Serbes qu'ont conquis les Albanais.

### 2.3.4  'Resumptive' and 'defective' relative clauses

An alternative to both the resumptive and the standard patterns is the so-
called 'defective relative', exemplified in examples like:

(28)   le colis que je te parlais (BM242)

(29)   y a une chose qu'il faut faire attention (BM242)

In each case there is a relative marker **que**, but no accompanying pronoun: the speaker leaves it to the hearer to deduce the grammatical relationship between **colis** and **parlais** or **chose** and **attention**. Hence the term *defective*. The corresponding resumptives (with the pronouns restored and the relationships made overt) would be:

(30)   le colis que je t'en parlais
(31)   [ . . . ] une chose qu'il faut y faire attention

With certain verbs (**parler, avoir besoin, se servir, être content, se souvenir**), defective relatives are in fact commoner than the resumptive type, and quite often occur in middle-class as well as lower-class speech:

(32)   Il faut accorder à l'athlétisme l'espace vital qu'il a besoin [*sports commentator*]. (ASA151)

(See also the quotations in Exercise 17 below).

A further type of defective relative is derivable from a standard sentence like:

(33)   l'ami avec qui je suis sorti

via a colloquial resumptive like:

(34)   le copain que je suis sorti avec lui

by omitting the pronoun **lui**. The result is the even more colloquial sentence-type seen in:

(35) le copain que je suis sorti avec

The parallel with English sentences ('my mate what I went out with') is of course striking, but it is only a parallel, not a result of English influence: **le copain que je suis sorti avec** emerges naturally from the relative clause structures that have been described. Moreover, the parallel is incomplete: in English *what* (or *who*) can be omitted; this is certainly not the case with **que** in French. A further difference is that in English any preposition can be involved, including *to* and *of* (*the lady I was talking to, the trip we were thinking of*), whereas in French of whatever variety, word-for-word equivalents of such sentences are out of the question.

The meanings of the defective relative clauses exemplified so far have been easy enough to deduce. But the fact that such clauses do not explicitly specify grammatical relationships like subject, object or indirect object means that some of them are ambiguous. **L'homme que je te parlais**, already quoted, allows of only one interpretation. This is not the case with:

(36)   l'homme que je parle (GFO115)

The missing pronoun here could be either **en** or **lui**, and the sentence could mean either 'the man I'm talking about' or 'the man I'm talking to'. As Françoise Gadet points out in her discussion of this example (Gadet 1997: 117), real-life sentences are used in a particular context, and the context would no doubt indicate which interpretation was appropriate. But their inherent ambiguity has made such sentences extremely suspect: many descriptive linguists (let alone normative grammarians) would regard them as ill-formed, even in terms of colloquial grammar.

On the other hand, the following are clear enough in meaning, but it is questionable whether **que** can be said to have the status of a relative marker at all:

(37)   des feux qu'il faut appeler les pompiers tout de suite (GFP96)

(38)   Mon voisin avait une voiture que en tirant sur le démarreur ça faisait du bruit (MB218)

All these very 'loose' examples, whether ambiguous or not, merge into the more general category of 'universal **que**', a conspicuous feature of colloquial French which is discussed further in 6.2.

## EXERCISES

9†   Arrange each group in order, from least to most colloquial. Indicate any familiar or popular sentences, and asterisk those which would be unacceptable in any register:

(a)   la canne qu'il sort jamais sans
le couteau qu'elle a commis le meurtre
le fusil avec lequel il a tiré
l'arme à feu il a utilisé

(b) le voyage dont je me souviens
le voyage que je m'en souviens
le voyage duquel je me souviens
le voyage je m'en souviens

10† Convert the following defective relatives into resumptives by supplying suitable pronouns. Then give standard equivalents.

(a) Mon mari que je suis toujours sans nouvelles [ . . . ] (RB)

(b) les associés que nous avons besoin (ASA151)

(c) le type que je te parle (FH)

(d) Le carambolage qu'on vous a beaucoup parlé ces derniers jours [ . . . ] [*news bulletin*] (BBE74)

11 Here are some further authentic examples. Most of them are of the resumptive type, but there are also one or two defectives. Comment on the structure and explain the meaning in all cases; then suggest standard French equivalents (sometimes these are not easy to provide: why not?).

(a) le crocodile que Tarzan il se bat avec (MB212)

(b) y en a que ça devient des amis [*local talking about tourists*] (FI)

(c) Il y a des dentistes que leurs doigts sentent le tabac. (AM142)

(d) c'est des petites bricoles que si on les fait pas, après on est mal (BBA104)

(e) sa mobylette qu'il manque la selle (BBE75)

(f) j'ai laissé passer toutes les voitures venant de ma droite que d'ailleurs il n'y en avait pas [*from letter to insurance company*] (EDJ)

(g) Elle me coûte cher ma salle de bains que je me sers pas d'ailleurs. (GFO118)

> (h) une mère qu'on exécute son fils devant ses yeux (GFP95)
>
> (i) Vous dites que vous le connaissez pas vous le fusil qu'il s'est tué avec? (LFCM456)
>
> (j) Y a que la maternelle que c'est mixte. (CR72)
>
> (k) des échalotes que nous allons tapisser le plat avec [*cookery demonstration*] (TF1)
>
> 12    Comment on the ambition expressed by a working-class immigrant teenager in an autobiographical novel:
>
> comme mon père, j'avais à coeur de parler comme il faut. De dire, par exemple: «C'est ce dont j'ai peur ...» Et pas: «C'est ce que j'ai peur ...» (PS24)

### 2.3.5   *How speakers handle relative clauses*

Not surprisingly, speakers who do not make habitual use of standard relative patterns encounter difficulties in situations where such use is required – in classroom exercises, for example. Here are some attempts by secondary-school pupils to make up sentences beginning with **le livre dont** ... (the original spelling errors have been retained):

(39)   Le livre dont Pierre a donné est bleus. (RB)

(40)   Le livre dont j'ai empreinté est à ma mère. (RB)

(41)   Le livre dont je tient dans mes deux mains appartient à un grand écrivaint. (RB)

(42)   Le livre dont je suis enttreint de lire appartenais à mon père. (RB)

Evidently **dont** is recognized as introducing a relative clause, but that is as far as recognition goes: it is treated as though it were merely a synonym of **que**. The following excerpt from a letter to an insurance company shows a speaker who feels obliged to use **lequel**, as befits the formal circumstances, but who uses it in a 'hypercorrect' way (in place of **où**):

(43)  Vous seriez bien aimable de réviser vos conclusions pour me remettre dans mon bon droit lequel je me trouve déjà par ailleurs. (EDJ)

As was suggested in 2.3.1, and as emerges from this example, elements of all three systems (standard, resumptive and defective) often co-exist in the usage of one and the same speaker – and even in the same situation. An illustration of this is to be found in D. François' extensive collection of spontaneous conversations involving upper-working-class speakers in the Paris suburb of Argenteuil (François 1974). A detailed analysis is given of the usage of one particular participant (a man in his late sixties).

The only relative pronouns in this speaker's repertoire are **qui, que** and **où** (however, **où** never occurs on its own: see below). In his various utterances during a single conversation with the author and other speakers, standard **qui** occurs alongside the colloquial contraction **qu'** in relative clauses like the following:

(44)  celui qui nous a vendu [ . . . ] (DF764)

(45)  c'était Béritaud qu'a vendu le champ (DF764)

(46)  voilà l'incendie qui prend feu (DF767)

There are no examples of resumptives of the **l'homme qu'il est là** variety (antecedent as subject), so this speaker's French, although colloquial, is evidently not of the most popular variety. There are also standard clauses with antecedent as object:

(47)  les jeunes filles là qu'on a vues dedans (DF769)

But before a consonant, **que** is often contracted:

(48)  le prix qu't'as payé (DF776)

And standard relatives like (47) alternate with the resumptive type:

(49)  si elle a un problème qu'elle arrive pas à le définir [ . . . ] (DF773)

There are a few defective relatives – for example:

(50)  c'est celle-là que j'parle (DF826)

(The context makes it clear that this means 'who I'm speaking about', not 'who I'm speaking to'.)

**Où**, finally, is either replaced by **que**:

(51)  à l'endroit que l'on est (DF834)

or else accompanied by one or other of various expansions:

(52)  le long de la maison où que c'est qu'y en avait eu un y a vingt et des années [*where there had been one twenty-odd years ago*] (DF785)

(53)  C'est la maison en descendant là, où c'est qu'habitait Fanny [*where Fanny lived*]. (DF825)

---

## EXERCISES

13   The corpus of conversations collected in Le Havre by F. Hauchecorne contains a mixture of different kinds of relative clause, like the conversation referred to in 2.3.5. Classify the following utterances and comment on them:

(a)  Et en face de chez moi y a euh y a une dame de 73 ans qu'a un fils qui s'appelle Druot [ . . . ] (FH)

(b)  les énormes machins comme, comme Le Havre où que c'est qu'y a encore 2 200 bonshommes [bɔnɔm] puis Marseille où qu'ils sont 2 500 [ . . . ] (FH)

(c)  en France y a un système de distribution qu'est vachement performant (FH)

(d)  les rayons de légumes, de fruits que tout le monde tripote [ . . . ] (FH)

14   Why are the following sentences examples of hypercorrection?

(a)  L'ami dont je vous en parlais [ . . . ] (RB)

(b)  La dame à qui vous lui avez prêté votre parapluie [ . . . ] (RB)

(c)  Tous les gens auxquels je leur en ai parlé [ . . . ] (GFP96)

15 What conclusions can be drawn from the following attempts by French schoolchildren to construct sentences beginning with **La forêt dans laquelle . . .** ?

(a) La forêt dans laquelle où je m'amuse j'ai vu un grand chêne. (RB)

(b) La forêt dans laquelle que je me promène elle est jolie. (RB)

16 The essential points of the discussion in this section are resumed in the following remarks by Claire Blanche-Benveniste, which hint in addition at certain widespread assumptions about the skill (or otherwise) of the 'masses' in manipulating relative clauses. Can you explain and comment?

> [ . . . ] c'est [le sujet] qui a le plus contribué à la notion de **syntaxe populaire** [ . . . ] L'idée générale était que, dans une structure réputée complexe, comme celle des relatives, le «peuple», ne pouvant maîtriser complètement cette complexité, la décomposait pour la simplifier, en utilisant deux processus majeurs: le «*que* passe-partout», qui éviterait de noter les marques fonctionnelles de sujet et de complément installées dans *qui, que, dont,* et le «décumul», qui ajouterait à ce *que* de subordination un pronom *il, le, lui* ou une préposition, assurant séparément le marquage des fonctions.
>
> Les romans et les chansons populistes utilisent très souvent, à titre d'indice de langage «peuple», ce décumul du relatif [ . . . ]:
>
> — c'est nous les pauvres Français *qu'on* paie la redevance (émission de radio comique [ . . . ])
>
> — c'est celle *que* je suis *avec* (chanson de Renaud). (Blanche-Benveniste 1997: 102–3)

17 The first of the following comments is by the opinionated and intolerant Lancelot du *Temps* (cf. 2.2.6), the second by a 1950s author of a number of guides to correct usage. What do they tell us about (a) normative prejudices and (b) the wide currency of certain colloquial relative-clause types?

(a) J'ai entendu de mes propres oreilles une dame chargée d'enseigner le français dans un collège de jeunes filles, et dont le mari est professeur de lettres dans un lycée, dire, ni plus ni moins qu'une épouse de gendarme: *Les livres que j'ai besoin.* (Hermant 1936: 327)

(b) Chacun connaît l'aimable formule des commerçants: *Est-ce tout ce que Madame a besoin?* Le français populaire dit: *C'est moi que je commande. Que* «ligature invariable» aurait ainsi toutes les fonctions qu'on veut. Ce serait commode évidemment. Mais ce confusionnisme serait la fin de toute syntaxe correcte. (Georgin 1951: 178)

# 3  Noun Phrases

## 3.1  Nouns, articles and modifiers

This section presents some colloquial aspects of the categorization of French nouns as masculine or feminine. It also shows how colloquial usage has certain distinctive ways of organizing the internal structure of noun phrases – in particular by means of the adverb **comme** – and attention is drawn to a few colloquial aspects of the use of adjectives and numerals. But see 7.2 and 7.3 for accounts of plural formation in nouns and gender marking in adjectives.

### 3.1.1  Gender of nouns

Divergences from the standard gender assignment occur from time to time, notably in the most popular varieties of French, but they are few and far between in relation to the total size of the vocabulary. As for familiar usage, normative grammarians list dozens of words which are liable to be 'miscategorized' (examples in Exercises 1 and 2 below) – but they are mostly quite rare and the meaning of some of them, let alone the gender, may be obscure even to educated speakers.

Particularly with rarer words, fluctuation is often due to analogies of various kinds with better-known items (for instance when **une épigramme** is treated as masculine because of **un gramme**). And nouns in **-ule**, which are evenly divided between the two genders, are especially liable to miscategorization.

In some cases, however, the change of gender is linked to the phonetic form of the noun in question. Although gender in French is notoriously unpredictable, it is more often than not the case that nouns are masculine if they end in a vowel (in pronunciation) and feminine if they end in a consonant (often followed by 'mute *e*' in the spelling). So, in popular usage, nouns like **auto**, **dynamo** or even **toux** [tu] may be made masculine, while **augure**,

**chrysanthème**, **orage**, **ovale** or **ulcère** can become feminine. **Incendie** (masculine in standard) moves in the opposite direction from **auto** and **dynamo**, following the pattern of the large number of feminine nouns in **-ie**. Reclassification of masculines as feminines is most likely to occur when, as in several of the examples just given, the noun begins with a vowel. The gender of vowel-initial nouns is less often indicated overtly: the definite article is an indeterminate **l'**, and if a masculine adjective precedes, it takes on a liaison form which is usually identical to the feminine in pronunciation: **un bel orage**, **un mauvais augure** ([mɔvɛ zogyʀ]). Though the feminization of common 'vowel-initial/consonant-final' masculines like **orage** is a characteristically popular phenomenon, one or two set phrases containing such *français populaire* genders have entered wider use: **de la belle ouvrage**; **une grosse légume** (*personnage important*). And the relatively uncommon noun **alvéole**, once masculine, is now usually feminine in standard French.

Note that in popular usage, feminine (especially inanimate) nouns, whether given a masculine article or not, are sometimes referred to by a masculine pronoun (accompanying predicative adjectives are affected as a consequence):

(1)   j'ai repiqué les tomates, i'n'ont pas, i'z'ont pas, ça va, i'sont encore verts, i'sont pas crevés hein [ . . . ] (DF778)

(2)   I' sont déjà fané les fleurs que je vous ai offert? (GFO 22)

Colloquial usage may also level out gender discrepancies between related words. Thus **un interligne** (*espace entre deux lignes*) is sometimes made feminine by analogy with **une ligne**. Similarly, masculine **hémisphère** and **bidonville** ('shanty town') are influenced by feminine **sphère**, **atmosphère** and **ville**. A few such gender changes have eventually been adopted by *bon usage*: **entrecôte** was once 'officially' masculine, but is now officially feminine. In many cases the analogy is reinforced by the fact that the noun is vowel-initial and consonant-final.

Other gender changes, or apparent changes, are due to grammatical, not phonetic or lexical, factors. Widely used familiar expressions like **un espèce de miracle** or **un espèce d'imbécile** are unanimously condemned by normative commentators, who insist on **une espèce de . . .** in all cases. In fact, **espèce** here can be regarded as having the status of a prefix or adjective (**un pseudo-miracle**, as it were), so that **un** 'goes with' the masculine noun. There is a similarity with **elle a l'air contente**, which, however, has long been accepted by the norm. Less polite usage offers various parallel examples: **ce putain d'appareil** for 'this bloody machine' (**une putain**: 'prostitute'), or **un vache d'accent italo-américain**: 'one hell of an . . . accent' (George 1996: see this article for further illustration).

---

## EXERCISES

1†   Why are the following nouns (feminine in standard French) sometimes made masculine?

acné, bodega, campanule, coquecigrue, écritoire, fourmi (see p. 139 for an example), interview, molécule, paroi, primeur.

2†   Why are the following nouns (masculine in standard French) sometimes made feminine?

automne, emblème, globule, haltère, indice, insigne, opuscule, planisphère, tentacule.

3†   Give the standard gender of the following nouns; then work out which of them are sometimes recategorized in colloquial usage, and which are not:

armistice, effluve, exutoire, héros, mandibule, marge, métro, molécule, orbite, portrait, tableau, tubercule, ustensile, vis.

---

### 3.1.2  Determiners: some colloquial aspects

(a)   In written and formal spoken usage, the indefinite article **des** (as in **des études intéressantes**) is replaced by **de** if there is an adjective before the noun: **d'immenses dégâts, de grands projets, de pénibles et difficiles décisions** – unless the adjective + noun combination is a set expression with a distinct meaning of its own: **des jeunes filles**. However, in much spoken and even written French, **des** is used in all cases:

(3)   Les éclipses ont permis de faire des grands progrès à la science. (FR3)

(4)   Si vous êtes des fidèles auditeurs de France-Inter [ . . . ] (FI)

(5)   J'ai toujours eu des bonnes places, moi. (IVR)

Except with **tel**: not ***des telles choses** but **des choses comme ça**.

(b)   The adverb **comme** is another characteristically colloquial feature of noun phrases. There are three main aspects to its use.

The first (and most widespread) is the substitution of sentences like **c'est une belle ville** by **c'est beau comme ville** (note that the adjective now modifies **ce** and not **ville**, and is therefore masculine). 'Restructuring' the noun phrase in this way places the intonation peak on **beau**. An equivalent English sentence might be 'It's a béautiful town' (stress on 'beautiful'), not 'It's a beautiful tówn'.

Secondly (and rather more colloquially), **comme** can occur with expressions of quantity: **comme fleurs il (ne) nous reste plus grand'chose**, corresponding to standard **il ne nous reste plus beaucoup de fleurs**. In the following the colloquial effect is enhanced by the use of the vocabulary items **vachement** and **paumer**:

(6)  J'ai vachement paumé comme argent. (FH)

This is equivalent to **j'ai perdu beaucoup d'argent**.

Thirdly (again with familiar overtones), **comme** can be used in questions containing **quel** or **quoi**:

(7)  Tu prends quoi comme apéritif? (RB)

(8)  Comme robe je mets laquelle? (GFO19)

The standard versions here would be **quel apéritif prends-tu?** and **quelle robe est-ce que je mets?**. Again, the prominence of particular sentence elements is the motivating factor: in these examples, restructuring with **comme** enables **quoi** or **laquelle** to be highlighted at an intonation peak.

(c)  Other familiar effects can be obtained by inserting **de** between modifier and noun. Corresponding to **elle a un beau chat** is:

(9)  Elle en a un beau, de chat.

Here the intonation peak is on **beau**, and **de chat** has a low, level tone: the English equivalent would be 'a béautiful cat', not 'a beautiful cát'. (Such noun phrases are closely related to sentences with 'dislocation': see 6.1.) A parallel example with a definite noun phrase is:

(10)  Elle a choisi la bleue, de robe.

This corresponds to **elle a choisi la robe bleue** or **c'est la robe bleue qu'elle a choisie**, and the same point applies about the intonational prominence of **bleue** ('the blúe dress'). Note that **en** is required in (9), where the article is indefinite, but not in (10), where it is definite, just as would be the case if there were no **de** phrase (**elle en a un beau, elle a choisi la bleue**).

In these cases the order of elements is 'modifier + **de** + noun'. In cases with the reverse order, the '**de** + modifier' element is equivalent to a relative clause:

(11)   J'ai ma mère de malade (= **qui est malade**).

The standard version of this is simply **ma mère est malade**: see 6.1.7 for colloquial sentences with 'presentatives' like **j'ai ... qui ....**

(d)   Characteristically colloquial is the use of **chaque** rather than **chacun(e)** after expressions indicating price: **ces oranges coûtent cinq francs chaque** (standard **cinq francs chacune**). This is regarded as unacceptable by normative commentators, on the grounds that **chaque**, being a determiner, needs to be followed by a noun (**chaque orange**): when there is no noun, a pronoun (**chacun**) is required, as in **chacune coûte cinq francs**. To which a descriptivist answer might be that **orange** is in fact there – though at the beginning of the sentence, admittedly.

---

## EXERCISES

4†   In standard French, which of the following would have **de** and not **des**?

  (a)   des bons résultats
  (b)   des petits pois
  (c)   des énormes problèmes
  (d)   des beaux films
  (e)   des gros fromages [*bigwigs*]
  (f)   des grands rassemblements
  (g)   des petits pains

5†   Rephrase more informally, using **comme** (and making any other adjustments that may be appropriate):

  (a)   C'est une émission très amusante.
  (b)   Quel train attends-tu?
  (c)   Il ne nous reste plus d'argent.
  (d)   C'était une plaisanterie de fort mauvais goût.
  (e)   Quelle sorte de vacances préfères-tu?
  (f)   Cela ne me semble pas une idée très originale.
  (g)   Combien de temps te reste-t-il?

6   Explain the use of **de** in:

(a)   Y'en avait au moins douze de mariages ce jour-là.
      (RS215)

(b)   Il faudrait du courage pour lâcher le trou où on vit, et le
      mien, de courage, je l'ai tout usé. (CE240)

(c)   [Après la guerre contre l'Iran] l'Irak il a eu le temps d'en
      faire une autre de guerre, au monde entier cette fois
      [ . . . ] (NO)

(d)   Y a pas mal d'efforts de fournis ici à Bordeaux [*football
      report*]. (FI)

(e)   Laquelle c'est de dent? (CR40)

(f)   Hum, j'en prendrais bien un, de pastis. (IZ117)

(g)   C'est toujours ça de gagné! (RB)

(h)   J'espère qu'y a encore un troquet d'ouvert. (TJ39)

(i)   Encore un carreau d'cassé!
      V'là l'vitrier qui passe!
      Encore un carreau d'cassé!
      V'là le vitrier passé! (Nursery rhyme)

### 3.1.3   *Adjectives and numerals*

The patterns of gender and number marking in adjectives are markedly
different in spoken and written usage: see 7.2 and 7.3. Otherwise there are
few divergencies between standard and non-standard usage.

(a)   The irregular comparative **pire** ('worse') is quite widely replaced in
familiar usage by **plus mauvais** or **plus mal**, though **plus bon** (instead of the
equally irregular **meilleur**) is rarer and restricted to popular French, or to
the usage of young children. Also popular is the use of **pire** as though it
simply meant 'bad', giving rise to comparatives like **plus pire** or **moins pire**,
which are tautologies from a normative point of view. A similar process
occurs with **plus mieux** and **plus meilleur**; again this is popular, though, like
**plus bon**, less often encountered. In the following excerpt from a detective

novel which makes extensive use of colloquial language, the superlative **le moins pire** is used rather incongruously alongside the past historic and negatives with **ne** – no doubt in order to evoke the 'tough' language characteristic of the residents of this and other high-rise estates:

(12)   Je garai ma R5 sur le parking de La Paternelle. Une cité maghrébine. Ce n'était pas la plus dure. Ce n'était pas la moins pire. (IZ52)

(b)   Another traditional feature of popular comparative structures is the use of **comme** for standard **que**. Like the popular formulae quoted in the previous paragraph, this seems to occur less often nowadays than it did fifty years ago:

(13)   Il est aussi grand comme lui. (PG74)

(c)   In familiar and popular French, a few adjectives (notably **facile, pareil**) are sometimes used adverbially – that is, they modify verbs without taking the characteristic **-ment** suffix:

(14)   Ça devrait s'arranger facile. (IZ134)

(15)   si ça aurait été le contraire (une auto qu'aurait venu par la gauche) il l'emboutissait pareil. (EDJ)

(16)   Le maire tout ce qu'il veut c'est dormir tranquille [ . . . ] (DZ138)

In the currently fashionable style inspired by *tchatche*, or 'youth language' (see 3.3.4 and 4.3.2), the pattern may be extended:

(17)   Alors là j'ai flippé sérieux. (EHA110)
(18)   je refuse les chiffres ils me blessent terrible (EHA129)

And it occurs in some expressions popularized by pseudo-colloquial advertising slogans: **s'habiller confortable** or **voter utile** (i.e. to vote for a large political party that might win, rather than a small one that cannot).

(d)   Two further points of usage involving adjectives (and adverbs) should be noted. Firstly, the widespread familiar use of **très** with certain nouns. Expressions like **j'ai très froid/très chaud** are standard: **froid** and **chaud** here are direct objects of **avoir**, but they are adjectives even so, and can therefore be modified by the adverb **très**. Understandably enough, this causes **très** to be adjoined to nouns like **faim, soif** or **envie** in the parallel expressions **j'ai très faim/très soif/très envie** (standard **j'ai grand' faim/grand' soif/grande envie**).

A further development is the still more familiar expression **faire très attention** (standard **faire bien attention**). Such uses are much criticized by normative grammarians, who see it as a breach of grammatical protocol for an adverb to modify a noun.

There is, however, less criticism of the 'adjectival' functions of **bien**. In familiar French this adverb can be used after a noun as though it were an attributive adjective, though only in the restricted sense of 'distinguished, morally decent or upright (of a person)'. Thus **un type bien, une fille bien, des gens très bien** (standard: **convenable, distingué, estimable**, etc.). But not *\*une excursion bien, \*un chien bien* or even *\*un étudiant bien*. When used predicatively, **bien** is less restricted in meaning (**il est bien, ce monsieur**, but also **c'était bien, ce film/cette excursion**, where it is simply a synonym of **bon**). Predicative **bien** is also a colloquial equivalent of **à l'aise, confortable** or **en bonne santé: installe-toi dans ce fauteuil – tu y seras bien**.

**Mal**, too, occurs predicatively, though only in the sense of **inconfortable** or **mal à l'aise (on est vraiment mal dans cette voiture)**. Except, that is, in negatives: while *\*il est mal (ce type)* and *\*c'était mal (ce voyage)* are not possible, **il est pas mal** and **c'était pas mal** ('it wasn't bad') are widely used colloquialisms (see 2.1.4). Negative **mal** is also frequently encountered attributively (**un type pas mal**). But the attributive use of positive **mal**, unlike that of **bien**, is not possible. So *\*un type mal* is ungrammatical whatever the level of language.

(e)    In all colloquial varieties, two numerals are often simply juxtaposed where standard usage would require them to be linked with either **à** or **ou**, according to the meaning:

(19)    un gosse de dix-douze ans (RB)

(20)    tu vois, y a cinq-six bateaux qui sont détournés d'Anvers, Anvers fait grève ce jour-là, bon ben ces cinq-six bateaux ils vont aller à Dunkerque pour être déchargés (FH)

## EXERCISES

7†   Reformulate in standard French the following traditional examples of popular comparatives:

(a)   C'est bien plus meilleur. (HB87)
(b)   C'est bien plus pire. (HB87)
(c)   C'est le plus pire de tous. (HB87)

(d)  A l'époque qu'on est il devrait faire plus bon. (HB87)
(e)  Il est aussi pire comme l'autre. (HB37)
(f)  C'est plus pire comme un enfant. (PG74)

8†  Insert **ou** or **à** into the following as appropriate:

(a)  cinq-six bateaux
(b)  dix-douze ans
(c)  quatorze-quinze ans
(d)  trois-quatre fois
(e)  cinquante-soixante francs

9  In what way would the descriptivist analysis of expressions like **plus pire** differ from a normative analysis?

## 3.2  Pronouns: nous and on

Personal pronouns are an area of informal usage where divergencies from the standard pattern are particularly noteworthy. This section focuses on the first-person plural pronouns, the equivalents of 'we' and 'us'. Other aspects of pronouns are presented in 3.3, 7.4 and 8.1.

### 3.2.1  Personal on

In informal speech, **nous** (and the accompanying first-person plural verb) is commonly replaced by **on** (together with a third-person singular verb) in utterances like: **on va au cinéma ce soir** (for **nous allons...**), **on habite en face de la gare** (corresponding to **nous habitons...**). The following account of a holiday is very typical:

(1)  On serait bien resté une semaine de plus. Le matin on allait aux bains. A une heure on déjeunait. A trois heures on prenait le sac et, hop, cinq kilomètres dans les montagnes des alentours. (PB105)

But this happens only if **nous** is the subject. It is never possible to use **on** in object position. So even in the most colloquial usage, there is no alternative to **nous** in **ils nous ont vus, ils sont partis avec nous**.

'Emphatic' or 'disjunctive' **nous** is not affected, either. It typically occurs side by side with an **on** that has replaced a non-emphatic **nous**. Thus **nous, on va au cinéma ce soir** (for **nous, nous allons...**), **nous, on habite en face de la**

**gare** (for **nous, nous habitons** . . . ). The following example is from an advertising slogan encouraging people to use the Paris Metro:

(2)  Voilà ce qu'on lui dit nous, à la pollution. (RB)

**Nous** is sometimes combined with **autres** (commonly pronounced **aut'**) if the group referred to does not include the person addressed: **eux ils sont allés au cinéma mais nous aut(res) on est restés à la maison.**

The possessive **notre/nos** also continues to be used, despite the presence of **on: nous, on prend notre voiture.** It is possible for **son/sa/ses** to serve as equivalents of 'our': **on prend sa voiture.** But there is an obvious potential for ambiguity here, in the absence of a clarifying context: 'we're taking our car' as against 'we're taking his/her car'. Perhaps as a consequence, **notre/ nos** tends to be preferred. In sentences like **on prend notre voiture**, the resulting clash between third-person **on prend** and first-person **notre** worries some grammarians, but speakers evidently find no contradiction: **on** is singular in grammatical form (it is followed by **prend**), but plural in terms of meaning – so **notre** can accompany it.

In the case of reflexive verbs like **se dépêcher** or **s'amuser**, pressures of form are dominant: **se** has to be used even with first-person **on: nous on va s'amuser, si on se dépêchait?.** By contrast, if an adjective or a participle follows, then meaning is the dominant factor: when such colloquial expressions are written down, there is most often a plural agreement: **on est contents, on s'est amusés** rather than **on est content, on s'est amusé.** And if the reference is to an all-female group, then **on** takes a feminine adjective – the difference in this case being audible, not simply visual (**on est contentes**).

Here is a summary of the relationship between first-person **on** and other personal pronouns, showing its somewhat anomalous place in the system (after Leeman-Bouix 1994):

- Like **je, tu, il**, it can function only as subject.
- Like **nous, vous**, it can be followed by plural adjectives.
- Like **il, elle**, it must be accompanied by a third-person singular verb.

Statistical investigations of the use of 'personal **on**' in conversations (Söll 1974: 115) showed that nine-year-old children used **on** to the total exclusion of **nous**; politicians speaking on camera (and presumably monitoring their own speech carefully as a result) used **on** three times for every two they used **nous**; in more general middle-class use, the **on:nous** proportion was five to one. So, although personal **on**, like many other features of colloquial French, has often been labelled 'popular', this is clearly contrary to the facts of usage. Indeed, the earliest examples of it are found in the works of classical writers like Racine and Madame de Sévigné.

## EXERCISES

1† Distinguish between:

   (a)  on nous fait payer trop d'impôts
   (b)  nous on paie trop d'impôts

2† Rephrase in more formal French:

   (a)  on a été plusieurs à protester
   (b)  on est fiers de notre équipe
   (c)  Nous on se regarde [ . . . ] et on se lit nos horoscopes en
        déconnant [ . . . ] (EHA146)

3† Rephrase in less formal French, using **on** as much as
   possible:

   (a)  Nous sommes allés jusqu'à Paris pour faire nos achats.

   (b)  L'agent nous a dit que nous n'avions pas le droit de
        laisser nos vélos dans le parking.

   (c)  Nous, nous apprenons le français, mais vous, vous
        étudiez l'allemand.

### 3.2.2  *The versatility of* on, nous *and* tu

**On** has of course retained its more traditional uses as an indefinite pronoun. In colloquial speech it often refers to a vague higher authority (**on nous fait payer trop d'impôts**), and in addition can have the same generic, impersonal senses as those found in the standard language (**on n'est jamais si bien servi que par soi-même; on a apporté le café à la fin du repas**). So it can be translated into English by 'one', 'we', 'they' or 'you', according to the context (or else by a passive: 'coffee was served').

Moreover, in certain situations it can be an informal equivalent of **je** (**on arrive**: 'I'm on my way'), or of **tu** (**on se calme!**, a rather peremptory equivalent of **calme-toi!**).

Ironically, its versatility is rivalled only by that of **nous**, which also has a wide range of applications, even in standard French:

   (3)  Dans ce chapitre, nous [= **je**] montrerons que . . .

   (4)  Bonjour! Nous [= **tu/vous**] avons bien dormi?

(5)  (A speaking about B to a third party) Excusez-le: nous [= **il**] sommes de mauvaise humeur, ce matin!

(6)  Aujourd'hui nous sommes jeudi [*impersonal use*].

This parallelism between **on** and **nous** may well have favoured their inter-changeability (see Leeman-Bouix 1994 for some discussion of this idea). And it does seem that the objections sometimes made to first-person **on** on the grounds that (unlike other pronouns) it is 'ambiguous' are somewhat misplaced.

In informal conversation, **tu** often takes over the indefinite function char-acteristic of **on** in standard French. This can occur when instructions are being given:

(7)  Tu desserres les boulons et tu enlèves la roue. (RB)

Or when hypothetical situations or general truths are being evoked:

(8)  Tu mets des fleurs [ . . . ] dans un bureau de chef de station. Au bout d'une heure, tu les vois clamser. Alors le chef, faut voir quel air il respire. (PB27)

(9)  T'es commissionné au bout d'un an, si t'as pas commis de connerie. (PB61)

Perhaps a tendency to relieve **on** of some of its burdens can be detected in such examples? Or perhaps it is merely that the impersonal use of **on** is too closely associated with formal register to be appropriate – in which case there would be a close parallel with the use of 'you' as opposed to 'one' in English.

---

## EXERCISES

4†  Say why the underlined uses of **on** have to be interpreted as 'we' in the following excerpts from interviews with Paris Metro train drivers:

(a)  La grève des balayeurs, nous <u>on</u> s'en occupe pas. (PB174)

(b) Si on n'avait pas la retraite à cinquante ans et un rythme de travail pas trop dur, on crèverait tous à trente ans. (PB48)

(c) Ça a changé en huit ans. Avant on était deux, on discutait . . . Maintenant les gars sont seuls. (PB77)

(d) On veut savoir si on est normaux. (PB83)

5† Suggest appropriate translations of the various occurrences of **on** in:

On ne peut jamais faire assez attention en conduisant. L'autre jour on était partis se promener en voiture, Jacques, Henri et moi. Jacques a brûlé un feu rouge, un policier a surgi, on a tous été amenés au poste, et on a retiré son permis de conduire à Jacques.

6 Is **on** best interpreted as 'we' or 'they' in the following quotation, and how can you tell? Context: an interview with a coal miner conducted not long after a left-wing election victory.

«Depuis le 10 mai, on a au moins stabilisé le chômage», dit un mineur de Liévin. «On». L'utilisation de ce pronom personnel montre à quel point les militants s'identifient au gouvernement. (EXP)

### 3.2.3 *The views of commentators*

Here are some further views about this extension of the use of **on**. The first is from a guide to 'better' (i.e. less colloquially influenced) French.

Le pronom indéfini *on*. Son emploi généralisé à la place du sujet *nous* est tout à fait condamnable. A la rigueur, on peut comprendre que des garnements préfèrent dire: «*On* a fait une bêtise» plutôt que: «*Nous* avons fait une bêtise» dans l'intention d'esquiver leur responsabilité. Mais il n'est pas du tout logique que, après avoir gagné un match, les joueurs d'une équipe disent: «*On* a gagné» au lieu de: «*Nous* avons gagné». (Capelovici 1990: 227)

The second account is from a more academic study of the structure of the spoken language:

La langue parlée présente [ . . . ] une nouvelle substitution: 'je', 'tu', 'il', 'elle', 'vous', 'ils', 'elles' ne sont généralement pas remplacés, mais 'nous', pour sa part, fait de plus en plus souvent couple avec 'on'. La pluralité sentie dans la première personne du pluriel 'nous' s'efface à la troisième du singulier 'on' qui donne une vision globale. En outre, les formes du singulier ont des terminaisons verbales plus faciles à conjuguer que celles du pluriel [ . . . ] (Burdin 1981: 30)

Some examples of generic **tu**, together with a rather improbable (and 'politically incorrect') explanation of them, were offered many years ago by a normative grammarian:

Les phrases à allure générale conviennent peu aux esprits simples; ils savent mal les manier et mal les comprendre. Savourez cet exemple:

  – Je suis allé hier à la campagne. Il pleuvait. Le terrain était une éponge. Quand *tu* marchais, *tu* enfonçais jusqu'aux genoux.

Or, *tu* n'est pas allé à la campagne; *tu* n'as pas enfoncé dans la boue. C'est à *je*, auteur du récit, que l'aventure est arrivée, ainsi qu'à tous ceux qui, ce jour-là, ont suivi le même chemin que lui. Régulièrement, il faudrait recourir au pronom indéfini *on* pour désigner les personnes (y compris *je*) qui ont pataugé dans les marécages: quand *on* marchait, *on* enfonçait. Cela, c'est la formule abstraite. Un esprit simple, faisant une première étape vers la «concrétisation», dira: «Quand *je* marchais, *j*'enfonçais». Une seconde étape le conduira à l'emploi de *tu*. Il associera l'interlocuteur à ses impressions; il les lui fera partager en imagination. *Tu* est amené à s'intéresser vivement à l'histoire. D'auditeur, il devient acteur par la pensée. Il comprendra mieux: le but est atteint! (Moufflet 1935: 202–3)

---

**EXERCISES**

7 Summarize the explanations given by Capelovici and Burdin, and say how plausible you find them.

8 Compare the views of these two commentators.

9 Comment on the ideas expressed by Moufflet.

## 3.3 Other aspects of pronoun use

This section is mostly concerned with third-person pronouns, which have
been subject to a good deal of restructuring in colloquial French: **ça** is
frequently used as a personal pronoun and the range of **il(s)/elle(s)** has been
restricted. But first some clarification regarding the relationship between **ça**
and **ce**, and between both of them and **cela**.

**Cela** is not used in colloquial French. Conversely, its informal equivalent
**ça** is absent from *français soigné* and is relatively rare in *français courant*. **Ce**
occurs in all registers, of course. Its relationship to **ça** is as follows:

- **Ce**, not **ça**, is used with **est** and **était** (i.e. **c'est, c'était**).
- **Ce** and **ça** are both possible with **sera** and **serait** and in some expressions
  with **devoir** or **pouvoir** (**ce/ça doit être . . .** , **ce/ça pourrait être . . .** ). **Ça** is
  always the more colloquial of the two.
- Otherwise **ça**, not **ce**, is used (standard French would have **cela**): **ça me
  plaît, ça marche bien, ça l'inquiète, ça arrive, ça sert à rien d'insister**, etc.

Many colloquialisms with **ça** have no direct standard equivalent. **Ça va?**, for
example, could not simply be replaced by \*cela va? or even \*est-ce que cela
va?. An appropriate expression would be **comment allez-vous?**.

### 3.3.1 Impersonal expressions

In standard French, in the absence of a specific noun subject denoting a
person, place or thing, **il** serves as a 'dummy' subject – a token place-filler,
corresponding to 'it' or 'there' in English. This occurs:

(a)  with adjectives preceded by **être** and followed by a specifying clause: **il
     était impossible (de traduire cette phrase)**;
(b)  with 'impersonal' verbs or expressions (used only in the third-person
     singular): **il faut (que), il s'agit (de), il y a**;
(c)  with other verbs in 'impersonal' uses: for example **il arrive (que)** ('it
     happens that . . .'), **il paraît (que), il reste (que/de), il suffit (de/que), il
     vaut mieux**;
(d)  with 'weather' verbs or expressions: **il pleut, il fait du vent, il neige**, and
     with time expressions like **il est dix heures, il va être midi**.

Note with reference to category (a) that when there is no clause following
the adjective, **c'est**, not **il est**, must be used, even in standard French: **Avez-
vous réussi à traduire cette phrase? – Non, c'était impossible.**

In colloquial usage, **il** has lost almost all of these functions. Either it is omitted altogether, or it is replaced by **ce/ça**. Here are the counterparts of the above four categories, arranged in ascending order of colloquialness.

- With adjectives and a following clause, **ce/ça** is always used, even sometimes in written French: **c'est difficile de le faire; c'était impossible de traduire cette phrase; ça serait ridicule de partir maintenant; ça va pas être facile de le réparer.**
- **Il** is omitted with impersonal verbs: **faut essayer; s'agit pas de ça; y a un petit problème.**
- In the case of impersonal uses of many other verbs, **il** is again omitted: **paraît qu'il n'était pas là; reste plus grand'chose; suffit d'attendre; vaut mieux pas** ('better not'). In some instances, though, the gap is filled by **ça**: **ça arrive qu'il neige sur la Côte d'Azur** (not *\*arrive qu'il neige*).

Structures like **il est venu beaucoup de monde** ('many people came'), where impersonal **il** 'stands for' a subject that occurs later in the sentence, are restricted to formal style, and have no direct colloquial counterpart.

- In very familiar usage, **ça** can replace **il** as the subject of impersonal 'weather' verbs: **ça pleut, ça a gelé pendant la nuit,** etc. Indeed, the colloquial equivalent of **faire froid** never has **il**: people always say **ça caille!.** But note that this does not apply to 'weather' expressions with **il fait** (where impersonal **il** is simply omitted: **fait beau hein?**), or to time expressions: *\*c'est dix heures, \*ça va être midi.*

If the level of language is colloquial enough for impersonal **il** to be omitted, this means that it is colloquial enough for **ne** to be omitted also: **\*ne faut pas oublier** is not a possible variant of **il ne faut pas oublier.** Here are some examples of the combined effects of the omission of **il** and **ne**:

| STANDARD | COLLOQUIAL |
|---|---|
| **Il ne faut pas oublier** | **Faut pas oublier** |
| **Il n'y a pas de problème** | **Y a pas de problème** |
| **Il n'y a qu'une solution** | **Y a qu'une solution** |
| **Il n'y a pas que Jean qui joue** | **Y a pas que Jean qui joue** |
| **Il n'y a qu'à changer de côté** | **Y a qu'à changer de côté** |

(In order, presumably, to provide a more 'popular' flavour, an unjustified apostrophe is sometimes inserted between **y** and **a** when such forms are used in written texts: **y'a pas.**)

Sentences like **y a qu'à changer de côté** (equivalent to 'all you need to do is . . .' or 'you just have to . . .') have given rise to a new noun, exemplified in the following remark by the Mayor of Lyon, Raymond Barre:

(1)  On ne gouverne pas avec des y'a qu'à. (FI)

(Des) y'a qu'à (phonetic transcription [jaka]) refers to 'saloon-bar' remedies to complex problems: **Y'a qu'à les bombarder/les expulser/les incarcérer/les fusiller tous** .... So (1) might be paraphrased as: 'You can't run a country on the basis of simplistic solutions'.

Note, finally, that unlike **il** in its impersonal uses, *personal* pronouns are rarely omitted in colloquial French, for reasons discussed in 8.1. The exceptions involve, on the one hand, phrases expressing indifference (**m'en fous**, etc.) and, on the other, a restricted group of 'verbs of knowledge and perception' when used negatively in the first-person singular: **connais pas**, **comprends pas**, **pense pas**, **sais pas** (the latter being an alternative to the equally familiar **ché pas**).

---

### EXERCISES

1†  Give two reasons for the asterisk in:

   *Est-ce facile de faire une omelette? – Oui, il est facile.

2†  Arrange in ascending order of informality:

   (a)  Ce serait prudent de faire attention.
   (b)  Il serait prudent de faire attention.
   (c)  Ça serait prudent de faire attention.

3†  Which one of the following should be asterisked?

   (a)  Il va être dur d'abandonner.
   (b)  Ce va être dur d'abandonner.
   (c)  Ça va être dur d'abandonner.

4†  Which one of the following is doubly inappropriate, and why?

   (a)  Cela a été possible de les sauver.
   (b)  Il a été possible de les sauver.
   (c)  Ça a été possible de les sauver.

5†  Only two of the following are likely. Which?

   (a)  Crois pas.
   (b)  Conduis pas.
   (c)  Fume pas.
   (d)  Voyage pas.
   (e)  M'en fiche.

### 3.3.2  *Ce/ça/cela* **and** *il/elle*

Even in standard French the **ce** of **c'est** can refer to a preceding noun (**Paris, c'est bien loin**). In the familiar and popular registers this use is extended to other verbs. If the subject noun is inanimate, **ce/ça** can be a straightforward alternative to **il/elle**. For example:

(2)  La Bibliothèque, comment ça marche? [*notice in Centre Pompidou library*] (RB)

(3)  Cette maison, ça a été construit il y a un an. (TF1)

(4)  y a une émission c'est c'est sur les sciences ils nous font montrer des expériences. J'sais pas comment ça s'appelle. (CR8)

Note how **il** is used in the following very similar utterance from the same conversation:

(5)  C'est un musée mais j'sais pas comment il s'appelle ce musée-là. (CR8)

In each of these examples, the noun in question refers to a specific, individual object. But the use of **ce/ça** can favour a generic or collective interpretation if the context or the meaning of the noun makes this plausible. In such cases, **ce/ça** and **il/elle** are not interchangeable:

(6)  La soupe, elle est bonne.
(7)  La soupe, c'est bon.

**Elle** refers to soup on a particular occasion (**la soupe que tu nous a préparée**); **ce** refers to soup in general ('soup is a good thing').
    Here are some further examples of 'generic' **ce/ça**:

(8)  Je te sers des épinards? – Non merci, j'ai horreur de ça.

(9)  Quelles sont les inconvénients de la voiture?
     –  Premièrement, c'est une menace pour l'environnement.

Generic reference is particularly common with indefinite and with plural nouns (in the latter case, the singular verb adds to the colloquial effect):

(10)  Ça peut se perdre, un dossier? (FI)

(11)  Un voyage ça ne s'achète pas partout [*travel advertisement*]. (RB)

(12)  les devoirs [*homework*] ça doit être obligé [ . . . ] (CRE62)

The following pairs (adapted from Cadiot 1988 and Carlier 1996) illustrate further subtle contrasts between specific reference and generic, 'collective' or 'group' reference:

(13)   Les légumes ils sont où?
(14)   Les légumes c'est où?

(15)   Tes livres ils sont lourds.
(16)   Tes livres c'est lourd.

The reference in (14) would be to the vegetable section of a supermarket (or some comparable grouping of vegetables). In (16) **c'est** focuses on the combined weight of the books.

With animate nouns, **ce/ça** is usually to be interpreted generically. The effect is more colloquial than with inanimates, but, contrary to a widespread assumption, is not necessarily derogatory:

(17)   Les riches c'est instruit, ça fréquente des députés, ça sait des choses. (FCR73)

(18)   Les docteurs sont toujours intrigués par les anomalies. Ça aime ça. (LBN)

(19)   Un prof c'est intelligent. (Cadiot 1988)

(20)   Un ministre ça ferme sa gueule ou ça démissionne. (J.-P. Chevènement)

The following example, on the other hand, does show a derogatory use:

(21)   Y a vraiment que ces cons de bourges [*bourgeois*] pour croire que les artistes peuvent créer que dans le dénuement. Je te foutrais ça au pain sec [*I'd put the bastards on bread and water*] pour voir s'y nous pondraient des chefs-d'oeuvre. (EHA97)

And **ça** is undoubtedly derogatory, or at best very condescending, in those relatively infrequent cases where it refers to a specific individual (who is thereby demoted to the status of an inanimate object):

(22)   –   T'as fini de déconner? demanda Gabriel.
           Le gérant poussa un cri de rage.
       –   Et ça [*Gabriel*] prétend causer le français, qu'il se met à hurler. (RQ176)

In all the above cases, **ça** replaces a subject pronoun. Note that in addition, it can occur as a direct object in cases where standard French would have **le/la/les**, particularly when an indirect object is also present (**on va leur**

**montrer ça** rather than **on va le/la/les leur montrer**), or in commands (**prends ça** for **prends-le** or **prends-les**). This is evidently part of a more general trend away from accumulating object pronouns before verbs, or placing them after verbs. For some discussion, see 8.1.1 and 8.1.2 (also Gadet 1992: 65).

---

## *EXERCISES*

6† Give more formal equivalents for the following, avoiding the use of **ça**. A simple substitution of **cela** for **ça** is possible in only one case: otherwise quite different expressions will have to be used.

   (a)   ça y est!
   (b)   ça ira?
   (c)   comme ça
   (d)   ben ça alors!
   (e)   ça va?
   (f)   ça va pas?

7   The following examples are from a collection of conversations involving ten- to twelve-year-old children. Classify the types of reference of **il/elle**, **ce/ça** (specific? generic?), and comment if appropriate:

   (a)   Les gâteaux secs c'est drôlement bon. (CR29)

   (b)   Ben oui puis elle est foutue ta télé. (CR74)

   (c)   Qu'est-ce t'as comme comme comme goûter? – D'la confiture d'abricots avec du pain. J'aime pas ça. (CR33)

   (d)   On croirait qu'elles sont à l'envers tes chaussettes? (CR51)

   (e)   Ah ben non mais c'est mieux les chaussons de maison quand même ça rentre mieux. Parce que tu sais c'est mes chaussons marrons. – Oui oui j'les ai vus. – Alors ils sont légers et on peut danser avec eux. (CR47)

   (f)   moi j'vais gagner un lapin puis je l'mettrai dans l'aquarium avec mon poisson [ . . . ] Remarque le lapin il se noierait et puis le le poisson sera dans son estomac. J'sais pas si ça mange des poissons? – Non, c'est plutôt herbivore. (CR70)

> **8**    M. Yaguello gives the following further examples (Yaguello
>     1998: 37).
>
>     (a)    Le lapin, j'aime ça.
>     (b)    Le lapin, je l'aime.
>     (c)    *Le chat, j'aime ça.
>
>     Comment on these, accounting in particular for the asterisk in
>     (c).

### 3.3.3   *Ça in questions and* ça *without an antecedent*

The original use of **ça**, as a demonstrative pronoun equivalent to 'that'
rather than as a personal pronoun equivalent to 'it', is still perfectly current
(**qu'est-ce que c'est que ça?**: 'what's that?'). Moreover, 'demonstrative **ça**'
often occurs in questions like (23) and (24), where it gives more substance to
the WH-words **où** and **pourquoi**:

(23)   Cet été on va beaucoup voyager. – Où ça?

(24)   Je suis vraiment furieux ce matin. – Pourquoi ça?

The antecedent here is the preceding statement. But demonstrative **ça** does
not always have as readily identifiable an antecedent as in (23)–(24) or the
examples discussed in 3.3.2.

Thus in (25)–(29) it refers rather vaguely to a situation or an ongoing
activity:

(25)   Ça bouchonne [*there are a lot of traffic hold-ups*] sur la Nationale
       90. (FI)

(26)   Tout d'un coup ça a freiné [*anti-drink-driving advertisement*]. (FI)

(27)   Et ça danse; ça danse partout d'ailleurs [*description of nightclub
       district*]. (NO)

(28)   En classe ça a beaucoup participé [*student referring to debate on
       terrorism*]. (FI)

(29)   A Marseille, ça causait déjà un curieux français. (IZ63)

Replacement of **ça** by **on** or **ils** would be possible in (27)–(29), but would
give a less strong impression of mass, almost orchestrated activity.

In (30)–(31) the reference of **ça** is even vaguer – it is little more than a 'dummy' subject:

(30)  Ça va barder [*there's going to be a hell of a row*].

(31)  Ça baigne; ça déchire; ça mousse; ça roule [*everything's fine*].

In (32), an antecedent is present in the form of an infinitive phrase:

(32)  Etre tout seul au milieu de la foule, ça craint [*youth employment advertisement*]. (RB) [*is a grim experience*]

But with **craindre** too, **ça** most often has no specific antecedent. In (33), it does not refer to **Olga**; the meaning is something like 'it's a bad situation':

(33)  Olga. Essoufflée. La trouille dans la gorge. Des mots entrecoupés. Ça craint. (LA153)

---

### *EXERCISES*

9†  Give English equivalents of the following 'ça questions', with suitable reinforcement of the WH-words:

(a)  Où ça? (b)  Pourquoi ça? (c)  Quand ça? (d)  Qui ça?
(e)  Comment ça?

10  Suggest English translations for:

(a)  Ça se drogue là-bas?
(b)  Comment ça va? – Ça gaze.
(c)  Ça coince du côté du boulevard périphérique.
(d)  Ça dérape sur l'autoroute du Nord.
(e)  Dépêche-toi: ça urge.
(f)  Passer une semaine chez eux, ça dose [*c'est désagréable*].
(g)†  Garçon, un sandwich au kangourou! Et que ça saute!

11  One or two of the verbs in the sentences considered in this section only ever occur after **ça**. Some have other uses, but then 'behave' in a different way grammatically. Identify as many verbs as you can that fall into these categories.

### 3.3.4    *Object pronouns in commands; 'ethic' uses;* nous deux . . . ; -zigue *pronouns*

#### (a)    Commands

In both standard and colloquial French the equivalents of 'take some' and 'touch it' are, respectively, **prends-en** and **touches-y** (pronounced with a liaison -*z*: *prends-z'en, touches-z'y*). But when a further pronoun (e.g. **me, te**) is added, there is a divergence. In standard French 'give me some (another)' and 'hold on to it' are, respectively, **donne-m'en (un autre)** and **tiens-t'y**. The rule is that **moi** and **toi** are contracted to **m'** and **t'** before **en** and **y**, but retain their full form otherwise (**donne-moi le journal, tiens-toi droit, donne-le-moi**). Colloquially this difference is disregarded, and the full forms are used in all cases. But, no doubt because of the influence of forms like **prends-en**, a liaison -*z* is, in the most popular usage, inserted into **donne-moi-en** and **tiens-toi-y**, so these commands are actually pronounced *donne-moi-z'en* and *tiens-toi-z'y*. (Sometimes the order of the pronouns is reversed: **donne-z'en-moi, tiens-z'y-toi**.) In fact, **z'en** can occur with other object pronouns too: **donne-lui-z'en un peu**, etc.

Again in the most popular register, a further levelling out of anomalies takes place in that **donne-le-moi** is sometimes replaced by **donne-moi-le**. This means that the same pronoun order is used as in statements (**il me l'a donné**: first person before third person).

It has to be said that, while **donne-m'en (un autre)** is undoubtedly stilted, **donne-moi-z'en** and, even more so, **donne-z'en-moi** have very popular overtones. Unfortunately, **donne-moi-en** (without the -*z*), far from being a satisfactory compromise, has a distinctly unnatural feel to it. So the usual way of expressing such commands in familiar (as opposed to popular) French is by abandoning the imperative altogether and using alternative structures like **tu m'en donnes!** or **tu vas m'en donner un autre!** (see also 8.1.3).

#### (b)    'Ethic' uses

The **moi** in **regarde-moi-ça!** is neither a direct object (like the **moi** in **regarde-moi!**), nor an indirect object (like the **moi** in **donne-moi-ça!**). Its purpose is simply to make the speaker's appeal to the listener more dramatic ('do it for my sake'). An English equivalent might, even more dramatically, involve the Almighty: 'Look at that, for God's/heaven's sake'.

In a somewhat more colloquial register, and in statements rather than in commands, **te** and **vous** can also be used as 'expletive' or 'ethic' pronouns. Here, too, the aim is simply to involve the listener – or in (36) and (37) the reader – more closely:

(34)   Qu'est-ce qu'il fout ce con-là que je vais te le redépasser [*car driver to passenger*]. (RB) [*you just watch me overtake him again!*]

(35)   [de la propagande] comme à l'époque de Goebbels qui t'balançait n'importe quoi dans la gueule des pauvres Berlinois qui suivaient comme des panurges [*moutons de Panurge*]. (FH)

(36)   Y a vraiment que ces cons de bourges [*bourgeois*] pour croire que les artistes peuvent créer que dans le dénuement. Je te foutrais ça au pain sec pour voir s'y nous pondraient des chefs-d'oeuvre. (EHA97)

(37)   nos missiles de l'Otan qui vous grillent les gens tout vifs. (NO)

## (c)   **Nous deux mon . . .**

Like **ti** interrogatives, the expression condemned in the following quotation belongs more to the mythology of *français populaire* than to the reality: everyone has heard of it, but it is not often encountered – these days, at any rate:

> *Nous deux mon chien, nous deux mon frère*, sont des expressions mal construites du français populaire ou *chien* et *frère* ne jouent aucun rôle grammatical. Il faut dire: *Moi et mon chien* (en se citant le premier parce que le second est un animal), mais, par tradition polie: *Mon frère et moi*. (Georgin 1959: 177)

## (d)   **-zigue** pronouns

There are a number of alternative personal pronouns in popular French, often used in a somewhat jocular way. The best known form a series based on the colloquialism **zig** or **zigue**, a rather dated equivalent of **type** or **mec**. Thus: **mézig(ue)**, **tézig(ue)**, **sézig(ue)** (or **cézigue**) for the first, second and third persons singular, respectively. There are parallels here with the use of 'yours truly' in English as an alternative to 'I/me', although this is familiar rather than popular. Like **ti** interrogatives and the **nous deux** expression just referred to, **-zigue** pronouns are more likely to be encountered today in written 'pseudo-popular' usage than in actual conversation. The first of the following examples is from a thriller, the second from a comic book:

(38)   Chez cézigue [*chez lui*] ça avait évolué différemment ce virus. (ASM30)

(39)   A la basse Deg le vautour, à la batterie Freddie le chat, à la rythmique Gérard le lézard, et mézigue Kebra à la gratte solo [*on solo guitar*]. (TJ24)

The tradition of alternative pronouns lives on in the *verlan* ('backslang') of teenagers on suburban estates. **Ouam, ouat** and **uil** are, respectively, **moi, toi** and **lui** with consonants and vowels reversed.

(40)   Ils sont déjà chez ouam, mes frères. (GD135)

(41)   Seca-ouat [*casse-toi*]. (GD135)

(42)   l'est vraiment chtarbé [*fou*], uil [ . . . ]. (GD135)

---

## EXERCISES

12†   Classify the phrases in each of the following groups as standard, familiar or popular:

(a)   (i) parlez-lui-en; (ii) parlez-lui-z'en; (iii) parlez-z'en-lui; (iv) tu vas lui en parler.

(b)   (i) accompagne-moi-z'y; (ii) accompagne-m'y; (iii) accompagne-z'y-moi; (iv) tu m'y accompagnes!

(c)   (i) sers-toi-z'en; (ii) sers-z'en-toi; (iii) sers-t'en; (iv) tu t'en sers!

13†   Identify ethic and non-ethic uses of pronouns among the following:

(a)   La vérité, je vais te le dire.
(b)   Mes cadeaux, je vais te les montrer.
(c)   Ce type, je vais te lui flanquer une baffe.
(d)   Au juge, je vais te lui dire toute la vérité.
(e)   Mon frère, je vais te présenter à lui.
(f)   Le petit déjeuner, je vais te le préparer.
(g)   Cette baraque, je vais te la ficher en l'air.

14†   Suggest non-colloquial equivalents for:

(a)   Nous deux ma bourgeoise.
(b)   Nous deux mon fiston.
(c)   Nous deux mon chat.

15   Deduce from the following the grammatical contexts in which
     **-zigue** pronouns can occur. Is **mézig(ue)**, for example, an
     equivalent of **moi, je** or **me** – or all three, or none of them?

     (a)   Quand je paume, mézig [ . . . ] ça rate jamais (MM22)

     (b)   Y a un gonze [*homme*] en bas pour tézigue (MM36)

     (c)   mais mézigue, chez Charlot, ce qui me botte le plus,
           c'est encore la Lucie (MM56)

     (d)   aller se pager [*coucher*] avec tézigue pour que dalle
           (MM60)

     (e)   monter sur l'affaire avec cézigue (MM64)

     (f)   j'ai pour tézigue une combine de première (MM108)

     But not:

     (g)   *mézigue vais y aller
     (h)   *dépêche-tézigue
     (i)   *on a vu cézigue

# 4 Verbs

## 4.1 Tenses and moods

When referring to past and future time, colloquial usage has a tendency to favour compound tenses (formed with auxiliary verbs: **j'ai fait**, **je vais faire**) over simple tenses (those without a 'helping' auxiliary: **je fis**, **je ferai**). But, contrary to what is sometimes assumed, the subjunctive mood continues to be an important feature of all varieties.

### *4.1.1* Passé simple

Probably the best-known difference between oral and written French concerns the past historic (*passé simple*) and the imperfect subjunctive (*imparfait du subjonctif*), and their absence – or alleged absence – from spoken usage. However, it would be wrong to place the two tenses on the same footing: the imperfect subjunctive has to a large extent fallen into disuse in the written language too; the past historic, on the other hand, retains a foothold in speech as well as continuing to be a conspicuous feature of much French writing.

One indication of its tenacity is the widespread convention whereby novelists who make extensive use of colloquial dialogue – note the *verlan* in (1) – nevertheless put verbs into the past historic in the accompanying narration, sometimes with literary inversions:

(1) Le grand black s'approcha.
    – Pourquoi y t'ont pécho, les keufs? [*pourquoi les policiers t'ont-ils arrêté?*] dit-il à Mourrabed. (IZ181)

And colloquial verbs in colloquial contexts routinely take past historic endings:

(2) Ella rigola, se foutant en caisse [*se moquant d'elle-même*] toute seule [...] (EHF82)

However, the past historic is far from being an obligatory feature of the written code. Alongside texts like those just quoted, there are large numbers of others in which the perfect (*passé composé*) or the present either systematically replace it, or occur in alternation with it.

Conversely, the past historic is by no means unknown in oral French: even children are capable of using it – at least in the third person, and with a varying degree of accuracy. (Children's books contain numerous examples of the past historic.) In the following, a six-year-old tells the story of a dog which has lost its owner:

(3) [ . . . ] un jour il ne revenut [*revint*] pas. Il avait fait un accident, il attendut [*attendit*] des heures et des heures, pauvre petit chien, il attendit des nuits et des nuits, des matins, des après-midi, des nuits et nuits, mais il ne revenait pas. Alors un jour, le pauvre petit chien mourut de faim . . . mais un jour on l'enterra [ . . . ] (DH149)

(Note the speaker's problems in forming the past historic of **revenir** and **attendre**.)

The oral past historic typically occurs in narrative discourse like this, especially if the setting is felt to be not quite that of an ordinary conversation. An example is given by Blanche-Benveniste (1997): the speaker has been asked to talk about her honeymoon – in front of a microphone, which she finds intimidating. The perfect alternates with the more 'ceremonial' past historic:

(4) Je vais vous raconter comment s'est passé mon voyage de noces. Après notre mariage, qui se déroula le 14 octobre 1990, euh, nous partîmes – c'était un samedi – et nous partîmes le lundi matin en avion. (BBA52)

A little later, after a few more verbs in the past historic, she reverts to the perfect, having by this time become accustomed to the microphone.

Moreover, some speakers are prone to insert the past historic of **être** or **avoir** (especially) into discourse that otherwise is not especially literary. This may be for dramatic effect:

(5) Ça s'est passé en 1715. – Ah, 1715: ce fut l'hiver cruel où il y eut tant de morts [ . . . ]! (RB)

Or it may mark a temporary switch to a more formal mode, as when newsreaders or reporters are providing background biographical information about a figure otherwise referred to in the perfect or the present:

(6) A 13 heures nous parlons au général Schmidt qui fut le commandant français durant la guerre du Golfe. (FI)

## EXERCISES

1†  Identify and comment on the past tenses used in the following
    excerpt from a child's narration of the story of *Little Red Riding
    Hood*:

> Puis après [le loup] se metta dans le lit [ . . . ] Et puis il
> enleva ses vêtements. l'les, i'les prit et il se mit dans le
> lit. [ . . . ] Puis après il y a le petit chaperon rouge, i'sortit
> de la chambre, il prit des grosses pierres et les mit dans
> le ventre du loup. Alors le loup alors le loup quand il
> s'est réveillé, il avait vu, il avait vu les trois personnes.
> Il a voulu, il avait voulu les manger. Il a sauté et puis
> tellement qu'il était lourd il retomba sur son cou. Il sortit
> et puis il est, il est tombé sur le cou alors i's'est tué sur
> le coup. (CR9–10)

2   Here are some comments made by children when asked about
    the past historic (Pazery 1988: 138). What light do they shed
    on their attitudes towards this tense, their knowledge of it, and
    their use of it?

> (a)  le passé simple c'est très joli à l'écoute mais [ . . . ]
>      quand je l'emploie c'est dur dans les rédactions, ça ne
>      me vient pas à l'esprit, mais c'est très joli: ça évoque
>      le passé, les contes de fées. Le passé simple, c'est
>      beau mais snob, riche, distingué, drôle, amusant
>      parfois, je ne sais pas.

> (b)  Le passé simple 'Quel nom'! On aurait dû l'appeler
>      *passé dur*. Ce n'est pas 'simple', c'est 'dur'.

3   Not only children have problems in forming the past historic,
    as the following suggests:

> – M'autorisez-vous donc à de nouveau formuler la
>   proposition interrogative qu'il y a quelques instants
>   j'énonça devant vous?
> – J'énonçai, dit l'obscur.
> – J'énonçais, dit Trouscaillon.
> – J'énonçai sans esse.
> – J'énonçai, dit enfin Trouscaillon. Ah! la grammaire
>   c'est pas mon fort. (RQ218)

What humorous point is Raymond Queneau making here?

### *4.1.2* **Passé surcomposé**

In literary French the past historic of **être** or **avoir** forms part of a compound tense known as the past anterior (*passé antérieur*), used after conjunctions like **quand**, **lorsque**, **dès que** or **aussitôt que** when the main verb is in the past historic:

(7) Quand il <u>eut terminé</u>, il se coucha (past historic of **avoir** + past participle = past anterior).

(8) Quand il <u>fut sorti</u>, il monta dans sa voiture (past historic of **être** + past participle = past anterior).

If the main clause is in the imperfect, then the pluperfect is used after **quand**, not the past anterior:

(9) (Tous les jours) quand il <u>avait terminé</u>, il se couch<u>ait</u>.

Just as **<u>eut</u> terminé** goes with **se coucha**, so **av<u>ait</u> terminé** goes with **se couch<u>ait</u>**. And similarly with verbs taking **être**: **Quand il ét<u>ait</u> sorti, il montait** ....

In more colloquial varieties, where the main verb is in the perfect not the past historic, then, logically enough, so is **avoir**:

(10) Quand il <u>a eu</u> terminé, il est sorti

and even **être**:

(11) Quand il <u>a été</u> sorti, il est monté dans sa voiture.

This tense is known as the *passé surcomposé* ('double compound past') and, like the past anterior, occurs typically after time conjunctions (**dès que**, **quand**, etc.):

(12) Une fois qu'il a eu tiré, moi j'ai tiré [*shopowner recounting a hold-up*]. (FI)

(13) Alors quand il a été parti, j'ai dit à Roger [ . . . ] il a pas l'air facile le p'tit pépère. (IVR)

(14) Quand je les ai eu mangées, elle me dit: «Tu sais combien qu'ça coûte?» (DF776)

In the last example, **dit** can be assumed to be a present tense (this speaker makes no use of the past historic). But as it refers to a past event, it is equivalent to **a dit**, so the use of **ai eu mangées** is compatible with the pattern given above.

In fact, usage is by no means fully consistent. Instead of the *passé surcomposé*, the pluperfect or perfect are at least as likely to be heard in conversation, even though such uses depart from the tense sequence required by strict logic:

(15)  Dès qu'il est parti, il s'est rappelé que ... (HF157)

(16)  Après qu'il a terminé il est parti. (HF157)

---

## EXERCISES

4†  Insert the tenses of **boire** and **appeler** appropriate to the level of formality indicated:

(a)  Quand il _____ son vin, il _____ le garçon (formal).

(b)  Quand il _____ son vin, il _____ le garçon (conversational with strict tense sequence).

(c)  Quand il _____ son vin, il _____ le garçon (conversational with loose tense sequence, first possibility).

(d)  Quand il _____ son vin, il _____ le garçon (conversational with loose tense sequence, second possibility).

5  How useful and realistic is the advice offered in the following (from a guide to the correct use of French)?

> *Le passé surcomposé.* Cette forme, qui n'est pas un modèle de légèreté, consiste en un curieux redoublement de l'auxiliaire *avoir*, comme dans: «Dès qu'elle a eu fini de parler, son frère a dit ce qu'il pensait». Ici encore, c'est le *passé antérieur* qui s'impose: «Dès qu'elle eut fini ... » De la même façon, on évitera de dire: «Sitôt qu'ils ont eu terminé ... » au profit de: «Sitôt qu'ils eurent terminé» ... pour autant qu'on ne considère pas hâtivement ce temps comme mort et enterré! (Capelovici 1990: 257)

### 4.1.3   Future and conditional

Statistical surveys, as well as informal observations, suggest that the simple future (**je verrai**) is being overhauled by the compound future (**je vais voir**). Investigations conducted in the 1950s and 1960s show that, in written usage, there were between nine and fifteen uses of the simple future for every one use of the compound, whereas in spoken French of a not particularly colloquial kind, the proportion was only two to one (Muller 1985). In the conversations analysed by Denise François (1974), her principal informant uses the simple future nineteen times as compared with twenty-nine times for the compound.

Even so, the process of replacement still has a long way to go. And, despite a large area of overlap, the two future tenses are by no means interchangeable. Thus, as Blanche-Benveniste (1997) points out, a statement like **une femme sera toujours une femme**, which expresses a general 'truth', could not be replaced by \***une femme va toujours être une feme**. Conversely, while **on va avoir un enfant** is a plausible utterance, it is difficult to ascribe any very clear meaning to **on aura un enfant**.

This suggests that, in standard French at any rate, events designated by the compound future need already to be on their way to happen at the time of speaking. This is in accordance with the literal meaning of **aller**, and is reflected in examples like **il va être midi** ('it's nearly midday') or **il va avoir douze ans** ('he's just coming up to twelve'), and in peremptory commands like:

(17)   Vous allez me donner votre nom, votre âge et votre adresse. (FI)

The speaker 'takes it for granted' that the action requested is about to happen.

According to Blanche-Benveniste, predictable events of this sort are the kind most commonly referred to in conversation, hence the prevalence of the compound future. On the other hand, when the events in question are hypothetical or longer-term, the simple future is more natural:

(18)   Si c'est complet, où c'est que t'iras? (DF791)

Predictability is, however, a rather elastic concept, and many colloquial examples can be found with a compound future where the standard language would use the simple tense. Sometimes the two alternate:

(19)   Pour de Gaulle de toute façon je crois qu'il va falloir qu'il se retire, on arrivera pas à le . . . le supprimer. (JE102)

(20)    La Cinquième va faire des émissions pour notre connaissance et
        tout ça, mais nous on sera en classe quand ça va passer, c'est pas
        très logique. (LFM70)

In (20) the compound future occurs after a time conjunction (**quand**), something which would not be possible in standard French. Further examples:

(21)    Ils vont bondir dans leur fauteuil dès qu'ils vont lire ça. (NO)

(22)    C'est pour Bernard, quand il va sortir de taule. (TF1)

And sometimes it is used of events which seem quite remote or hypothetical:

(23)    un jour on va trouver une belle cité dans ce coin-là, et ils seront
        bien hein (DF830–1)

(24)    Le maire [ . . . ] il fait faire des piscines et des salles de sport pour
        les jeunes, pour être sûr qu'ils vont voter pour lui plus tard.
        (LFM147)

So the difference between the two tenses is increasingly a matter of register
rather than one of meaning. A contributory factor to the decline of the
simple future is no doubt the relative complexity of its forms (see 7.4 and
8.1).

Turning to the conditional, note that standard sentences like **si j'étais toi,
je la mettrais à la porte** can be reformulated familiarly by using the conditional itself to mark the hypothetical assumption ('if I were you'). This
makes it possible to omit **si**. The result is a sentence with a conditional in
both clauses:

(25)    Je serais toi, j'la foutrais dehors. (PS62)

The same applies to past conditionals:

(26)    On l'aurait pas dit, je l'aurais pas deviné. (EXP)

In popular usage, **que** can be used to link the two clauses (paradoxically,
this possibility is also available in formal literary French, but not in intermediate registers):

(27)    On l'aurait vu qu'on l'aurait pendu à un arbre. (RFC30)

In the most popular varieties, **si** can be retained despite the conditional:

(28)   Si j'aurais su [standard: *si j'avais su*], j'aurais pas venu. (Catchphrase from the film *La Guerre des boutons*)

(29)   si ça aurait été le contraire [ . . . ] il l'emboutissait pareil [*letter to a motor insurance company*] (EDJ)

The last example, with an imperfect instead of a conditional in the main clause, shows a complete reversal of the standard pattern, which would be: **si cela avait été le contraire, il l'aurait embouti . . . .**

---

## EXERCISES

6† Why is the compound future acceptable in standard as well as in colloquial French in the following?

(a)   Mais c'est un fou; mais il va se tuer hein [*reference to a car being driven at excessive speed*]. (DF821)

(b)   Nous allons passer le pont d'Argenteuil [*passenger on bus approaching a bridge*]. (DF821)

(c)   Elle va s'écrouler cette maison [*reference to a dilapidated building*]. (RB)

(d)   J'vais t'dire, j'vais t'dire, quand on a été à Thionville hein [ . . . ] [*introductory conversational formula*] (FH)

7† In which of the following does the compound future have colloquial overtones, and why?

(a)   Le blé qu'on met dans le pain, c'est sacré pour les Français. Va y avoir une révolution s'ils déconnent avec ça. (LFM44)

(b)   Attendez, je vais voir. (RB)

(c)   Maintenant la mère, dès qu'elle va se voir dans un miroir elle va pleurer parce qu'elle verra les yeux de son fils [*reference to a mother who has been given a corneal graft from her dead son*]. (LFM11)

(d)   C'est lui qui va s'en aller, comme ça ils vont avoir peur quand ils vont être seuls, et ils vont établir la paix [*reference to a possible departure of the President, leaving rival party members to settle their quarrels*]. (LFM84)

(e)   On va être trempé. – Oui. – Ben dis donc on ferait mieux de rester pour voir l'autre, l'autre film, le même quoi parce que ça va recommencer [*speakers emerging from cinema into a downpour*]. (CR93)

(f)   Dépêchons-nous, le train va partir. (CR94)

8†   Rephrase as standard conditional sentences:

(a)   On l'aurait pas dit, je l'aurais pas deviné. (EXP)

(b)   Yves Montand il aurait été SDF, personne n'en voudrait [ . . . ] (LFM16)

(c)   Il se serait agi de Karajan, on aurait agi autrement. (NO)

(d)   Tu partirais une semaine que tu manquerais pas. (CE227)

(e)   j'ai plus de rétro [*rétroviseur*] gauche, ça serait le droit je m'en foutrais complètement, mais c'est le gauche hein [*bus driver radioing HQ*] (JE65)

9†   Reconstruct the original colloquial form of:

(a)   Si j'avais été seule, ça n'aurait pas eu d'importance.

(b)   Si je n'étais pas chez moi, le logement serait dans son nom à lui.

(c)   Moi, si j'étais président [ . . . ] je serais triste [ . . . ]

(d)   Si tu avais remonté la rue [ . . . ] jusqu'à la grille, arrivé là, tu aurais vu, sur le côté à droite, que la rue continue.

### 4.1.4 *Indicative and subjunctive*

According to Henri Bauche, in his 1920s study of colloquial French: 'Le subjonctif tend à disparaître du langage populaire'. As far as the imperfect subjunctive is concerned, this process has been completed – and not only in popular usage. But eighty years on, the situation of the present subjunctive (and the perfect: **qu'elle soit venue**) seems considerably more healthy than Bauche's comment would imply, despite some encroachment by the indicative.

There is of course a good deal of variation between speakers, as some are more strongly influenced by the standard than others. But the patterns of usage in themselves seem fairly systematic: it is not the case that the use of the subjunctive is simply becoming haphazard and unpredictable.

After expressions of volition and necessity (**elle veut que, j'ordonne que, il faut que, il est nécessaire que**), the subjunctive is as widely used in all varieties of colloquial French as in the standard language. Its continued viability is also demonstrated by the fact that it occurs after many newly coined familiar expressions:

(30)   ce serait idiot qu'ils fassent la guerre (LFM140)

(31)   Elle n'était pas très chaude que je vienne l'aider. (BBA90)

Indeed, colloquial French sometimes uses a subjunctive after **dire**, whereas the norm requires the infinitive:

(32)   Il m'a dit que j'aille le voir. (ASA92)

Moreover, some *français populaire* speakers add [j] to certain subjunctive forms, thereby differentiating them from the indicative, from which they would otherwise be indistinguishable. For example, **qu'ils croyent** [kil kʁwaj] instead of standard **qu'ils croient** [kil kʁwa]. Similarly with **voir** and, indeed, **être**:

(33)   un film dangereux qu'il fallait pas qu'il voye (JS304)

(34)   Alors, je disais comme ça, c'est pas possible que Maurice y soye déjà arrivé. (AM190)

However, after expressions of feeling ( **je suis content que, ils ont peur que, ça m'étonne que**), there is a certain amount of fluctuation:

(35)   C'est embêtant qu'il est pas là. (BM242)

(36)   Evidemment, c'est embêtant qu'il y ait autant d'inégalité. (LFM40)

(37)   Je suis heureux qu'il y a une pièce de plus. (BBA41)

And the subjunctive has certainly lost ground in its more recondite uses – notably with various negative expressions (**je ne pense pas que**, **il n'y a pas ... qui ...**), after superlatives and associated adjectives like **seul** or **premier** (**le seul ... qui ...**, **le plus grand ... qui ...**), or with reference to antecedents the existence of which is hypothetical (**je cherche un singe qui sache parler**):

(38)   la plus grosse boîte qu'il y a ici, à Caen (JS309)

(39)   je ne crois pas qu'on peut faire grand'chose (JS309)

The other main use of the subjunctive in the standard language is after conjunctions like **pour que**, **bien que**, **avant que**, **jusqu'à ce que**, etc. Here the situation in colloquial French varies from one conjunction to another. The indicative is quite often used with **bien que** and **jusqu'à ce que**, especially when a factual situation is referred to (this is understandable enough, and in fact resembles pre-seventeenth-century usage):

(40)   bien que je savais que cette possibilité existait (L. Jospin)

**Pour que** and **avant que**, on the other hand, are almost always followed by the subjunctive. Indeed, so engrained is its use with **avant que** that it very often occurs with **après que** as well, in defiance of the recommendations of the normative grammarians:

(41)   après que deux coups durs ne soient portés contre la police (FI)

Note also the 'hypercorrect' use of expletive **ne** in this example.

An analysis of recordings of conversations involving apprentices and college students in Caen (Sand 1983: 311) reflects the various tendencies presented in 4.1.3. Here are some of the findings. The figures show the number of occurrences in the corpus: in standard French the indicative column would show zero for all the categories.

|                                    | Subjunctive | Indicative |
|------------------------------------|-------------|------------|
| verbs of volition/necessity        | 111         | 7          |
| verbs of feeling                   | 6           | 6          |
| negative verbs of saying/believing | 12          | 17         |
| after superlatives/negatives       | 2           | 11         |
| clauses with **bien que**          | 9           | 14         |
| clauses with **pour que**          | 41          | 1          |

## EXERCISES

10† What is non-standard about each of the following?

(a) France-Inter est la seule radio qu'on peut capter à bord du *Foch*. (FI)

(b) La seule remarque qu'on peut faire. (FI)

(c) il y a qu'un pigeon qui peut accepter ça! (LFM105)

(d) il faut au moins en manger deux morceaux, [c'est] le moins que tu peux faire [ . . . ] (DF777)

(e) Il faut faire des routes où on peut dépasser les 130 [*à l'heure*]. (LFM154)

(f) bien que des giboulées sont toujours possibles. (FI)

(g) Bien que nous sommes tous pollueurs, nous ne sommes pas tous sensibilisés aux problèmes environnementaux. (LG48)

(h) Je ne pense pas que c'est le cas. (FI: head teacher)

11† What do the following tell us about the viability of the subjunctive in everyday speech?

(a) Moi, je trouve ça lâche que les Serbes soient si violents sur des gens qui ne se défendent pas. (LFM140)

(b) C'est pas normal qu'on ait si peu de moyens. (FI)

(c) C'est logique qu'il y ait une répartition. (FI)

(d) des fois qu'ils fassent pareil pour nous (DF785)

(e) ça m'emmerde qu'il revienne (RB)

(f) je crois que j'aurais préféré qu'elle puisse passer (DF772)

(g) Dis-leur qu'ils viennent pour me purger mon circuit d'eau [ . . . ] et qu'ils amènent quand même de la flotte en même temps [*driver of broken-down bus to HQ*]. (JE65)

## 4.2 Past participles, agreement, auxiliaries

The intricate rules about past participle agreement are one of the thornier areas of standard French grammar, and another example of the legacy of the seventeenth- and eighteenth-century grammarians. One or two other aspects of agreement are also considered in this section, and so is the use of **avoir** and/or **être** in compound tenses involving the past participle.

### 4.2.1 Past participle agreement

Basically the rules require past participles to agree in number and gender with the preceding direct object when the auxiliary is **avoir**, and with the subject when the auxiliary is **être**:

- **il a écrit les lettres** (the direct object **les lettres** follows the verb, so **écrit** does not agree).
- **il les a écrites** (the direct object **les**, referring to **les lettres**, precedes the verb, so the past participle takes the feminine plural form, **écrites**).
- **elle est arrivée** (**elle** is subject and **être** is the auxiliary, so **arrivée** agrees).
- **elle a écrit** (**elle** is subject again, but this time the auxiliary is **avoir**, so no agreement).

In spoken French, there is usually no audible difference between masculine and feminine, singular and plural past participles: **envoyé, envoyée, envoyés** and **envoyées** are all pronounced [ɑ̃vwaje], making the rules of agreement irrelevant. But there are a small number of verbs where there *is* a difference in pronunciation, with a final consonant present in the feminine but not in the masculine (see 7.3). **Ecrire** [ekʀi, ekʀit] is one example; others include **faire** [fɛ, fɛt] and **prendre** [pʀi, pʀiz].

The tendency in familiar and popular French is to treat these verbs like the others, and dispense with the agreement in all cases:

(1) Ces lois contraignantes que le peuple n'a jamais vraiment admis. (F. Mitterrand)

In the following, both occurrences of **mis en (application)** were pronounced [mi ɑ̃ . . . ], not [mi zɑ̃ . . . ]:

(2) ils savent pas exactement si la fameuse réforme portuaire a vraiment été mis en application, elle a été mis en application dans les tout petits ports [ . . . ] (FH)

However, when a past participle directly modifies a noun (**une documentation écrite**) it is being used as an adjective and is made to agree like one – in colloquial as well as in formal usage.

The influence of the norm (and the importance attached to the standard rules by the education system) means that usage fluctuates: the more formal the circumstances, the more likely speakers are to monitor themselves and to make the agreements. But as (1) shows, the tendency to non-agreement affects the highest in the land – even in the fairly formal situation of a broadcast interview.

Although social and situational factors are uppermost in determining whether speakers follow the standard rules or not, there is some evidence that purely grammatical factors play a part too (M. Gibier, quoted by Blanche-Benveniste 1990: 202–6).

For example, assuming equivalence of register, a participle is (even) less likely to agree when it is within a sentence than when it is at the end (**la nouvelle que j'ai appris hier** as compared with **. . . que j'ai apprise**). Whether the participle comes last or not, agreement is more likely with third-person **la** and **les** (**je l'ai prise, je les ai prises**) than with other persons (**me, te, nous, vous**). So **on m'a admis** is often used by female as well as male speakers. But the presence of **lui** inhibits agreement, even when **le** or **la** is present (**il la lui a appris**).

The same investigator detects a strong tendency for the past participle of **faire** actually to agree if it is followed by the infinitive (e.g. **je l'ai faite bouillir**). This is doubly paradoxical, since such an agreement is impossible in standard French. Other commentators have suggested that it is a case of 'hypercorrection' (see 1.6). But why hypercorrection should be triggered by **faire** + infinitive in particular is unclear.

---

## EXERCISES

1†  Here are some further examples of past participles used on television by well-known public figures – with no agreement. Give the standard forms in each case. (All examples are taken from Pastre 1986: 148–9.)

(a)  Une expression que l'on a repris. (Valéry Giscard d'Estaing: former President of the Republic)

(b)  Les chansons qu'il a fait pour vous [ . . . ] (Frédéric Rossif: singer)

(c)  La lettre que vous m'avez écrit [ . . . ] (Robert Sabatier: novelist)

(d)  Les concessions que j'ai fait au propos de [ . . . ] (Jean-Claude Bourret: television presenter)

(e)  C'est une chose que j'ai appris. (Jacques Chirac: at the time Mayor of Paris)

(f)  pour dire les choses que le Président a dit (Paul Quilès: government minister)

(g)  C'est comme ça qu'il m'a séduit. (Anne-Marie Carrière: broadcasting personality)

2†  The participles in the following sentences all agree in the approved fashion. So why are the sentences inauthentic?

(a)  Où tu les as mises mes gommes?

(b)  Au moins on voit qu'il l'a écrite tout seul sa lettre.

(c)  Pourquoi qu'il l'a pas prise sa voiture?

3†  The following are from the data which form the basis for Monique Gibier's investigation (see above). What grammatical factors lie behind the agreement or non-agreement in each case?

(a)  la pile que tu as fait là (bank clerk)

(b)  pour les raisons que j'ai dites (student)

(c)  elle s'est faite remarquer (primary teacher)

(d)  ils l'ont mise à l'hôpital la fille (student)

(e)  ils emmènent leurs parents et ça ça m'a surpris (schoolmistress)

(f)  des tableaux qu'elle s'était faite donner (art teacher)

### 4.2.2   The views of commentators

Non-agreement of the past participle is one of the areas of colloquial French which has been most strongly criticized by upholders of the norm.

The collector of the sentences in Exercise 1 comments on them as follows:

Affligeant, et d'autant plus que bon nombre de ces gens célèbres publient des livres. Cette accumulation d'exemples entachés de fautes grossières montre bien que trop de personnes en vue, de personnages même, ignorent la règle du participe passé des verbes conjugués avec l'auxiliaire *avoir*. Elle est pourtant simple: on fait l'accord avec *le complément d'objet direct placé avant le participe passé.* (Pastre 1986: 149)

This may be contrasted with the view of a descriptive linguist writing in the 1960s:

La distinction du genre a été retenue dans la langue écrite en ce qui concerne le participe passé employé dans certaines constructions (lorsqu'il vient après le complément direct du verbe). On doit écrire, et l'on devrait dire: *Il n'a pas reçu la lettre que je lui ai écrite, les lettres que je lui ai écrites*, etc. [ ... ] Mais, dans trop de cas, l'accord est purement graphique: *son arrivée l'a bouleversée, les a bouleversées*, etc., aussi, comme c'est le cas de le dire, il demeure lettre morte. Pour cette raison et d'autres encore sur lesquelles il n'y a pas lieu de s'arrêter ici, l'accord du participe passé a fait son temps. Il ne s'entend pratiquement plus dans la langue parlée, même celle des personnes cultivées [ ... ] En épluchant les colonnes des quotidiens, par exemple, on peut faire tous les jours une ample moisson de ces fautes d'orthographe et même parfois de prononciation qui ne choquent plus personne parce qu'elle sont devenues universelles. (Sauvageot 1962: 87)

### EXERCISE

4   Compare and contrast the views of these two commentators.

### 4.2.3   Other agreement issues

In standard French, **ce sont, ce seront**, etc. are used if a plural noun is referred to: **Ce sont mes amis qui m'ont donné ce cadeau.** In informal usage,

**être** usually agrees with **ce** in such cases, not with the noun: **C'est mes amis qui m'ont donné ce cadeau**. Other examples:

(3)  Il y a des fois des femmes musulmanes qui commandent leur mari et c'est eux qui obéissent [ . . . ] (LFM34)

(4)  Ça c'est pas des pizzas qu'on achète dans le commerce. (RL33)

(5)  Les zonards [*jeunes voyous*], c'est des mecs cool. (IZ53)

One or two less widely encountered cases should also be noted, in which the most popular French in particular shows different agreement patterns from the standard language.

Firstly, a divergence affecting number agreement. This involves cases where a singular collective noun (e.g. **la majorité**) refers to a plurality of people or things – in other words is singular grammatically, but plural in terms of meaning (semantically). In such cases, the standard rule is for grammatical agreement to take precedence over semantic, and for the verb to be singular (**la majorité est**).

Even in quite formal usage, however, semantic agreement is sometimes preferred, and it invariably is in colloquial French: **la majorité sont, le plus grand nombre sont, la plus grande partie sont**. The standard language follows this pattern itself in the case of **la plupart**: **la plupart sont**, not *\*la plupart est**.

In the most colloquial French, things are taken still further. Semantic agreements like the following are regarded as serious deviations from the norm:

(6)  Malheureusement elle était toute seule de sa famille, le reste sont en Belgique et en Hollande. (PG36)

(7)  Tout le monde sont venus. (GFP60)

Some divergencies of person agreement should also be noted.

In standard French relative clauses, the person of the verb matches that of the antecedent. Usually the third person is involved: **l'homme qui a, ceux qui vont**. But there are a few cases where the first or second person occurs: **c'est moi qui ai, c'est nous qui sommes, c'est toi qui as**. Informal French extends the third-person pattern to these cases too: **c'est moi qui a gagné** and (more colloquial) **c'est nous qui sont partis**.

(8)  C'est pas moi qui va tout changer. (PB131)

As was explained in 2.3.3, alternative formulations are also available: **c'est moi que j'ai gagné** or **c'est nous qu'on est partis**. And in a large number of cases, there is of course no audible difference between the standard and colloquial forms (**c'est toi qui a/as**).

Similarly, standard French requires a first-person verb in **Jean et moi (nous) sommes partis**, but the third person is sometimes used in popular speech: **Jean et moi sont partis** – no doubt because of the analogy with **Jean et Pierre sont partis**. However, it has to be said that **Jean et moi on est parti(s)** is a great deal more likely, whatever the degree of informality.

---

## EXERCISES

5† The linguist Pierre Guiraud, discussing 'le reste sont en Belgique', gives the following example sentences (Guiraud 1965: 36):

(a) Aucun de ses camarades ne l'ont vu.

(b) La foule qui remplit les rues observent un silence absolu.

(c) Plus d'un ministre n'ont pas caché l'impression produite.

Though there is no reason to doubt the general tendency that is being illustrated, these particular sentences might be considered slightly suspect. Why?

6† Insert into the following frame (i) appropriate colloquial and (ii) appropriate standard forms of the verbs indicated (present tense). In which cases is there no audible difference between the two forms, and in which cases is there no audible or visible difference?

C'est moi qui _____
(a) aller
(b) sortir
(c) décider
(d) être
(e) finir
(f) mettre
(g) vouloir

### 4.2.4 *Auxiliary verbs* avoir **and** être

In standard French, the great majority of verbs form their perfect tense with **avoir**, only a dozen or so taking **être**. Occasionally, both auxiliaries are possible, with the choice of one or the other corresponding to a difference of meaning. For example, **il a divorcé** and **il est divorcé**. The first of these focuses on the event ('he got divorced'), the second on the resulting state ('he is divorced'). Similarly with **il a disparu** ('he disappeared' – and may or may not have reappeared) and **il est disparu** ('he has disappeared' – and has not reappeared).

In popular French **avoir** is sometimes found with verbs which take **être** in standard and, for that matter, familiar usage:

(9)    une auto qu'aurait venu par la gauche [*letter to insurance company*] (EDJ)

(10)    C'est un ancien ouvrier [ . . . ] il a monté en grade. (PB146)

(11)    Si j'aurais su, j'aurais pas venu. (Catchphrase from the film *La Guerre des boutons*)

This tendency can also affect reflexive verbs:

(12)    Elle s'en a racheté un autre. (JE36)

(13)    Depuis que je m'ai rencontré au carrefour avec M.X [ . . . ] [*letter to insurance company*] (EDJ)

Needless to say, such uses are particularly stigmatized by all normative commentators. In fact, the use of **avoir** as an auxiliary instead of **être** is one of those stereotypical features of working-class usage which in reality occur less systematically than is sometimes supposed. In the following 200-word stretch of discourse, for instance, the speaker makes one non-standard choice of auxiliary (underlined) and five standard choices, namely:

(14)    ils s'sont dit [ . . . ] <u>ils ont arrivé</u> [ . . . ] je me suis dit [ . . . ] qu'était plongée dans la Seine [ . . . ] moi j'étais rentré [ . . . ] il est p'être noyé [ . . . ] (DF819)

In the following conversation, some hesitation can be observed before the speaker finally opts for the non-standard form:

(15) – les leaders i' n'ont pas, i' ne sont pas [ ... ]
 – i' sont pas encore dans le [ ... ]
 – non, non, i'z'ont pas encore entré totalement dans les réformes
 [ ... ] (FH)

And further fluctuation can be seen in:

(16) Une fois on a rentré dans un couloir [ ... ], on pouvait plus sortir,
 on a resté au moins plus d'une heure [ ... ] on est retombés dans
 l'aut' bout d'la rue [ ... ] on est rentrés à deux heures du matin.
 (IVR)

However, for some speakers (though not for all by any means), this kind
of usage is not a straightforward replacement of **être** by **avoir**, or a random
fluctuation between the two, but an extension of the standard difference
(mentioned above) between **a divorcé** and **est divorcé**.

Thus **il a tombé** can mean 'he fell down (some time ago, and may well
have got to his feet by now)', as against **il est tombé**: 'he fell down (and is
still on the ground)'. **Il est tombé** in standard French is ambiguous as between these two interpretations. Popular French has reintroduced (or main-
tained) a distinction parallel to 'he fell down' versus 'he has fallen down' in
English – or to **il tomba** versus **il est tombé** in literary French.

A similar choice is available for **monter, descendre, partir** or **sortir**. In each
case there is the same 'event' versus 'state' distinction of meaning. The
distinction applies of course to other tenses formed with **avoir**, not just to
the perfect: **j'aurais (serais) sorti**, etc.

## EXERCISES

7† Say what different English equivalents correspond to the
standard French verbs in:

(a) Il n'est pas rentré à midi/Il n'est pas rentré encore.
(b) Il est mort en 1900/Il est mort depuis cinquante ans.

8† In the following popular examples, can the speakers' use of
**avoir** instead of standard **être** be justified in terms of meaning,
and if so how?

(a) Alors j'ai parti à Lyon pour voir le professeur X. (BBA42)

> (b) et là j'ai pas resté deux jours chez eux j'ai resté une journée quoi pour leur faire plaisir (BBA42)
>
> (c) j'sors une fois par an, j'ai même pas sorti cette année (DF817)
>
> 9 Explain the following quotation and characterize the author's standpoint:
>
> > Ce système qui caractérise les verbes à deux auxiliaires est [ . . . ] étendu à ceux qui ne se conjuguent en principe qu'avec *être* par les personnes qui disent *J'ai tombé* ou *J'aurais pas venu,* formes non ambiguës pour exprimer l'action, *Je suis tombé* ou *Madame est sortie* étant de ce fait réservés à l'état. On ne devrait que louer cet effort qui, quoique populaire, va dans le sens de la clarté de la langue . . . (Leeman-Bouix 1994: 91)

## 4.3 Transitive and intransitive; active and passive

In all registers of French, there is a distinction between intransitive, directly transitive and indirectly transitive verbs. And the majority of verbs are allocated to one or other category (or to more than one) in the same way, too. But there are a few well-known differences – and also some differences in the ways in which prepositions like **après**, **pour** or **contre** are used (or not used) with verbs. Similarly, all registers use both active and passive sentences, though their relative frequency varies. But only colloquial French has a 'pseudo-passive' involving **se faire** plus an infinitive.

### 4.3.1 Standard and non-standard transitivity patterns

A number of verbs in standard French can be used both intransitively and transitively:

**Je comprends** (intr)
**Je comprends le français** (tr)

**Il mange** (intr)
**Il mange un hamburger** (tr)

**Je pense** (intr)
**Je pense le monde/l'histoire** (tr)

The last of these is a fairly recent (twentieth-century) extension used mainly in academic discourse: otherwise **penser** takes pronouns, not nouns, as objects (**ce que je pense**). Perhaps because of its academic associations, this use of **penser** has had no difficulty in being accepted by normative commentators. Other changes to verb transitivity have encountered much more resistance from defenders of the standard language. Here, together with some remarks by grammarians, are the most common examples.

### débuter

Non-standard use: directly transitive (**débuter la séance**). Standard use: intransitive.

> '... mais quand est-ce qu'il faut débuter les travaux?' Ce *débuter* transitif est très à la mode, mais contraire au bon usage [...] Débuter des travaux est une faute indigne même d'un ... débutant. (DLF)

### invectiver

Non-standard use: directly transitive (**invectiver quelqu'un**). Standard use: with complement introduced by **contre**.

> Dans un texte soigné, préférons [...] la forme *invectiver contre* qui aura toujours une allure plus recherchée. (Dupré 1972: 1,867)

### pallier

Non-standard use: indirectly transitive (**pallier à un problème**), no doubt because of the influence of the synonym **remédier à**, which is standard and also more usual. Standard use: directly transitive.

> *Pallier*, qui signifie étymologiquement couvrir d'un [...] manteau (du latin *pallium*, manteau), est un verbe transitif qui doit s'employer sans préposition. Mais la construction fautive *pallier à un défaut* s'explique par l'analogie, *pallier* ayant pris le sens de porter remède à, ce qui a entraîné l'emploi de la préposition à. (Georgin 1959: 58)

### se rappeler

Non-standard use: indirectly transitive (**se rappeler de quelqu'un**). Standard use: directly transitive.

> Une de mes lectrices est agacée par l'éternel «je m'en rappelle» qu'elle entend continuellement et lit même assez souvent. Je ne puis que partager son agacement, et ... rappeler que ce verbe est transitif direct [*je me le rappelle*]. (Mourlet 1996: 88–9)

### réussir

Non-standard use: directly transitive whatever the complement (**réussir son permis de conduire**). Standard use: indirectly transitive with certain complements.

> Il faut absolument distinguer entre le tour correct *réussir un dîner* et le tour incorrect *réussir un examen* [ ... ] On n'emploiera comme complément d'objet direct de ce verbe qu'un nom indiquant ce que le sujet a créé, fabriqué, organisé, réalisé: *la cuisinière a réussi son soufflet.* Mais le candidat à un examen est en présence de cet examen, qui existe déjà, c'est une situation dans laquelle il se trouve. On dira donc: *il a réussi au baccalauréat.* (Dupré 1972: 2,284)

### sortir

Non-standard use: directly transitive in the sense of 'take out (e.g. for a walk)':

(1)  Alors, tu me sors au cinoche? (TJ19) [*are you going to take me out to the cinema?*]

Standard use: directly transitive only in the sense of 'take out (e.g. of a drawer)'.

> Admis par l'usage comme verbe transitif, au sens de 'faire sortir, tirer' mais avec un nom de chose comme complément: *sortir un couteau de sa poche.* Le tour est moins acceptable si le verbe a le sens de 'promener' et un nom d'être animé pour complément [*sortir un visiteur*]. (Georgin 1951: 72)

The directly transitive use of **profiter** (without the usual **de**) falls into a somewhat different category, as its use is restricted to a small number of expressions like **occasion à profiter** ('a bargain not to be missed'). Maurice Rat, in common with other normative commentators, recommends replacing **profiter** here by **saisir**, and states:

> *Profiter* n'étant pas un verbe transitif (on *profite* d'une occasion, mais on ne saurait *profiter* une occasion), ce tour de langage boutiquier et populaire est à proscrire. (Rat 1978: 48–9)

**EXERCISE**

1†  Give (i) standard and (ii) non-standard French equivalents of:

(a)  start the work
(b)  put a defect right (using **pallier**)
(c)  take the dog for a walk
(d)  pass one's A-levels
(e)  remember someone's address
(f)  hurl abuse at a rival

### 4.3.2  Recent developments

The cases discussed in 4.3.1 represent long-standing – one might almost say 'time-honoured' – differences between standard and non-standard usage. More recent developments have so far received little attention from normative commentators. But a number of transitive verbs have taken on colloquial intransitive uses (or, less commonly, the reverse).

(2)  Ça énerve un peu. (LJ107)

(3)  Quand ils ont vu arriver les CRS, ils ont dégagé [*pris la fuite*] vite fait. (DU403)

(4)  Qu'est-ce qu'il a dégusté/reçu! [*he didn't half cop it!*]

The following examples involve fashionable pseudo-psychological vocabulary items that originated in the *français branché* ('switched-on media French') of the 1980s and seem to have found a permanent place in the language.

(5)  Marie culpabilise [*se sent coupable*]. (LJ108)

(6)  J'assume complètement [*j'accepte ma condition*]. (RB)

(7)  Elles assurent [*ont l'air compétent*] en Rodier [*advertisement for pullovers*]. (RB)

(8)  Bordel, devant tous ces groupies faut qu'on assure [*qu'on montre sa capacité*]. (TJ26)

Other uses are found in the variety of French known as *le parler jeune, le tchatche*, or *le langage ado(lescent)*. This originated in the speech patterns

of immigrant suburban teenagers, but various elements have been dis-
seminated more widely by the media in recent years. In (9)–(10), as well as
an example of intransitive **abuser**, there are some colourful *verlan* ('backslang')
vocabulary items (**péta, turvoi, reup, meuf**).

(9)    T'as abusé, t'aurais pas dû péta la turvoi à mon reup [*tu as exagéré,
       tu n'aurais pas dû voler ('taper') la voiture de mon père*]. (PPA9)

(10)   Elle assassine, la meuf! [*cette femme est belle*] (NO)

(11)   Etre tout seul dans la jungle des métiers, ça craint [*ce n'est pas
       agréable*] [*youth employment advertisement*]. (RB)

(12)   Allez, activez un peu! [*dépêchez-vous*] (TJ38)

(13)   Le premier qui m'regarde, j'calcule pas, j'l'éclate [*frappe*]! (GD87)

Often the grammatical change has been accompanied by a quite striking
change in the meaning of the verb – most particularly perhaps in the case of
**assassiner, assumer, assurer** and **craindre**.

---

### EXERCISES

2†   For each of the verbs **abuser, activer, assassiner, assumer,
     assurer, craindre, culpabiliser, dégager, déguster, éclater,
     énerver** and **recevoir**, as used in (2) to (13), say whether the
     new development replaces an intransitive use by a transitive
     one, or vice versa.

3    Attempt to specify the links in meaning between the standard
     and the colloquial uses of the verbs.

---

### 4.3.3  Passives in colloquial speech

It is often stated that passives occur less often in familiar spoken French
than in the standard written language. For instance, as A. Sauvageot has
pointed out (Sauvageot 1962: 133), a written passive sentence like:

(14)   Le représentant de commerce a été assassiné par une personne de
       sa connaissance

would most probably be formulated as an active in conversation (for the 'topicalized' structure, see 6.1):

(15)   Le représentant de commerce, c'est une personne de sa connaissance qui l'a assassiné.

Statistical investigations support this view. According to Ludwig Söll, for example (Söll 1974: 112–13), passives occur twice as often in written as in spoken usage – and four times as often if, like (13), they contain an 'agent phrase' introduced by **par**. It is relevant to this latter point that, despite the presence of several passives in the large corpus of utterances collected by Denise François from her Argenteuil informant (see 2.3.5), there is no example of one with an agent phrase.

The difference between standard and colloquial French passives relates essentially to this question of their relative frequency. The same structural patterns occur in both varieties, as the following conversational examples show:

(16)   ben j'avais été agressé par un jeune (BBE51)

(17)   Ils savent pas exactement si la fameuse réforme portuaire a vraiment été mis en application, elle a été mis en application dans les tout petits ports. (FH)

(18)   la sonorisation avait été cassée la veille, paraît-il (JE21)

(19)   il a été traité de nazi et de tous les noms alors qu'en fait c'était un déporté de . . . en Allemagne (JE96)

However, a distinctive colloquial passive structure does occur with the verbs **commencer** and **finir**:

(20)   ma 2CV elle est pas finie de payer (EDJ)

Similarly, **la maison est finie de construire** (corresponding to **on a fini de construire la maison**). Not only is **finir** itself passive in such examples, but the accompanying verbs **payer** and **construire** also have passive meaning: 'to be paid', or, more idiomatically, '(finished) being paid for', 'being built'. Although this construction has been condemned by many purists, examples like **fini de construire/de bâtir/de payer** occur widely and are accepted these days by the more tolerant *dirigiste* grammarians. Curiously, this does not apply to the parallel construction with **commencer**, and popular connotations still attach to:

(21)   La soupe n'est pas commencé de manger [*hasn't begun to be eaten*].
       (LB25)

Otherwise the most noticeable standard/non-standard contrast is to be found
not in the passive as such, but in the fact that familiar and popular registers
make widespread use of a 'pseudo-passive' structure involving **se faire** plus
an infinitive:

(22)   Je me suis fait attraper [*I got caught*].

(23)   Tu t'es fait avoir [*you've been cheated/had*].

(24)   Trois jours plus tard, alors qu'il est à un cocktail à la Tour
       Montparnasse, Papa se fait voler la voiture [*had his car stolen*].
       (PA155)

(25)   Le Paris-Saint-Germain [*football team*] s'est fait battre [*were beaten*]
       par Laval. (FI)

A **se faire** construction also occurs in standard French, but is restricted to
situations where there is an element of volition on the part of the subject,
who can therefore be said to be the 'cause' of the event: **il s'est fait couper les
cheveux, elle s'est fait conduire à l'aéroport en taxi**. No 'causative' implication is present in (22)–(25). Indeed, the events typically have adverse consequences for the subject, who is therefore unlikely to have instigated them.
    The context and the meaning of the verb itself usually make it clear
whether **se faire** is 'causative' (standard and colloquial) or 'passive' (colloquial only). The same applies to English sentences like 'He got his hair cut'
as opposed to 'He got his foot run over'.

---

## EXERCISES

4†   Convert into the pseudo-passive form with **se faire**:

     (a)   Le chat a attrapé la souris.
     (b)   On lui a marché dessus.
     (c)   On lui a volé son auto-radio.
     (d)   On l'a prié de rester.
     (e)   Quelqu'un lui est rentré dedans ('ran into him/her').

5† Are the following examples of 'causative' or 'passive' **se faire**, and how can you tell?

(a)  Il s'est fait arracher une dent.
(b)  Il s'est fait arracher le bras.
(c)  Il s'est fait refuser l'entrée.
(d)  Il s'est fait retirer son permis de conduire.
(e)  Il s'est fait servir le petit déjeuner dans sa chambre.
(f)  Il s'est fait accorder une prolongation de huit jours.
(g)  Il s'est fait cambrioler sa cave.

# 5 Conjunctions and Prepositions

## 5.1 Subordinating conjunctions

All registers of French have a noteworthy facility for forming conjunctions by combining **que** with a wide range of nouns, participles, prepositions and other items. Some of these are restricted to use in informal contexts, however.

### 5.1.1 Conjunctions with and without que

**Que** (as in **on m'a dit que...**) is not only the most commonly occurring French subordinating conjunction in its own right: it is also a component part of all other conjunctions in the language apart from **quand, comme, si, où, comment** and **pourquoi**. It figures, for example, in **puisque, parce que, afin que, pourvu que, sans que, à condition que, sous prétexte que, étant donné que**.

There is, however, considerable variation in the extent to which **que** is bound to the rest of the conjunction of which it is part. In the case of **puisque**, the link is so close that the unit as a whole is unanalysable: what exactly does **puis** mean here? (The single-word spelling is a reflection of this.) **Parce que** and **afin que** (always spelt as two words), though perhaps not immediately obvious either, are not difficult to break down more or less meaningfully into their component parts: **par + ce + que; à + fin + que** ('to the end that', i.e. 'in order that'). **Pourvu que** and **sans que** are much more transparent. **A condition que** and **sous prétexte que** come close to being phrases rather than subordinating conjunctions. But **condition** and **prétexte** are not preceded by articles and therefore cannot be followed by adjectives (as is the case in 'true' phrases like **à la condition expresse que** or **sous le prétexte absurde que**), so they can still be regarded as conjunctions. It is a moot point, though, whether **étant donné que** should be considered a single unit or not. Some examples will be given in 5.1.2 to show how readily such phrase-like conjunctions can also be formed in colloquial French.

**Que** figures in so many of these items that in popular usage it comes to be added to the 'simple' conjunctions themselves: hence **comme que**, **comme si que**, **quand que**, **comment que**:

(1)   des repas froids, j'avais toujours des [ . . . ] oeufs durs comme si que j'faisais un un camping, hein (FH)

(2)   Regardez-moi les virages comment qu'il les prend. (DF817)

(3)   Je le ferai quand que j'aurai le temps. (PG73)

This is parallel to the use of **que** with **quand, où, pourquoi, comment** and **qui** when they introduce direct WH-questions like **où que tu vas?** (see 2.2.2). And some examples were given in 2.2.3 of the use of **où que** and **pourquoi que** to introduce indirect questions. The tendency is evidently for **que** to become a component of all subordinating conjunctions and all interrogative adverbs and pronouns. Over and above this, it can be attached to **plus** (as used in the standard structure **plus . . . plus**, 'the more . . . the more') and to **tellement**:

(4)   Plus qu'on est mort depuis longtemps, plus qu'on vaut! (NO)

(5)   Sa bagnole, on dirait un cendrier, tellement qu'on fume là-dedans. (RB)

Despite these extensions (and others to be presented in 5.1.2), **que** has lost ground in the adverbial 'exclamatory' use seen in **que c'est affreux!**. This does not occur in colloquial French unless a theatrical effect is being sought, and even in the standard language it is often replaced by **comme** (**comme c'est affreux!**). More familiar in register, and much criticized by normative grammarians, are formulae like the following (in ascending order of colloquialness, and with an appropriate vocabulary substitution): **ce que c'est moche!**, **qu'est-ce que c'est moche!**, **ce que ça peut être moche!**.

---

## EXERCISES

1   Which of the following are more 'phrase-like' and which more 'conjunction-like', and why?

> **une fois que, chaque fois que, de sorte que, au fur et à mesure que, à proportion que, en attendant que, de peur que.**

> **2**    On the evidence of the conjunctions mentioned so far, and any others which occur to you, specify which parts of speech can combine with **que** to form subordinating conjunctions.
>
> **3†**   Arrange in order, from more formal to less formal:
>
>    (a)   Ce que ça flotte!
>    (b)   Comme il pleut!
>    (c)   Qu'est-ce que ça flotte!
>    (d)   Ce qu'il pleut!

### 5.1.2  Colloquial conjunctions

Here are some conjunctions which are not part of the standard repertoire.

#### à cause que

This is based, logically enough, on the standard preposition **à cause de**. But as a conjunction, **à cause que** is frowned upon by many purists, is generally stigmatized as typical of uneducated speech, and is frequently used in dialogues in 'populist' novels.

(6)   Si ce genre de trucs arrive, c'est à cause, sans doute, que les gens regardent trop la télévision. (LFM104)

(7)   On l'appelle le Sarrazin, à cause qu'il fait une drôle de tête quand il se fâche. (RS229)

#### des fois que

**Des fois** is a colloquial equivalent of **quelquefois** and **parfois**. In the following, it approximates in meaning to **par hasard**, and the conjunction as a whole might be paraphrased as 'pour le cas où':

(8)   Regarde bien dans ton sac, des fois que t'aurais pas prêté attention. (CE63)

(9)   Je vais voir ce qu'il fait, des fois qu'il voudrait se jeter dans la Loire. (TF1)

#### histoire que

This is parallel to the colloquial preposition **histoire de**, an equivalent of standard **afin de** (see 5.3.3). **Histoire** conveys the idea of a 'pretext' or 'reason' for carrying out an action.

(10) il m'aide un peu au ménage histoire que je vienne me coucher avant qu'il soit endormi (LBN)

## malgré que

Like its synonym **bien que** (in informal use), **malgré que** is found with the indicative as well as the subjunctive.

(11) Eux, ils s'aimaient bien, malgré qu'ils se disputaient tout le temps. (AB106)

Though a logical enough development from the standard preposition **malgré**, this conjunction is particularly disapproved of by normative grammarians:

*Malgré que* a suscité des discussions passionnées. Peut-on l'employer au sens de «quoique, bien que, encore que»? En raison même de ces discussions, qui continuent à opposer grammairiens et écrivains, il vaut mieux éviter de se servir de cette locution et l'abandonner à la langue familière. (Thomas 1956: 250)

## même que

In standard French, **que** can replace **si** in certain situations (**si nous avons le temps et qu'il fait beau, nous irons nous promener**). In colloquial French, **que** is equivalent to **si** in:

(12) Même qu'on y aurait pensé, ça nous aurait avancé à quoi, hein? (JC20)

More commonly, though no less colloquially, **même que** is equivalent to **il est même possible que** ... or simply **même**:

(13) Demain douze heures trente mon train décolle, même que je passe par Venise, même que, si ça se trouve [*possibly*], j'refoutrai jamais les pieds à Malakoff. (JC125)

(14) les piquets de grève [ . . . ] ont envahi l'amphi complètement même qu'ils sont arrivés avec des tambours et des tam-tam (RL34)

## pour pas que

When **pour que** is followed by a negative clause (**pour que ça tombe pas**), there is a strong tendency in colloquial usage for it to 'attract' **pas** (**pour pas que ça tombe**), the result being a colloquial conjunction with negative value:

(15)  Ils font tout pour me bloquer, pour pas que je prenne le vol Paris-Pékin. (FI)

(16)  Il faut qu'il s'occupe des choses graves comme les malades pour pas qu'ils meurent. (LFM119)

**surtout que**

This equivalent of **d'autant plus que** is another conjunction which has attracted much criticism from normative commentators. However, attitudes have probably softened somewhat since the following was written some twenty years ago, and today **surtout que** can be heard in conversations of all kinds:

D'un quotidien: «Surtout que la résistance de Clara au divorce est tenace et dur». [ . . . ] nous estimons que cette locution, fort usitée chez les gens peu instruits, doit être évitée par les journalistes dont la mission est d'élever leur public et non de le maintenir dans son ignorance. (DLF)

**vu que**

This equivalent of standard **étant donné que** is only slightly colloquial, and indeed is sometimes included in lists of *bon usage* conjunctions.

(17)  des chiottes [ . . . ] sans chasse d'eau vu qu'il y a pas l'égout (FCT163)

The freedom with which complex conjunctions can be coined is further illustrated by the 'one-off' use of **avec ça que** in the following, where it has the sense of 'what's more' (cf. the shopkeeper's ritual question: **Et avec ça, Madame?**):

(18)  Avec ça que ces gens-là n'écrivent pas comme nous autres [ . . . ] (DP29)

**A ce que** falls into a different category from the preceding items, as it is well established in standard usage (**tenir à ce que**, **veiller à ce que**). However, in familiar French a wider range of verbs can be followed by it:

(19)  Je demande à ce que l'Etat cesse de prélever des taxes aussi exorbitants. (ASA152)

(20)  Les particuliers cherchent à ce que leurs avoirs rapportent le plus possible. (ASA152)

But examples in which **à ce que** occurs after a verb not otherwise followed by **à** are probably the result of hypercorrection, **à ce que** being felt to be more 'literary' or 'correct' than simple **que**:

(21)   Il faut éviter à ce que les gens s'ennuient. (ASA152)

In all these cases, the norm would have **que**, not **à ce que**.

---

### EXERCISES

4†   Give English translations of each of the colloquial conjunctions illustrated in examples (6) to (17).

5    Probably the commonest sources of new colloquial French conjunctions are existing prepositions or prepositional expressions. Find some examples above.

---

### 5.1.3   *Comme quoi, si jamais* **and** *quand même*

In spite of the dominance of **que** in this chapter, note should be taken of three colloquial conjunctions in which **que** is not an element, or at least not an essential one. One of these is exemplified by:

(22)   une théorie comme quoi il s'agit d'un complot (TF1)

(23)   des gens [ . . . ] qui donnent des leçons à la télé comme quoi il faut être honnête (LFM42)

*Bon usage* would use alternatives like **une théorie selon laquelle** or **des leçons qui montrent comment** . . . . Predictably no doubt, **que** can 'infiltrate' this conjunction too:

(24)   Il a téléphoné comme quoi qu'il pouvait pas sortir. (RB)

Some further examples of **comme quoi** are to be found in the following (hostile) commentary:

   – Le patron a établi un certificat *comme quoi* l'ouvrier a reçu une blessure en service commandé.

*Comme quoi* veut dire: de quelle façon, dans quelles conditions, en quelle qualité. Il ne peut pas suivre immédiatement un substantif. Dans la phrase citée, il manque un verbe: «... un certificat *établissant* que la blessure de l'intéressé est imputable à une circonstance de service». Un employé de mairie m'a dit une fois:

– Vous apporterez une pièce d'identité officielle ...

Pris d'un scrupule et redoutant que je n'eusse pas compris ces mots hermétiques, il eut la bonté d'ajouter:

– ... *comme quoi que* c'est vous, enfin!

L'emploi de *comme quoi* est très répandu dans le langage populaire, qui estime que cette locution est noble, par rapport à *que*:

– C'est marqué su' l'journal *comme quoi que* le thermomètre a monté hier à 35,8. (Moufflet 1935: 201)

These uses of **comme quoi** had long been current when the above comments were published. However, a type of usage that was unknown in those days was reported by the linguist Marina Yaguello in 1998. Teenagers, it seems, are increasingly liable to use the composite conjunction **si jamais** in a way not possible either in standard French or in other colloquial varieties (Yaguello 1998: 110–13).

Normally, **jamais** reinforces **si** only when unlikely eventualities are referred to (**si jamais je gagnais le gros lot, je ferais le tour du monde**). In other words, it is an equivalent of **si par hasard**, or English 'if ever'. It would therefore not be used, for example, in stating general truths about the world: **si deux droites sont perpendiculaires à une troisième, elles sont parallèles entre elles** ('straight lines perpendicular to another line are parallel to one another'). However, Yaguello's youthful informants produce utterances like:

(25) Si jamais tu cliques sur l'icône, le document s'ouvre.

(26) Si jamais tu as du citron, on peut faire une tarte.

Indeed, they rarely if ever use **si** on its own to form a conditional clause. This leads her to conclude:

Tout se passe comme si *jamais* était agglutiné avec *si* pour constituer un seul mot et donc une conjonction nouvelle. On dirait que *si* tout seul ne suffit plus à poser une condition logique. Faudra-t-il un jour réécrire les manuels de géométrie? (Yaguello 1998: 113)

Finally **quand même**, which, when used as a conjunction, is an alternative to
**(même) si**, but is in no way restricted to younger speakers (for the conditional in the following example, see 4.1.3). It, too, is sometimes followed by
**que** in popular usage:

(27)   Quand même que ce serait vrai. (PG75)

---

## EXERCISES

6†   Suggest English translations for **comme quoi** in (22) to (24)
and in the examples given in the excerpt from A. Moufflet.

7   What is Moufflet's view of colloquial **comme quoi** – and those
who use it?

8   How seriously should M. Yaguello's predictions about **si
jamais** be taken?

---

## 5.2   Extending the role of que

The various uses of 'subordinating' **que** outlined so far are not the end of
the story. In colloquial French, a solitary **que** can link clauses or sentences
in a range of other circumstances – as though it was not 'overloaded' enough
already! (The following account is mainly based on the detailed discussion
and exemplification in Gadet 1997: 125–9.)

### 5.2.1   Que *as a substitute conjunction*

In cases like the following, a **que** clause is used with a verb (**laisser, accuser**)
in a way which would be impossible in the standard language:

(1)   Ne laisse pas que Dolly le mange. (GFO125)

(2)   J'accuse pas qu'elle ait fait ça. (GFO125)

Instead, *bon usage* would make use of the infinitive: **ne laisse pas Dolly le
manger; je ne l'accuse pas d'avoir fait cela.**

In other examples where colloquial French has **que**, standard French, too,
would use a conjunction, but a more explicit one:

(3)   T'en reveux un deuxième que tu l'as laissé bouillir? (GFO125)

**Que** here is equivalent to **puisque**, or **étant donné que**, and the meaning is something like: 'do you want another one now that/seeing that you've let the first one boil?'.

(4)   et les copains arrivèrent en masse qu'on se serait cru au *Vendôme* le jour qu'ils ont sorti *Les Parapluies de Cherbourg* (G. Perec, quoted in Gadet 1997: 126)

In this case **que** might be expanded into **au point où** ('to the extent that'): 'they turned up in such large numbers that you'd have thought . . .'.

(5)   Elles viennent discuter avec moi que je leur suggère des trucs pour le dossier quoi. (GFO126)

The relevant part of this could be translated as 'to have a chat with me so that I can suggest . . .', with **que** equivalent to **pour que**.

There is a further use of **que** in which it could almost be said to be a substitute for inversion. Standard French uses **dit-il, ai-je demandé** and similar *incises* after direct quotations («**Bonjour**», **m'a-t-il dit**). The general avoidance of inversion in familiar French results in the use of affirmative word-order instead: «**Bonjour**», **il m'a dit**. In the most colloquial styles, however, **que** can be inserted before the *incise*: «**Bonjour**», **qu'il m'a dit**. But even in popular speech, contrary to what is sometimes believed, this is not the dominant type of *incise*, as can be seen from the following typical examples (underlined):

(6)   Y m'a dit: t'en fais pas, d'ici là, qu'y dit, j't'aiderai un p'tit peu. J'dis oui, mais, pis j'dis j'aurai droit à tous mes trucs, j'dis, t'en fais pas. Alors y'm'dit: si tu t'trouves l'occasion, sans t'marier qu'y dit, tu peux trouver quelqu'un, un p'tit vieux, y dit, qu'a une bonne retraite. (IVR)

Over several minutes of discourse, this working-class Parisian speaker uses **il dit** more than twice as often as **qu'il dit**, and **je dis** about ten times as often as **que je dis**.

---

### *EXERCISE*

1†   Standardize the following by replacing **que** with one or more of: **afin que, pour que, si . . . que, au point que, puisque, parce que**, or with inversion:

(a)  Y avait pas de raison qu'on ait faim. (JE19)

(b)  Elle est bête que c'est à pas y croire. (HF154)

(c)  Qu'est-ce qu'il a donc qu'il ne dit plus rien. (HF154)

(d)  Tu la mets dans la terre et tu fais ressortir un bout qu'ça fait racine. (DF783)

(e)  ah moi, j'dis, j'peux pas, j'dis, j'suis occupée toute la journée, que j'lui fais moi [ . . . ] (IVR)

(f)  Mais y a rien, que j'te dis. (IZ182)

### 5.2.2  *Que as a 'universal' conjunction*

Sometimes it is less easy to specify standard conjunctions equivalent to **que**. For example:

(7)  Tu es prête que je te serve? (GFO125)

This translates very naturally into English ('are you ready for me to serve you?'). But in standard French, the closest literal rendering would be the dubiously grammatical **est-ce que tu es prête pour que je te serve?**. Otherwise a major reformulation has to be resorted to, e.g. **si tu es prête, je te sers**.

Similarly with:

(8)  C'est pas le moment que j'en ai encore un troisième [mari]. (IVR)

This might be paraphrased as: 'this isn't the right time for me to get married for a third time'.

In fact, in colloquial usage, it is not unusual for **que** to connect two clauses in a way which it is hard to express with *any* standard conjunction. Such uses are sometimes condemned as 'vague', but usually they are far from being so vague that the intended meaning is obscure. Maybe 'condensed' or 'concise' would be a better characterization:

(9)  La semaine de l'action contre le sida, c'est pour faire peur aux jeunes qui ont pas acheté des préservatifs et que, s'ils n'ont pas d'argent, ils arrêtent la sexualité, et qu'ils fassent du sport. (LFM114)

In this case, standardization would involve introducing another verb: **pour les encourager à arrêter**, perhaps.

Another example is:

(10)   Tu sais à qui tu n'as pas téléphoné depuis et que c'est pas sympa? (GFO125)

This might be paraphrased as: 'There's someone you've not phoned for ages, and you know who it is. It wasn't very nice of you, was it?'
   In the following utterance (by a car driver), the exact shade of meaning needs to be supplied by the context:

(11)   Qu'est-ce qu'il fout ce con-là que je vais te le redépasser? (RB)

(See 3.3.4 for the use of **te** here.) Possible paraphrase: 'What the hell's he doing? He's doing something so stupid (annoying? dangerous?) that I'm going to overtake him again'. As in the previous example, the clumsy English reformulation falls far short of the elegantly terse original.
   The 'universal' use of **que** is a good example of an unstable area of grammar in which the 'open-endedness' of usage makes it very difficult to lay down hard and fast rules about what is possible and what is not. Can **que** replace any conjunction at any time? Surely not. So can the restrictions be described in a systematic way? Or are some at least of the sentences quoted merely 'one-off occurrences' and therefore outside any system?
   This would seem to apply to the following, which, unlike the cases given above, is uninterpretable as it stands:

(12)   Il est venu que j'étais malade. (HF154)

**Que** here could be equivalent either to **parce que** or to **pendant que**.
   The following seems equally uninterpretable (though it no doubt made sense in the context in which it was uttered):

(13)   Il a réussi que je puisse vraiment pas le faire. (GFO126)

---

## EXERCISES

2†   Show the meaning of the following by giving standard paraphrases:

(a)   elle avait mis quatre ans à faire couper ces tilleuls qu'on y voyait plus rien, on avait pratiquement les branches dans la salle (DF780)

(b) J'ai plein de choses à vous dire qu'on est pas contents du tout. (GFO126)

(c) Je pourrais t'aligner [*te jeter à terre*] que ça f'rait pas une vague. (IZ175)

(d) [ma fille] elle est difficile [*finicky*] que j'sais pas quoi lui donner (DF777)

(e) T'as besoin de rien que je monte? (GFO126)

3   The following quotation resumes some of the points that have just been made about **que**. You should now be in a position to explain what the writer is saying here:

[ . . . ] *que* continue bien à jouer dans la langue populaire ce rôle de conjonction minimum, de terme générique impliquant tous les autres; on mettra un simple *que* là où la norme exigerait *parce que, puisque, sans que, au point que*, etc., le seul contexte précisant la nature de la corrélation. (Guiraud 1965: 72)

## 5.3   Prepositions

Although colloquial French has fewer distinctive prepositions than distinctive conjunctions, there are a number of instances where colloquial and non-colloquial usage diverge: in colloquial French, for instance, it is possible to end a sentence with a preposition! One or two of the conjunctions discussed in 5.1.2 reappear in this section in prepositional guise.

### 5.3.1   'Preposition stranding'

It is acceptable in standard French for the prepositions **avant** and **après** to be used adverbially, i.e. at the end of the clause or sentence, and without a noun object (this being 'understood'):

(1)   Le spectacle s'est terminé à minuit, mais nous sommes partis avant [*avant minuit*].

In familiar usage this can be extended to other prepositions, notably **avec**, **sans**, **contre** and **pour**:

(2)    Le prince s'est dit: Quelle jolie princesse – j'coucherais bien avec. (FI)

(3)    Il avait eu quelqu'un, il s'était mis en ménage avec. (IVR)

(4)    Tu es Noir: j'ai rien contre. (LBN)

(5)    La libéralisation des moeurs, je suis pour, moi. (RFB185)

Such sentences can be converted into standard form by providing the preposition with an object: **lui, elle, eux, ça/cela** for example, or a suitable noun phrase. Note in this connection the common idiomatic expression **il faut faire avec** ('You've just got to put up with it/go along with it'). Here the 'missing' object is **cette situation, ce malheur**, or an equivalent expression.

A similar pattern was discussed in 2.3.4 with reference to relative clauses like the one in **le copain que je suis sorti avec**. However, supplying an object **(lui)** in this case would not result in a *bon usage* sentence, but in an equally colloquial 'resumptive' relative (see 2.3.2), so the resemblance is in some respects superficial. Another difference is that the parallelism with English is lacking in the case of (2)–(5): 'who I went out with' is acceptable, but '*I've nothing against' and '*I'd like to sleep with' are not.

'Stranding', as this process is sometimes called, is also possible with **sur**, **sous** and **dans**, provided they take the adverbial form **dessus, dessous** and **dedans** respectively:

(6)    L'assassin est apparu: les soldats lui ont tiré dessus.

(7)    Le taxi traversait le carrefour, quand un camion lui est rentré dedans [*collided with it*].

And stranding can occur with **après** in the non-temporal sense found in expressions like **crier après** ('shout at'), **aboyer après** ('bark at') or the colloquial **attendre après** ('wait for'), **demander après** ('ask for someone'):

(8)    Un gros clebs de merde, qui t'aboie après. (PS73)

**Dessus, dessous, dedans** and non-temporal **après** are usually accompanied by a pronoun placed before the verb **(lui, t'** in the examples just given). This is not possible with the **avec/pour/contre** group of prepositions: ***j'y suis contre**, ***il lui a couché avec**. This is because expressions like **tirer sur, aboyer après**, etc. function as units, whereas **coucher avec** and **être contre** do not: **aboyer-après/toi**, as opposed to **coucher/avec-elle**.

A further difference between the **avec/pour/contre** group and the **après/ dessus/dessous/dedans** group is that the adverbial, 'stranded' use is distinctly more colloquial with the first group than with the second. **Il lui a tiré dessus** (unlike **il faut faire avec**) is actually quite acceptable in *français courant*, though probably not in *français soigné*. If a stranded **après** or **dessus** does sometimes have familiar or popular overtones, this is not so much due to grammatical considerations as to the fact that the verb used is itself colloquial. For example:

(9)   Avec quoi que j'y tape dessus? (RFC67)

(**Y** here is a contraction of **lui** (see 8.1.1); **taper sur** is a familiar equivalent of **frapper**: so an equivalent standard sentence would be **Avec quoi est-ce que je le frappe?**.)

There are, finally, many French prepositions that do not allow themselves to be stranded under any circumstances. This applies in particular to **à, chez, de, en** and **vers**. Stranding does occasionally occur with **autour, entre** and **parmi**, but can be considered marginal.

---

### EXERCISES

1† 'Rescue' the stranded prepositions in the following by providing them with suitable noun or pronoun objects:

   (a)   On a eu le charbon, le pétrole, qui sont bougrement sales, et on a vécu avec. (FI)

   (b)   Elle a pris la voiture et elle est partie avec. (FI)

   (c)   Ça c'est des cons! [ . . . ] Je vais finir par me fâcher avec. (RFB108)

   (d)   Ces mesures ont été adoptées avec l'accord, car il n'est pas intervenu contre, du ministre de la justice. (FI)

   (e)   J'ai le pot d'échappement qui est tombé, je peux pas continuer avec parce que [ . . . ] il traîne par terre [*bus driver to HQ*]. (JE64)

   (f)   Vittel, on vit tellement mieux avec [*advertisement for mineral water*]. (RB)

2† 'Strand' the prepositions in the following:

   (a)   Les enfants ont crié après lui.

   (b)   Les gendarmes ont sauté sur lui.

> (c)   Quant à la protection de l'environnement, je suis totalement pour cette politique.
>
> (d)   La conservation de la chaleur est essentielle, et cette maison est étudiée pour la réaliser.
>
> (e)   Ses amis sont allés voir Marie, mais elle n'a pas voulu sortir avec eux.

### 5.3.2   Colloquial uses and innovations

#### (a)   histoire de

This prepositional expression, an informal equivalent of **afin de**, has already been referred to in connection with the even more colloquial and less widely used conjunction, **histoire que** (see 5.1.2). Its use is illustrated in the following account of a police operation to defuse a suspected bomb:

(10)   Les artificiers accourus d'urgence neutralisent l'objet suspect en édifiant autour un mur de sacs de sable. Et lancent une grenade au milieu, histoire de vérifier. (NO)

Similarly:

(11)   Tu vois, Pérol, des soirs, on devrait se faire des virées, nous deux. Histoire de pas perdre de vue la réalité. (IZ237)

#### (b)   'concerning'

Both formal and informal French possess a large number of phrases equivalent to 'concerning' 'as regards', 'as far as . . . is concerned'. The following are the main possibilities, arranged in three groups according to register. The phrases in Group 1, though often encountered, have rather pretentious and/or administrative overtones; those in Group 2 are standard; those in Group 3 are familiar or popular (arranged here in ascending order of colloquialness):

*Group 1*

**au niveau de**
**s'agissant de**

*Group 2*

| | |
|---|---|
| **sur le plan de** | **concernant** |
| **en ce qui concerne** | **du point de vue de** |
| **à propos de** | **quant à** |
| **au sujet de** | |

*Group 3*

**point de vue** (familiar): point de vue fric, j'ai des problèmes
**côté** (familiar): côté santé, ça va?
**question** (familiar): j'ai eu des ennuis, question assurances
**rapport à** (popular): c'est rapport à vot' dame que je vous cause ('I'm speaking to you about your wife')

Note that **rapport à** can also be equivalent to **à cause de**:

(12) J'ai pas voulu me marier une deuxième fois rapport à ma fille. (IVR)

**Rapport à** should not be confused with standard **par rapport à**, which in some contexts can correspond to 'in respect of', but more commonly means 'compared with'.

### (c) **sur**

When used with nouns referring to places, the preposition **sur** has undergone some noteworthy developments of meaning in informal French. Though often encountered in writing as well as in speech, this kind of use continues to be regarded as familiar or popular by many commentators.

One set of examples shows **sur** to have developed a 'directional' sense:

(13) Moi je rentre sur Courbevoie [*taxi driver*]. (FI)

(14) La Russie n'arrive pas à exporter sur l'Europe de l'ouest autant de pétrole qu'elle souhaiterait. (FI)

(15) Les blessés ont été évacués sur le centre hospitalier d'Aubagne. (FI)

It is possible to detect connotations of rather purposeful, targeted movement in cases like these, where **sur** corresponds to standard **à** in the first sentence and standard **vers** in the second and third. With a less 'dynamic' verb such as **aller**, this use of **sur** is less likely (not **\*un taxi qui allait sur**

**Courbevoie**, but **un taxi qui allait à Courbevoie**). So a new distinction of meaning seems to have emerged, differentiating **à** and **sur**: it is not a simple matter of one being substituted for the other (cf. Yaguello 1998: 78–84).

In the second kind of example, **sur** has taken on a 'territorial' sense:

(16)   des jeunes qui, sur un quartier, ont un sentiment d'être propriétaires (FI)

(17)   il existe des centaines d'entreprises de plomberie sur la région parisienne (TF1)

(18)   Moi je te dis franchement, tout ce que j'ai appris c'est dans la cité et en bougeant sur Paris. (GD57)

(19)   Sur Paris les 126 praticiens de SOS-Médecins ont effectué l'an dernier plus de 300 000 visites. (NO)

The standard language would have **dans** in (16)–(18) and **à** in (19). The focus is on influence extending over, or activity taking place in, a particular demarcated territory. With a more neutral verb like **habiter**, the preposition **à** is more likely (not ***habiter sur Paris**, but **habiter à Paris**).

Finally, with reference to the traditional sense of **sur**, it should be noted that the widespread familiar expression **sur le journal** ('in the paper') is frequently condemned by normative grammarians, according to whom the 'correct' form is **dans le journal**.

---

## EXERCISES

3†   Suggest suitable English translations of **histoire de** in (10) and (11).

4    Attempt to reconstruct the way in which the nouns **point de vue**, **côté**, **question** and **rapport** have taken on prepositional uses or become incorporated into a prepositional phrase.

5†   Can you justify the use of **sur**, and say whether the 'directional' or the 'territorial' sense is uppermost, in:

(a)   Trois grands incendies se sont déclarés sur Marseille. (FI)

(b)  Nous avons maintenant un résultat sur la Nouvelle Calédonie. [ . . . ] Nous avons une estimation sur Marseille [*election broadcast*]. (FI)

(c)  Elle me demandait si elle pouvait téléphoner sur Paris [*depuis la Normandie*]. (FI)

(d)  L'hôpital psychiatrique de Clermont couvre dix secteurs sur l'Oise, trois sur les Hauts-de-Seine. (NO)

(e)  un périodique gratuit diffusé sur Paris (LBN)

(f)  des retours difficiles sur la capitale. [ . . . ] seules les entrées sur Bordeaux sont difficiles (FI)

(g)  J'avais demandé un poste sur Paris. (FI)

### 5.3.3  *Some traditional* bêtes noires

This sub-section presents some further aspects of preposition use which for many decades have attracted condemnation from a majority of normative commentators, including some *dirigistes*. However, with the sole exception of 'possessive à', they are widespread in conversation and even in writing, and it is doubtful whether most speakers feel them to be particularly colloquial. So it could be that in time the purists will relent and accept most of them as standard, just as they have come, over the last half-century or so, to tolerate **ne . . . pas . . . que** (see 2.1.3).

The data here are presented in the format characteristic of the *guide du bon usage*:

*NE DITES PAS:* (followed by the use being criticized)

*MAIS DITES:* (followed by the recommended use)

A typical comment is quoted in the first five cases. The uses (a)–(f) are arranged in roughly ascending order of colloquialness.

(N.B. Prepositional use is involved also in one or two other classic *bêtes noires*, discussed in 4.3.1: **pallier à**, **se rappeler de**, **invectiver contre**.)

(a)  Ne dites pas: **neuf à dix personnes**
Mais dites: **neuf ou dix personnes**

On peut dire: ce livre coûte de neuf *à* dix francs (car il peut coûter neuf francs cinquante, neuf francs quatre-vingt-dix, etc.). Mais on ne saurait parler de neuf élèves et demi ou de neuf élèves trois quarts. (Rat 1978: 23)

(b)   Ne dites pas: **partir à Paris**
      Mais dites: **partir pour Paris**

Faut-il rappeler que *partir* dans cet emploi, c'est quitter un lieu, et qu'on ne quitte pas un lieu *à* mais *pour* un autre lieu? (Mourlet 1996: 118)

(c)   Ne dites pas: **en bicyclette/en vélo**
      Mais dites: **à bicyclette/à vélo**

[ . . . ] *en* équivalant à *dans* accompagné d'un article, on ne saurait dire qu'on va *en* bicyclette comme on va *en* voiture, puisqu'on va *sur* la bicyclette, comme on va *à cheval* ou *à pied*. (Rat 1978: 24)

(d)   Ne dites pas: **causer à quelqu'un**
      Mais dites: **causer avec quelqu'un**

*Causer à quelqu'un*, dû à l'analogie avec *parler à quelqu'un*, est très vivant dans la langue populaire ou familier; cette construction tend à se répandre dans la langue littéraire, mais dans l'usage actuel, elle reste suspecte d'incorrection. (Grevisse 1964: 928)

(e)   Ne dites pas: **aller au coiffeur/au dentiste**
      Mais dites: **aller chez le coiffeur/chez le dentiste**

*Aller au coiffeur, au dentiste*, etc. est considéré comme du langage populaire. *Aller chez le coiffeur, chez le dentiste*, etc. est seul correct, *aller à* ou *au* étant réservé aux choses (*aller à la messe*, [ . . . ] *au bois, au bain*, etc.). (Thomas 1956: 24)

(f)   Ne dites pas: **le vélo à Marcel**
      Mais dites: **le vélo de Marcel**

This use, unlike (a)–(e), *is* widely felt to be colloquial and rarely occurs in writing, or indeed in middle-class conversation. Like **j'ai monté**, l'homme que je le connais or où que tu vas?, 'possessive à' is popular rather than familiar in register, and seems likely to remain so.

Two points should be made about it, though (for more extensive discussion, see Leeman-Bouix 1994: 129–33). Firstly, it is a logical enough development, given that **le vélo est à Marcel** and **à qui est le vélo?** are both perfectly standard. Secondly, the replacement of **de** by **à** is restricted to cases involving ownership of an object, or a family relationship of some sort. As a consequence, the 'possessor' has to be a person: **la voiture à mon père** or **la femme à l'épicier**, but not *****la mort à Marcel** or *****les roues au vélo**.

Various other non-standard uses of prepositions are occasionally commented on by normative grammarians. These, too, have popular associations and are accordingly less often encountered than (a) to (e) above: (g) **se promener alentour la ville**; (h) **la clef est après la porte**; (i) **aussitôt son retour**; (j) **en face la mairie**; (k) **en outre de cela**.

Also often condemned, but – unlike the last five cases – very widespread and in no way restricted to *français populaire*, is the omission of the prepositions in time expressions involving the names of months: **à la fin de mai**, **au début d'octobre**, etc. This gives rise to contracted colloquial variants like **fin mai** (or **à la fin mai**), **début octobre**.

---

## *EXERCISES*

6† Which of the following should be asterisked, and why?

    (a)  le livre à Henri
    (b)  le roman à Emile Zola
    (c)  le pantalon à mon cousin
    (d)  la jambe à mon cousin
    (e)  l'anniversaire à Marie
    (f)  l'appartement à Marie

7† Why are the following acceptable?

    (a)  Nous <u>partons à</u> midi.
    (b)  Ce magasin est bien fourni <u>en bicyclettes</u>.
    (c)  Nous sommes allés <u>au marché</u>.
    (d)  <u>Dix à quinze</u> personnes étaient présentes.

8† Replace the prepositions in expressions (g)–(k) above by appropriate standard choices from the following: **à part**, **autour de**, **dès**, **en face de**, **sur**.

# 6 Sentence Structure and Organization

## 6.1 Topic structures and *reprise*

The stereotypical French sentence consists of a subject noun phrase followed by a verb followed by an object noun phrase (**le gros chat a attrapé la petite souris**). But in colloquial usage, nouns are often duplicated by pronouns, and the word-order is not necessarily 'subject-verb-object'. This section explores these features.

### 6.1.1 *Variations on the basic sentence pattern*

The following example illustrates a kind of structure that occurs frequently in all varieties of colloquial French:

> (1)   Marie, elle est partie.

(Such sentences occasionally occur in literary usage too, but have traditionally been regarded as 'loose' or 'redundant' forms of expression which are better avoided.)

The subject noun phrase here (**Marie**) is 'duplicated' by a pronoun (**elle**). This variant of **Marie est partie** is a single intonational unit, with no break between **Marie** and **elle**. In fact there is no real need for the comma: **Marie elle est partie** gives a more accurate representation of the intonation pattern. Sometimes, though, a comma can be useful because it reveals the grammatical structure more clearly.

The subject noun phrase can be located at the end of the sentence instead of the beginning:

> (2)   Elle est partie, Marie.

(Again, no comma is needed: **elle est partie Marie**.)

Indeed, there can be a considerable 'distance' between the noun phrase and the pronoun/verb unit:

(3)   Marie, ça fait plusieurs mois, sinon plusieurs années, je t'assure, qu'elle est partie.

Moreover, there is no particular limit on the length of a 'duplicated' NP:

(4)   La vieille marchande de journaux de la rue St-Pierre, elle est décédée ce matin.

The duplication of noun phrases by pronouns is known in French as *reprise*: the noun is 'taken up again' by the pronoun, so to speak. (Sometimes this term is restricted to cases where the relevant NP is placed at the beginning of the sentence, *anticipation* being used when it occurs at the end.) The process of moving the NP – in either direction – is called *detachment* (*détachement*), and the resultant sentences are *dislocated sentences* (*phrases disloquées* or *phrases segmentées*).

Specifically, (1) is a case of *left detachment* (or *left dislocation*), with the NP occurring before the pronoun, while (2) illustrates *right detachment* (or *right dislocation*), with the NP following the pronoun. The terms *left* and *right* derive, of course, from Western conventions of writing – rather inappropriately, given that detachment is essentially a spoken phenomenon.

The frequency of dislocated sentences in familiar and popular French can be as high as 50 per cent. Subject noun phrases undergo detachment much more often than direct objects, and direct objects more often than indirect objects (see 6.1.2 for examples of detached objects). Left detachment is about a third more frequent than right detachment for subjects, but right is more frequent than left for direct and indirect objects.

However, the frequency of occurrence varies greatly according to the level of formality and the identity of the speaker: *reprise* is, for example, a particularly noteworthy feature of the usage of younger speakers of whatever social category – evidence perhaps of a growing tendency to use this type of pattern.

---

## EXERCISE

1† Detach the underlined noun phrases first to the left, then to the right:

(a) La terre tourne autour du soleil.
(b) Je crois que notre planète tourne autour du soleil.
(c) La troisième planète du système solaire tourne autour du soleil une fois par an.
(d) Il y a des milliards d'années que la patrie de l'espèce humaine tourne autour du soleil.

---

### 6.1.2  Detachment of objects; multiple detachment

Here are some examples of detached direct objects (5)–(7) and indirect objects (8)–(9):

(5)  Marie, je la connais bien.
(6)  Je la connais bien, Marie.
(7)  Les voyages, Marie adore ça.

(For the use of generic ça, see 3.3.2.)

(8)  On lui a offert un beau cadeau, à Marie.
(9)  Marie, on lui a offert un beau cadeau.

At the beginning of a sentence, à is most often omitted from the indirect object noun phrase, as in (9). But it is possible to retain it:

(10)  A Marie, on lui a offert un beau cadeau.

A 'prepositionless' indirect object at the end of the sentence is unacceptable, however:

(11)  *On lui a offert un beau cadeau, Marie.

The pronouns y and en are involved in cases like:

(12)  Du vin, Marie en boit tous les jours.
(13)  Il lui en faut beaucoup, de nourriture.

(14)  J'y vais deux fois par an, à Paris.
(15)  (A) Paris, j'y vais deux fois par an.

And left (but not right) dislocation can affect the objects of other prepositions. For example, j'aimerais partir avec Jean can be rearranged either as:

(16)   Jean, j'aimerais bien partir avec lui

or, more colloquially, without **lui** as:

(17)   Jean, j'aimerais bien partir avec.

(See the discussion of 'preposition stranding' in 5.3.1.)

A phrase like **la soeur de Jean** can of course be detached as a unit: **elle est arrivée, la soeur de Jean**. But it is also possible to extract the 'possessor' from the rest of the phrase and detach it to the left:

(18)   Jean, sa soeur est arrivée.

A similar arrangement enables an adjective or numeral to be separated from an accompanying noun (see 3.1.2):

(19)   Hélène en a un beau de chat.

(20)   J'en ai acheté cinq de journaux.

But in these cases, only rightwards movement can occur: **\*de chat Hélène en a un beau** is not possible.

*Multiple detachment* (involving more than one noun phrase) is possible, but unusual, even in the most colloquial French, unless one of the noun phrases is a pronoun (**moi je le connais Jean**). Like the **ti** interrogative, simultaneous detachment of two nouns is one of those 'mythological' features of *français populaire* which are more often found in popular literature than in popular speech:

(21)   Marie, elle le déteste, Pierre.

The information about who hates whom in this sentence is conveyed by the pronouns, not by the position of the nouns. Marie hates Pierre whatever the permutation:

(22)   Pierre, elle le déteste, Marie.
(23)   Pierre, Marie, elle le déteste.
(24)   Elle le déteste, Marie, Pierre.

If both nouns have the same gender, then of course this kind of flexibility is less readily available. Unless there is a clarifying context, the following are not interchangeable:

(25)   Marie, elle la déteste, Sophie.
(26)   Sophie, elle la déteste, Marie.

## EXERCISES

2† Carry out *reprise* in as many different ways as you can on the underlined items in the following. State in each case which type of detachment results (left, right or multiple).

(a) On va mettre <u>ces fleurs</u> dans un pot.
(b) Il y a <u>des survivants</u>.
(c) On connaît <u>l'ordre du jour de ce matin</u>.
(d) Marie a présenté un bouquet de fleurs <u>à la reine</u>.
(e) <u>Bernard</u> a trompé <u>Sophie</u>.
(f) Je crois que <u>Pierre</u> a rencontré Chirac à une réception.
(g) Je crois que Pierre a rencontré <u>Chirac</u> à une réception.
(h) Ils ont eu <u>de la chance</u>.
(i) <u>La nièce des Dupont</u> a été reçue au bac.
(j) La nièce <u>des Dupont</u> a été reçue au bac.
(k) On est contre <u>la peine de mort</u>.
(l) Marianne portait <u>un chapeau</u> ridicule.

3† Convert the following into standard form (with vocabulary and other grammatical changes when appropriate):

(a) Le Tibet je peux manifester pour, ça changera rien. (LBN)

(b) Nous ça on s'en fout. (LBN)

(c) La Suisse on y mange pas très bien. (CR81)

(d) La propreté, je suis pas contre. (RFB108)

(e) Les caniveaux, il y a tout le temps des nouilles dedans. (FCT188)

(f) Il en a mangé trois de pommes. (KL85)

(g) A l'Odéon, j'y suis pas allée. (JE20)

(h) Moi mon père les roses lui donnaient le rhume des foins. (TF1)

(i) Moi ma soeur sa dent elle tenait pas bien. (CR109)

### 6.1.3 Previous mention; topic and comment

What is the reason for these rearrangements? Generally the referent of a detached NP has already figured in some way in the conversation or in the situational context. The most typical examples are those in which the detached NP itself is occurring for the second time in a short stretch of discourse:

(27) Nous avons eu deux mille appels de consommateurs et ces consommateurs ils nous disent que [ ... ] (FI)

(28) Vous êtes des mômes et les mômes ça joue pas avec les armes. (FR3)

(29) Si elle a un défaut il faut le trouver ce défaut. (MBD47)

On its first, non-detached, occurrence, the NP is 'new' to the discourse (not mentioned before). By the time of its second, detached, occurrence, it has become 'familiar' to the hearer and the speaker proceeds to say more about it. The effect of the detachment is to signal the difference between familiar and new information, and to foreground the latter.

In English, new information is usually highlighted simply by being given the main sentence stress. Thus 'kids don't pláy with guns' would be the equivalent of the second clause in (28). Individual words cannot be stressed in this way in French, so alternative methods of emphasis and de-emphasis are used.

The same mechanism of 'previous mention' can be seen at work in the following example of multiple detachment (underlined). Here a small boy (**le petit**) is punished by his teacher (**la [bonne] soeur**) for climbing a tree. In this case, both protagonists have already been referred to: the new information is contained in the verb phrase **courir après**:

(30) Eh ben son frère il a reçu une fessée par la [bonne] soeur. Parce qu'il montait sur un arbre [ ... ] Alors tu penses bien qu'il y en avait déjà un qui était tombé une fois. Alors <u>la soeur elle lui a couru après au petit</u> qui était descendu [ ... ] parce qu'elle voulait pas qu'il recommence. (CR57)

A noun phrase which, in a particular sentence, incorporates 'familiar' or 'given' information is known as a *topic*. The 'unfamiliar' information is called the *comment*. The term *to topicalize* is used to designate processes like *reprise* in French, which serve to mark topics overtly. Topics do not have to be subjects, though most often they are. In (29), **défaut** is an object topic.

## EXERCISES

4† If Jean meets Marie and says to her: **Bonjour, quoi de neuf?**, which of the following is more likely to be her reply, and why?

(a) Le chien de mon propriétaire a été écrasé par un camion.

(b) Le chien de mon propriétaire il a été écrasé par un camion.

If, instead, Jean asks how the animals at Marie's house are getting on, which of the above replies is more likely, and why?

5† Account for the multiple detachment (underlined) in:

Rufus [ . . . ] a commencé à expliquer que c'était l'histoire d'un corbeau qui tenait dans son bec un roquefort [ . . . ] 'Mais non, a dit Alceste, c'était un camembert. – Pas du tout, a dit Rufus, <u>le camembert, le corbeau il n'aurait pas pu le tenir</u> dans son bec, ça coule et puis ça sent pas bon! (SGN45–6)

6 Detachment of three NPs is a real curiosity. People do not normally 'talk about' three things simultaneously! However, the linguist Lucien Tesnière quotes the following, which he says was uttered by a student in 1936 (he provides no context, unfortunately):

(a) Il la lui a donnée à Jean son père sa moto. (LT175)

Analyse the structure of this sentence, explaining why it is clear even without a context, and give a standard French equivalent.

From a more recent conversation, Françoise Gadet quotes:

(b) Tu comprends Jacqueline sa mère la bonne elle la lui refile. (GFP76)

Why is this difficult or impossible to interpret out of context? What kind of contextual information would facilitate interpretation?

### 6.1.4 *Links between topic, discourse and situation*

In some cases the link between a topic and the preceding discourse is less direct than in the examples given so far. It may merely be *related in meaning* to an earlier NP:

(31) Il fait un froid de canard en ce moment, je regarde dans le jardin, je regardais la salade ce matin, la laitue ça fait huit jours qu'elle est morte. (DF778)

**La laitue** is topicalized here because the lettuce itself has already been referred to – as **la salade**: these two nouns are near-synonyms.

In yet other cases, the topicalized NP *contrasts* with an earlier NP, but there is still a relationship of meaning:

(32) Oh! je ne suis pas en forme. J'ai mon plus jeune, il va falloir lui recasser le bras. L'opération a été mal faite. Et puis mon grand, à l'armée, ils l'ont hospitalisé. (PB81)

This speaker is not announcing that she has more than one son: the hearer can be assumed to have deduced this, so it is not new information. Rather, she is making the point that the elder son, as well as the younger one, has had to go to hospital.

Sometimes the topic need not actually have been mentioned at all: as long as it is part of the situational context, it is still possible to detach the NP that refers to it. During a televised cookery programme, for example, in which pots of jam are set out on a table in full view, one participant says to another:

(33) Tu les as goûtées les confitures? (TF1)

No reason for anyone to ask 'Quelles confitures?': they are on display and thus constitute familiar information. Similarly in the case of a waiter arriving with a tray of drinks and asking:

(34) Le café au lait c'est pour Madame?

Cases like (31)–(34) should be contrasted with situations in which detachment is inappropriate. If a telephone rings unexpectedly in another part of the house, the person breaking off the conversation to announce the fact is unlikely to say:

(35) Tiens, le téléphone il sonne.

The phone is an important element in the new information being provided, so a more appropriate form of expression would be:

(36)   Tiens, le téléphone sonne.

(See also 6.1.7.)

Cases are encountered, nevertheless, where the motivation for detachment is less clear. Generic NPs like **les gens** or **les mecs**, and NPs referring to close friends or relatives like **ma mère** or **ma soeur**, are often detached, even when used for the first time in the discourse, without an earlier related NP having been used and without the referent(s) being physically present. Presumably, close family members are present by proxy, as it were, if the speaker is. And **les gens** in the generic sense seems to be felt to include the speaker on the basis of some kind of solidarity:

(37)   Tu fais des choses pour les SDF et les jeunes, après tu dis bonjour en levant les bras, et les gens ils veulent bien voter pour toi. (LFM12)

In the following, the detachment of **les bus** is less easy to explain (the reference is to the visit of a foreign head of state):

(38)   Il a chamboulé tout Paris, alors que tout marchait si bien avant sa visite officielle. Les bus ils étaient bloqués, il a qu'à aller à pied! (LFM109)

Possibly the buses are subsumed under **tout** and therefore have effectively been mentioned already. Ultimately, speakers make their own decisions about what they are assuming their interlocutor to know, and individuals sometimes behave idiosyncratically. But there is a large area of consistency.

---

### EXERCISES

7†   Account, in terms of 'given' and 'new' information, for the detachment of the underlined items in:

(a)   Avec mon fils je suis parti au Japon. J'en parle plus, les gars ils croient que je bluffe. (PB104)

(b)   mais tu vois le cheval d'Aurélie, en reparlant de ça, sa selle elle est vraiment pas bien (MBD47)

(c) Alors la maîtresse lui a donné des lignes à faire, à lui aussi. Agnan, il a été tellement étonné qu'il n'a même pas pleuré. La maîtresse a commencé à les distribuer drôlement, les punitions. (SGN13)

(d) Figure-toi qu'il y avait des fourmis, il était plein de fourmis. Ah! je dis, je vais le traiter [ . . . ] Ah! je dis, les fourmis ils vont s'en rappeler, hein. (DF787) (See 3.1.1 for the gender of **fourmi** here.)

(e) De retour à la maison, Renée se regarda dans la glace. C'était un beau salaud, le père Etienne, pire qu'un flic. Mais elle avait deux mille francs et des conserves, du café, du sucre pour la semaine. (RFC45) [*Renée has just allowed herself to be seduced by Etienne, the local grocer, in return for the money and groceries referred to. Etienne is not present in this scene and has not been mentioned in the preceding discourse.*]

8   What is confusing and/or inaccurate about the following account of detachment (from a French grammar for anglophones)?

Under the stress of emotion, utterance begins before the mind has clearly surveyed the whole field of the thought to which it is about to give expression, and proceeds in short spurts, a bit at a time, the result being a *dislocation* of the elements of the sentence [ . . . ]

'Le café, je n'ai pas le temps, moi, pour y aller.'

[ . . . ] The direct object of the sentence may be stressed,

1. by isolating it at the beginning of the sentence: *Les cigares, je n'aime pas ça*;

2. by isolating it at the end of the sentence: *Je ne les aime pas, vos cigares.* [ . . . ]

[In] *Ce livre, Henri me l'a donné* [ . . . ] by a dislocation, *donné* is brought into a strong position, in which we may give it full vocal stress. (Mansion 1952: 14, 181, 180)

9    The following observations are by a normative grammarian of
     the 1930s. Comment on his view of detachment and its users:

     Le désir d'être bien compris inspire beaucoup de
     procédés du langage populaire et c'est pour lui une
     grande excuse [ . . . ] Dans la tournure suivante: «Il
     faudra bien que Jean il comprenne que . . . », cet *il*,
     grammaticalement superflu, est utile dans la pensée de
     celui qui parle.
       Ce pronom inutile a pour but d'indiquer, sans erreur
     possible, que *comprenne* est à la troisième personne et
     ne doit pas se confondre avec les formes, identiques
     pour l'oreille, des première et seconde personnes: que je
     comprenne, que tu comprennes.
       Le peuple veut être clair, et c'est pourquoi il réussit
     souvent à être obscur. Rien de tel que les mots superflus
     pour faire perdre le fil du discours et le sens du
     raisonnement [ . . . ] (Moufflet 1935: 201–2)

### 6.1.5   *Left versus right detachment*

In a right-dislocated sentence the detached noun phrase is characterized by
a low, flat intonation pattern, with the intonation peak falling on the phrase
before it:

(39)  Elle n'est pas contente, la directrice.

This contrasts with the left-dislocation pattern, in which the noun phrase is
included in the general rising tune of the first part of the sentence:

(40)  La directrice, elle n'est pas contente.

The fact that right-detached noun phrases lack intonational prominence
means that they also lack prominence in terms of the importance of the
information they convey. And this in turn means that there are tighter
restrictions on right detachment than on left. Essentially, a noun phrase can
be right-detached only if its referent is present in the situational context:

(41)  C'est pour Madame, le café au lait?

or if the NP itself (but not normally a related NP or a synonym) has previously occurred:

(42) Dans les ateliers on est mieux que les roulants [*train drivers*]. Ils ont pas de vie de famille, les roulants. (PB47)

Such arrangements have the effect of foregrounding the 'comment' particularly strongly (**pour Madame, vie de famille**): the right-detached NP is there simply to 'remind' the listener what the topic is. Right-detached NPs are therefore often encountered in exclamatory sentences like:

(43) Mais c'est pas normal, cette décision! (RB)

(44) Ils sont fous, ces Romains! (GU passim)

However, if a right-detached noun phrase is a term of abuse, it need not be identical to an earlier NP – the relevance of the term is taken for granted:

(45) La Lolotte elle était jamais là, j'ai su après où elle était cette salope. (DB94)

Right detachment is rare in the other cases that were mentioned in 6.1.4. The following variant on (31), for example, would be unnatural, because the expected repetition of the same NP (**la salade**) does not occur (and **la laitue** is not a term of abuse!):

(46) *Il fait un froid de canard en ce moment, je regarde dans le jardin, je regardais la salade ce matin, ça fait huit jours qu'elle est morte, la laitue.

Equally unacceptable is the following variant on (38), where the right-detached NP seems to appear 'from nowhere', with consequent difficulties of interpretation: 'what buses?', the hearer is likely to ask:

(47) *Il a chamboulé tout Paris, alors que tout marchait si bien avant sa visite officielle. Ils étaient bloqués, les bus, il a qu'à aller à pied!

The various differences are shown in:

(48) Juju escalada le talus et gagna les voies. Les voies, ça avait été son jardin d'enfant et sa promenade de poivrot. Il les aimait encore, les voies. (RFC208)

**Les voies** occurs three times here (underlined). First it is part of a comment (new information). Then it appears as a left-detached topic, introducing new information about the now 'familiar' railway tracks. Finally, it is detached to the right and reduced almost to an afterthought, allowing intonational prominence to be given to **encore** ('he still loved them').

---

## EXERCISES

10† Which types of detachment seem most appropriate in the following cases: left, right, either or none? (Examples adapted from Lambrecht 1981.)

  (a) The police officer points to an illegally parked car and says to a passer-by:

  Elle est à vous cette voiture?
  Cette voiture elle est à vous?
  Cette voiture est à vous?

  (b) A and B are conversing in a room; A happens to look out of the window and sees B's father at the front door. However, neither party has been thinking or talking about B's father. A says:

  Dis donc, ton père est à la porte.
  Dis donc, ton père il est à la porte.
  Dis donc, il est à la porte ton père.

11† In the following, is Jospin or Henri being referred to as a **crétin**, and what is the reason for the structure used?

  J'ai rencontré Henri ce matin. Il a voté pour Jospin, ce crétin!

12 Account for the successive non-detachment, left detachment and right detachment of the underlined NPs in the following:

  (a) Conversation about presents.
     – Elle voudrait bien ma mère, mais quand <u>ma chatte</u> sera morte.
     – Quoi?
     – Ben me donner une petite bête.
     – Quoi? Mais qu'est-ce qu'il y a?
     – Ben un petit chien un tout petit chien. Ou comme ça.

- On t'achètera un petit chien?
- Oui. Même quand ma mère, quand <u>ma chatte elle</u> sera morte elle vou ... elle veut bien m'acheter un petit chien.
- Pourquoi est-ce qu'<u>elle</u> va mourir <u>ta chatte</u>? (CR85)

(b)   Account of a conversation at the butcher's.
- [ ... ] i'm' dit prenez un ... tenez j'ai un p'tit bout d'épaule, euh, de veau, i'm'dit, <u>un p'tit ragoût</u>, vous savez, j'dis après tout comme elle [*his daughter*] est difficile que j'sais pas quoi lui donner, j'dis j'vais prendre ça, et bah j't'affirme hein, <u>mon ragoût</u> je crois qu'i'me revenait bientôt plus cher que l'bifteck.
- Oh oui, <u>c'est</u> cher <u>le ragoût</u>. (DF777)

### 6.1.6   *Moi, je ...*

The examples of left detachment considered so far should be distinguished from ones like:

(49)   Qui va accompagner Marie? – Jean, il va l'accompagner.

The intonation pattern here is different: **Jean** would have high pitch, and the rest of the sentence (which could in fact be omitted) has low, level pitch.

**Moi** (or **nous**) can have a similar intonation pattern to **Jean** in contexts like (49):

(50)   Qui va être dérangé? – Moi, je vais être dérangé.

This is the 'emphatic' or 'contrastive' use of **moi**. But there are other instances where **moi** or **nous** have a status comparable to that of the topic NPs in earlier examples, with the intonation peak occurring later in the sentence. Being a participant in the conversation, the speaker is inevitably 'given' or 'familiar'. Consequently, a left-detached **moi** (or **nous**) is often used to initiate an account of a speaker's opinions, feelings or activities. (In principle, the difference of intonation pattern could be signalled in transcriptions by the presence or absence of a comma after **moi**, but usage is inconsistent on this point.)

The following exchange is typical. The participants have been discussing the disadvantages of having too short a lunch-break in a building where the canteen is a long way from their workshop. Speaker C introduces his remarks with **moi je ...**, then uses **je** by itself with subsequent verbs.

(51)   A:   Oh puis y a les étages, dis donc.
       B:   On prend l'ascenseur hein.
       A:   Oui m'enfin tout de même.
       C:   Oui.
       B:   On prend l'ascenseur.
       C:   Une heure pour manger, le moins, le moins une heure
            pour manger, là, <u>moi j'aime</u> bien qu'en mangeant, je mange
            tranquillement, je commence à manger, il est midi, midi cinq,
            je finis à moins vingt, moins vingt-cinq, je prends mon journal
            ou une lecture [ . . . ] (DF811)

Omission of **moi** would not make C's sentence unacceptable, but its inclusion enables him to announce himself as the theme of the discourse, to set himself in the centre of the stage, as it were. (50), on the other hand, would be impossible without **moi**.

The 'turn-taking', non-contrastive use of **moi** is further illustrated in:

(52)   A:   [ . . . ] les Américains, bon ben, ils croient vraiment qu'ils
            sont gros. Y en a qui sont gros, hein.
       B:   Comme j'dis, c'est un problème d'obésité.
       A:   Oh oui.
       C:   Oh oui, parce que <u>moi</u>, la première fois qu'j'suis arrivée, j'ai
            vu des, surtout des femmes, ça des fois, c'est des monstres.
            (BKB38)

In the English equivalents of sentences with emphatic **moi** ( . . . **je**), the pronoun 'I' is stressed, but in the equivalents of (51) or (52), the main stress (and intonation peak) would fall on the comment that follows: 'I like to eat quíetly' (51) or 'I saw some . . . húge women' (52).

This use of **moi je** no doubt accounts for the fact that **moi** (and **nous**) are five times more likely to be left detached than right detached (as compared with other noun phrases, in the case of which the likelihood is only a third greater). **Toi** and **vous**, on the other hand, tend to be right not left detached. This encourages other participants to give a reply:

(53)   – T'es pas sportif toi. – Si quand même, je fais mon jogging tous les
       matins. (RB)

Left-detached **toi** is usually contrastive, serving to single out the person addressed:

(54)   A:   J'y suis jamais allé alors j'peux pas savoir. J'ai vu ça à la
            télévision.

B:  Et toi, tu y es allé?

C:  J'ai pas pu l'voir à la télévision parce que y a pas longtemps qu'je l'ai. (CR1)

Here, B listens to what A has to say, and then tries to find out what C's position is ('Have yóu been there?').

---

## EXERCISES

13†  Use English translations of the relevant parts of the following in order to ascertain whether **moi** (or **nous**) is being used contrastively or not.

(a)  Moi j'aime pas ce bruit-là.

(b)  Moi je pars, toi tu restes.

(c)  La maîtresse est entrée en classe toute nerveuse. 'M. l'Inspecteur est dans l'école, elle nous a dit, je compte sur vous pour être sages et faire une bonne impression.' Nous on a promis qu'on se tiendrait bien. (SGN39)

(d)  Et Alceste a pris le cigare et il a essayé de faire passer la fumée par son nez, et ça, ça l'a rudement fait tousser. Moi, j'ai essayé à mon tour [ . . . ] (SGN101)

14  Comment on the role of **moi ma femme** in the following:

A:  i' z'avaient un grand congélateur, il était plein . . .

B:  Oh dis, à la Résidence . . .

A:  Dis, pour quatre personnes . . .

B:  . . . les gens qui jetaient des gigots . . .

C:  Ah là là . . .

A:  Oui, c'est arrivé aussi ça, un grand machin rectangulaire . . .

B:  Ben tiens, quand t'étais à la boucherie c'était pareil hein, les gens qui, qui jetaient . . .

A:  Oui, oui

C:  Oh là là, mais moi, moi ma femme fait un rôti, on reçoit du monde, on fait un rôti [ . . . ] [*and a long anecdote follows*]. (FH)

### 6.1.7  *Indefinites and presentatives*

If the basic factor determining whether an NP can appropriately be detached is the extent to which its referent is 'familiar', 'given' or 'inferrable from the situation', then this explains why detachment is unacceptable with indefinite NPs:

(55)  *Quelqu'un il a frappé à la porte.
(56)  *Un agent il a frappé à la porte.
(57)  *Trois agents ils ont frappé à la porte.
(58)  *Il pleurait dans l'appartement voisin, un bébé.

**Quelqu'un, un agent, trois agents, un bébé** are not topics: they refer to un-specified individuals who are being mentioned for the first time. The only indefinite NPs which allow detachment are those referring to a general cat-egory, not to individuals:

(59)  Ça demande beaucoup d'attention, un bébé.

This sentence is equivalent to **ils demandent beaucoup d'attention, les bébés**, with a definite NP. (See 3.3.2 for the use of 'generic' **ça**.)

However, although acceptable, **un agent a frappé à la porte** (without **il**) is not particularly informal. Colloquial French avoids placing non-topic sub-jects at the beginning of sentences. Instead, they are commonly introduced by means of a 'presentative' expression like **(il) y a . . . qui**:

(60)  Y a un agent qui a frappé à la porte.

Similarly when the non-topic subject is a definite NP:

(61)  Salut! Quoi de neuf?
      –  Y a Pierre qui est malade.
      –  Y a mon grand-père qu'est mort.
      –  Y a le chien qui s'est fait écraser.
      –  Y a Jean à qui j'ai dit une bêtise.

In the following, the status of **cinq-six bateaux** evolves from one clause to the next:

(62)  tu vois, y a cinq-six bateaux qui sont détournés d'Anvers, Anvers fait grève ce jour-là, bon ben ces cinq-six bateaux ils vont aller à Dunkerque pour être déchargés [ . . . ] (FH)

The **y a** presentative introduces **cinq-six bateaux** as a non-topic noun phrase. (The prefatory **tu vois** is an additional signal that new information is about to be provided.) This NP then re-occurs as a left-detached topic: the new information now is that the ships are being taken to Dunkirk.

Another commonly encountered presentative is **j'ai**:

(63)  J'ai le pot d'échappement qui est tombé. (JE64)

(64)  j'ai mon plus jeune, il va falloir lui recasser le bras [ . . . ] (PB81)

Other persons of **avoir** can also act as presentatives:

(65)  ils sont stressés par leurs fins de mois comme tout le monde – mais ils ont moins de sollicitations – ils ont moins les magasins qui les attirent. (BBA91)

This is equivalent to standard **les magasins les attirent moins**. The literal meaning of **avoir** has been lost altogether in:

(66)  J'ai encore un formulaire que j'ai pas. (GFP77)

In standard French **il me manque encore un formulaire**, or an equivalent wording, would have to be used. However, in colloquial French (66) is not contradictory: presentative **j'ai** is a separate item from **j'ai** meaning 'I have'.

Other presentative expressions (though more restricted in use than **y a** or **j'ai**) include: **ça fait (trois cent francs qu'il me doit), voici (le train qui arrive)** and **voilà**:

(67)  V'là le brouillard qui s'amène. (TJ37)

## EXERCISES

15†  It was stated in 6.1.4 that, if a phone suddenly starts ringing, then **le téléphone sonne** (without detachment) is more appropriate than **le téléphone il sonne**, as **le téléphone** is not a topic. Can you suggest a still more natural formulation, which would avoid locating **le téléphone** at the beginning of the sentence?

16†  Show the meaning of the following by giving standard French equivalents of the parts of the examples containing presentatives:

(a) Y en avait qui avaient déjà commencé à faire la grève. (JE18)

(b) J'en ai un qui me manque. (AM199)

(c) on a des camions-double cabine – on a plus les gens qui sont dehors comme avant (BBA91)

(d) parce qu'une fois qu'y a que'que chose qu'a été écrit, signé et contresigné ratifié comme tu dis, [ . . . ] ça d'vient des . . . ça d'vient des conventions collectives, tu vois (FH)

(e) Tire-toi, y a des keufs [*policiers*] qui arrivent. Y en a qui matent [*regardent*] devant chez ta meuf [*femme*]. (IZ32)

(f) Ma soeur, y a son fourneau, quand on veut allumer, tu as rien à faire, y a un truc prévu pour. (AC292)

### 6.1.8 Clefts and pseudo-clefts

Reference was made in 6.1.6 to the emphatic or contrastive use of **moi** found in **moi je vais être dérangé**, in which **moi** represents 'new' information. The rest of this sentence is 'given' and has a topic-like function: it is known that someone or other is going to be disturbed – the question is, who.

An alternative (and quite standard) way of achieving the same effect is by means of a so-called *cleft sentence* – one in which the new information is introduced by **c'est** and the given information (**je vais être dérangé**) is placed in a following relative clause: **c'est moi qui vais être dérangé**. This allows **moi** to be highlighted intonationally. In informal usage the verb would be third rather than first person: **c'est moi qui va être dérangé** (see 4.2.3). Otherwise formal and informal French coincide on this point.

Clefts are probably more frequent in spoken usage than in written, and the same is undoubtedly true of *pseudo-cleft* sentences like **celui qui va être dérangé, c'est moi**. Here **moi** still represents new information, but the order of new and given is reversed, with the postponement of the new allowing a 'mini-surprise' to be built up. If the 'new' noun phrase is inanimate, then the given information is introduced by **ce qui**: **Ce qui me dérange c'est le bruit**.

Both cleft and pseudo-cleft structures make it possible to locate non-topic noun phrases away from the beginning of the sentence, i.e. to avoid sentences like **le bruit me dérange**. In this respect they serve a similar purpose to the presentatives just discussed in 6.1.7 (**y a un bruit qui me dérange**).

They also have the advantage of providing an alternative to rather cumbersome and non-conversational expressions like **le fait de/que** . . . . For example, instead of: **ils sont caractérisés par le fait qu'ils ont quatre pattes**, or **le fait d'avoir quatre pattes les caractérise**, it would be much more natural, and probably more elegant, to say:

(68)   Ce qui les caractérise, c'est qu'ils ont quatre pattes. (BBA99)

---

## EXERCISES

17†   Give (i) cleft and (ii) pseudo-cleft equivalents of:

    (a)   Je voudrais un kir royal.
    (b)   Le président a ouvert la séance.
    (c)   Un fou a inventé tout cela.

18†   Give pseudo-cleft equivalents of:

    (a)   Il a décidé de s'absenter.
    (b)   Elles préfèrent ne pas essayer.
    (c)   Il nous faut un nouveau gouvernement.

19†   Reformulate more colloquially by pseudo-clefting:

    (a)   L'incroyable, c'est qu'ils ne sont jamais chez eux.
    (b)   Qu'il ait pu commettre trois meurtres est étonnant.
    (c)   Le fait d'avoir à faire trois kilomètres à pied tous les jours m'agace.
    (d)   La possibilité qu'il y ait eu un accident nous inquiète.
    (e)   L'ivresse au volant a provoqué la collision.
    (f)   Je suis frappé par le fait qu'il est presque toujours absent.

---

## 6.2   Extending the range of grammar: 'macro-syntax'

Despite their frequency, topic structures like those described in 6.1 have been largely excluded from traditional grammars. So have various other typically colloquial utterance types which, in the view of many French linguists, are not just unsystematic or random deviations from the norm, but, like dislocated sentences, follow structured patterns of their own. More detailed accounts of what has come to be known as *macro-syntaxe* are given in Blanche-Benveniste (1990 and 1997), the source of many of the examples that follow.

### 6.2.1   *Topicalization without* reprise; *binary sentences*

It occasionally happens that **y a** or **j'ai** presentatives occur without any relative pronoun. So instead of:

(1)   Y a Jean qu'on le voit pas souvent

we find:

(2)   Y a Jean, on le voit pas souvent.

Similarly:

(3)   Il y a des gens, on leur confierait jamais son argent. (JDE105)

In terms of intonation, (2) is a single unit, with a rise, not a fall, on **Jean**. In terms of grammatical structure, the absence of a linking **que** means that it is a sequence of two independent units. However, the relationship between them is still indicated by the reference of **le**, or **leur** in (3).

*Reprise* pronouns are sometimes omitted from dislocated sentences in a parallel way. For example, instead of **le boulot on s'en plaint pas**, we find:

(4)   Le boulot, on se plaint pas. (GFP77)

This has the same single-sentence intonation pattern as (2). The fact that **le boulot** is the sentence topic is still indicated by the left detachment, but this time its relationship to the second part of the sentence (**on se plaint pas**) is not made explicit. The term *phrase binaire* (or *énoncé binaire*) has come to be used of sentences like (4), which are made up of two (or more) components that are simply juxtaposed.

Note that right detachment is impossible if there is no *reprise* pronoun:

(5)   *On se plaint pas, le boulot.

Right-detached NPs always need overt linkage to the rest of the sentence (**on s'en plaint pas, du boulot**).

In (5), a pronoun (**en**) can easily be supplied. In (6), on the other hand, it is not obvious what the pronoun could appropriately be. But the meaning is clear enough, even out of context:

(6)   ces souliers, j'écrase les pieds de tout le monde (JDE75)

In standard French (6) would have to be paraphrased (much less concisely) along the lines of **quand je porte ces souliers, j'écrase les pieds de tout le monde**.

A binary utterance like:

(7)   Claude Debussy ma soeur (note the absence of a verb)

seems cryptic when taken in isolation, even if it is explained that the reference is not to the composer but to a school named after him. However, if the conversational context is supplied, it becomes perfectly meaningful:

(8)   – Et ton frère il est à Marcel Roby?
      – Heu oui. Claude Debussy ma soeur, et Marcel Roby mon frère.
      (CR84)

Even exclamations or expletive can follow this type of pattern:

(9)   Ce mec, putain! (RB)

(10)   Ce voyage, oh là là! (RB)

(9) might be more elegantly expressed as **ce garçon est vraiment admirable**, and (10) paraphrased as **ce voyage a été bien pénible**. However, other interpretations would be possible, depending on the specific context.

## EXERCISES

1†  Add suitable *reprise* pronouns to the following, in order to bring out the relationship between the components:

(a)  Paris, j'ai jamais été. (RB)

(b)  la cantine, on a pas à se plaindre (GFO134)

(c)  L'Angleterre, hein, il pleut tout le temps. (CR80)

(d)　l'eau, on pouvait pas se baigner (CR80)

(e)　Le chocolat j'aime pas tellement. (RB)

2†　Explain the meaning of the following and supply standard
　　French equivalents or paraphrases. In which cases, if any,
　　could the topic NP be right detached?

(a)　mon métier, j'ai fait chauffeur-livreur (JDE100)

(b)　la dernière crise que j'ai eue, je suis allé voir le docteur
　　X (JDE100)

(c)　la moindre contrariété, je suis angoissée (JDE100)

(d)　ce métier, on se déplace tous les jours (JDB40)

(e)　il y a des gens qui disent que les camps [*de
　　concentration*] c'est faux (LFM85)

3　Suggest less colloquial equivalents of the following (you may
　need to narrow down the range of possible contextual
　meanings):

(a)　Paris bof!

(b)　Moi, la sauce béarnaise, beurk!

### 6.2.2　*Prefix, nucleus and suffix*

The examples so far suggest that binary sentences have a general resemblance to the 'topic + comment' structures presented in 6.1. In order to project the topic–comment kind of analysis on to this wider domain, some new terminology has been proposed by the Aix-en-Provence group of linguists (see 1.8). *Noyau* ('nucleus') designates the 'comment' (new information: underlined) in an utterance like:

(11)　<u>Amusant</u>, ce tableau. (RB)

This is equivalent to the standard **ce tableau est amusant** or **je trouve ce tableau amusant**, or indeed to the colloquial **ce tableau il est amusant**.

The equivalent of the topic may take the form of a 'prefix' or a 'suffix'. The analogy is with the structure of individual words, e.g. **in-compréhens-ible** (prefix + nucleus + suffix). **Ce tableau** in (11) is an example of a suffix; prefixes are exemplified by the non-underlined components of:

(12)   Des vacances, <u>pas question</u>. (RB)

(13)   Le lendemain, <u>grande surprise</u>. (BBA116)

Two such structures can be juxtaposed, making a larger 'macro-syntactic unit' than the binary structures considered so far:

(14)   En centre-ville d'accord, ailleurs non. (BBA116)

This falls into two symmetrical halves:

| **(en centre-ville** | **+** | **d'accord)** | **+** | **(ailleurs** | **+** | **non)** |
|---|---|---|---|---|---|---|
| (prefix | + | nucleus) | + | (prefix | + | nucleus) |

A grammatically more explicit (but less satisfyingly terse) paraphrase might be something like: **nous permettons que cela se passe au centre-ville, mais nous l'interdisons ailleurs**.

Symmetrical repetitions can also be found *within* individual nuclei, for example in the nucleus of the following 'prefix + nucleus + suffix' unit:

(15)   en général dans les maisons/<u>il y en a il y en a pas</u>/ça dépend [*sometimes there are some, sometimes not*] (BBE117)

And nuclei can be accompanied by more than one prefix or suffix (as can word-stems: **in-compréhens-ibili-té**). The prefix in (16) contains two adverbial expressions (**finalement** and **vu l'importance de l'enjeu**), which, in terms of traditional categories, might be labelled 'temporal' and 'causative'. Again, the overall arrangement is 'prefix + nucleus (underlined) + suffix', with the suffix **la Patagonie** fulfilling a similar role to the right-detached topics in earlier examples (the reference is to a project relating to Patagonia, rather than to the region itself – hence the masculine adjective).

(16)   finalement, vu l'importance de l'enjeu/<u>intéressant</u>/la Patagonie (BBE126)

The theoretical possibilities of this kind of concatenation are illustrated in a sentence invented by Blanche-Benveniste:

(17)   selon eux, chez leur père, quand c'était l'hiver, quand la neige
       arrivait, les femmes, quand elles travaillaient, des trucs comme ça,
       elles aimaient pas du tout (BBA120)

Here the nucleus **elles aimaient pas du tout** is preceded by successive prefixes
relating to: point of view; place; time; time (again); topicalized subject (with
*reprise*); topicalized object (without *reprise*). Some of these combine to form
smaller units within larger ones. Brackets help to make the groupings clearer:

(17a)   selon eux, chez leur père, (quand c'était l'hiver, quand la neige
        arrivait), (les femmes, quand elles travaillaient), des trucs comme
        ça, elles aimaient pas du tout

As Blanche-Benveniste points out, it is unlikely that such a unit would ever
actually be uttered (though parts of it might well be). But what is interesting
is that theoretical predictions can be made about types of utterance which
hitherto have been considered too chaotic ever to be systematized.

Indeed, it is even possible to identify 'ungrammatical' macro-syntactic
sequences. Thus, like **le boulot, on se plaint pas** in (4), most of the sentences
that have been quoted become unacceptable if right detachment is used
instead of left:

(18)   *J'écrase les pieds de tout le monde, ces souliers.
(19)   *On pouvait pas se baigner, l'eau.
(20)   *Pas question, des vacances.

## EXERCISES

4†   Suggest more explicit, standard paraphrases for the following
     sentences, which have already been quoted above:

     (a)   Amusant ce tableau.
     (b)   Des vacances, pas question.
     (c)   Le lendemain, grande surprise.
     (d)   en général dans les maisons il y en a il y en a pas, ça
           dépend.
     (e)   finalement, vu l'importance de l'enjeu, intéressant la
           Patagonie.

5    Analyse the following in terms of prefix, nucleus and suffix,
     then suggest English translations:

(a)  Les Cévennes, faut pas sous-estimer le temps [*weather*].
     (SM194)

(b)  Leurs cousins, les Becker, c'est la même chose. (KL55)

(c)  le suisse allemand faut se lever tôt alors [*conversation
     about language learning*] (KL55)

(d)  Moi c'est quatorze [*discussion about homework marks*].
     (CR83)

(e)  question jeunesse, au Vatican, ça manque [*discussion
     about the Catholic church and young people*] (LFM37)

(f)  Lui c'est la linguistique appliquée [*said when pointing
     someone out*]. (SM194)

(g)  Moi, mon frère, sa voiture, les freins i'déconnent. (AC292)

(h)  Mon père sa moto le guidon le chrome est parti. (JDB41)

### 6.2.3  *Parenthesis*

Written texts occasionally enclose material inside brackets (*parentheses*) as a
way of indicating information or observations which are relevant to the
surrounding discourse, but not linked to it grammatically. Parenthetical
material has a much more prominent role in the structure of colloquial
discourse, as recent research has shown.

Speakers make use of parenthesis (underlined in the following examples)
in a variety of circumstances. Sometimes the purpose is to include explanat-
ory information which, strictly speaking, should have been provided earlier:

(21)  Un jour sa gra-, sa, sa belle-mère lui dit: «Euh, euh, écoutez Hubert»,
      (parce qu'il s'appelle Hubert Litier, en plus) «Hubert, il faudrait
      que vous me, m'ouvriez le vasistas dans l'escalier» (elle habite un
      hôtel particulier, il y a des escaliers). Lui, il dit [ . . . ] (BBA122)

In this and many other examples, a parenthesis is introduced by **parce que**
(sometimes **puisque**). This is a noteworthy extension of its standard meaning: from 'because' to something more like 'the point is' or 'you see'. **C'est
que** . . . performs a similar function in standard French.

Sometimes the parenthetical material serves to reorientate the conversation. In the following, it might be paraphrased as 'to come back to what I was talking about':

(22) Alors à l'Electro <u>puisqu'on r'vient au à la à la base de la de la du machin</u> à l'Electro quand je travaillais pendant deux ans dans les années 61–62 bah j'me souviendrai toujours de l'oncle Jef [ . . . ] (FH)

Sometimes a comment is being made on the speaker's own discourse:

(23) Et y a un mec là <u>ché plus comment c'est son nom</u> qu'est passé à FR3 l'aut' jour [ . . . ] (FH)

Sometimes it takes the form of an aside which provides further relevant information:

(24) Tout le monde faisait (<u>j'en ai fait moi-même</u>) de l'aviron. (BBA122)

This example also illustrates how parenthetical material in colloquial discourse can occur at points within the sentence which would be unacceptable in formal French – in this case, between the verb and the object. But in colloquial French too, there are constraints on the insertion of parentheses – **j'en ai fait moi-même** could not be inserted before **faisait** in (24), for example. It is interesting, moreover, that in no case does the speaker have any difficulty in recovering the sentence structure embarked on before the parenthesis.

Those who have investigated discourse parentheses restrict the term to expressions containing a verb phrase. But colloquial speech contains large numbers of shorter pieces of inserted material. An appeal of some sort may be made to the interlocutor:

(25) Ma femme elle a son boucher sur la place de Bléville, e' va à son boucher, <u>attention</u>, ils nous soignent bien, ils nous donnent de la bonne viande. (FH)

The insertion may take the form of an expletive:

(26) Et y a un mec là ché plus comment c'est son nom qu'est passé à FR3 l'aut' jour c'est euh <u>merde</u> Loïc Hilaire ou que'que chose comme ça [ . . . ] (FH)

Or the intention may be to highlight a particular point:

(27) J'ai refusé parce que, <u>bon ben</u>, ça me disait pas grand'chose. (RB)

## EXERCISE

6† Rewrite, omitting all parentheses (no punctuation is provided).

(a) pour le moment je touche du bois ça a l'air d'aller (BBE147)

(b) alors il a donc écrit ce livre je l'ai dit tout à l'heure mais il a aussi relancé un petit peu l'idée du royaume de Patagonie (BBE149)

(c) pendant la guerre je vous l'ai pas dit j'avais créé une petite épicerie de campagne (BBE148)

(d) et on nous a obligés à devinez quoi vous ne devinerez jamais nous mettre tout nus (BBE147)

(e) Il y a bon de très rares cas mais ça existe quand même de malades parce que ce sont des malades qui n'ont dès la naissance aucune sensation de douleur (BBA123).

### 6.2.4 Structure and its absence in informal discourse

Here is a fairly typical short stretch of discourse, transcribed without any editing, but with some punctuation added in order to clarify the structure. The speakers are ten- and eleven-year-olds, discussing their friend Hélène, who, at a party, is more interested in card games (**jeux de société**) than in dressing up (**se déguiser**), and consequently falls behind the others.

(28) A: Hélène elle est pas encore déguisée alors.
   B: Ah ben non Hélène elle est en train de trier les les les jeux.
   C: Oui c'est c'qui l'intéresse le plus, elle vient chez des amies bon y a tous les déguisements qui sont sortis, elle est déjà à moitié déshabillée, puis alors elle aperçoit un jeu de société, alors elle regarde toutes les cartes l'une après l'autre, puis les filles elle sont toutes déguisées, il reste qu'elle elle est à moitié déshabillée. (CR58)

This illustrates a well-known (but sometimes over-emphasized) feature of spontaneous colloquial discourse. C's intervention consists essentially of a sequence of sentences linked by **alors, puis, mais** or **bon**, or simply juxtaposed.

The term *parataxis* (corresponding adjective *paratactic*) is often used to designate this kind of arrangement.

In more formal discourse, the links between sentences would be expressed by means of more specific connectors (**cependant, d'ailleurs, néanmoins**) or by greater use of subordination (**bien que, où, qui, après avoir** . . . ). The type of sentence structure that makes extensive use of subordinate clauses rather than sequences of main clauses is known as *hypotactic* (corresponding noun *hypotaxis*).

So speaker C's highly paratactic intervention might be rephrased more hypotactically as follows (with the narrative tense changed from present to perfect):

(28a)   Oui c'est ce qui l'intéresse le plus. Un jour elle est allée chez des amies qui ont sorti des déguisements. Après s'être à moitié déshabillée, elle a aperçu un jeu de société, dont elle a regardé les cartes l'une après l'autre. Par conséquent, lorsque les autres filles avaient fini de se déguiser, elle, elle est restée à moitié déshabillée.

If this seems stilted, then this is precisely because it lacks characteristic features of much spoken usage.

But it would be wrong to assume that colloquial speech is exclusively paratactic. The familiar and popular registers possess as wide a range of subordinating conjunctions as the standard language (see 5.1) – a fact that has sometimes tended to be overlooked. It is essentially a matter of the relative frequency of the two types of structure, and this can vary considerably from one user to another, both in more formal and in less formal discourse.

Now although conversational utterances may well be quite highly structured in various ways, the fact remains that speakers are normally improvising as they go along, and are not in a position to 'edit' what they have said. The result is that spontaneous colloquial speech contains a greater or lesser number of 'performance errors': hesitations, slips of the tongue, changes of construction 'in mid-stream', and various departures from the usual grammatical patterns – even from the ones described in this book. This is rarely imitated in dialogues in novels or plays, however colloquial they may otherwise be. In this respect, 'written spoken French' is almost always unnatural (cf. 8.2).

Even real speakers vary a good deal in the extent to which their utterances deviate from 'well-formedness': some are more fluent and articulate than others. The following excerpt illustrates some 'deviations', and also shows that it is not easy to divide informal discourse neatly into sentences, even 'loose' ones of the type described in 6.2.2. In the first half of speaker B's intervention there are nevertheless three clear breaks, justifying the full stops that have been inserted in the transcription.

In the second half ('Bah au Hav' . . .' onwards), the flow is more continuous and the speaker gets 'sidetracked' into talking about his own situation, rather than unemployment in general, which was the original point of the conversation. This results in a series of 'false starts' and changes of construction – not that these prevent the speaker from making his point very vividly. (The technical term *anacoluthon* is sometimes used to designate such breaks and discontinuities.)

(29)   A:   Tout ce qui est usine en général ça foire hein, dis, j'vais t'dire, j'vais t'dire quand on a été à Thionville hein, des des cités à l'infini hein des cités, des aciéries des aciéries tout ça . . .

   B:   Bah les mines de, les mines de fer de Longwy hein c'est connu hein, ben oui hein. Sept mille bonshommes qu'ont sauté d'un seul coup là-bas. Sept mille bonshommes ça veut dire . . . une femme ça fait quatorze mille, et deux gosses ça fait ça fait trente mille hein. Bah au Hav' i'sont en train de . . . depuis que le . . . moi depuis que . . . depuis six ans et demi qu'i' m'ont viré, parce que moi moi i'm'ont viré, j'emploie le terme viré en ce qui m'concerne, i'm'ont pas . . . i'm'ont pas évincé, i'm'ont viré moi hein. Parce que moi je voulais travailler. (FH)

However, even this excerpt is far from being totally unstructured. Alongside various examples of parataxis there are a number of hypotactic structures involving **quand**, **depuis que** and **parce que**. Moreover, a 'loose' sentence like:

quand on a été à Thionville hein, des des cités à l'infini

lends itself well to analysis in terms of a macro-syntactic 'prefix + nucleus' framework:

**quand on a été à Thionville + des cités à l'infini**

These two elements are linked by **hein**, which serves as a kind of topic-marker. Similarly with:

les mines de fer de Longwy hein c'est connu

(Taken in context, this means that the problems of the mines, not the mines as such, are well known.)
   Consider also:

une femme ça fait quatorze mille, et deux gosses ça fait trente mille

This is the kind of sequence which makes little sense in isolation, but in fact is coherently organized and symmetrical:

| Prefix | + | Nucleus |
|--------|---|---------|
| **une femme** | + | **ça fait quatorze mille** |
| | **et** | |
| **deux gosses** | + | **ça fait trente mille** |

The meaning is clear enough in context: if each of the 7,000 redundant steelworkers has a wife, then 14,000 people are affected – 30,000 if each couple is assumed to have two children.

---

## EXERCISES

7  Paraphrase the meaning of the following excerpts and identify as many of the following structural features as you can: parataxis, hypotaxis, anacoluthon, prefix + nucleus structures, parenthetical insertions.

(a)  A ten-year-old describes how her friends tried to dry their clothes during a skiing holiday.

Alors on a suspendu une ficelle. Et on étendait les anoraks et tout ça parce que elles les lavaient pas mais après le ski elles les . . . on les . . . on les suspendait, elles les . . . elles les étendaient, c'étaient la même chose dans la chambre à trois. Et puis au bout d'un moment elles mettaient un anorak deux trois, euh, des culottes, des chandails, des pulls, de tout; et puis à euh, à peu près à la vingtième chose, elle met la vingtième chose crac! (CR190)

(b)  A dock worker has to leave a wedding reception in order to go on night shift.

A:  L'après-midi j'étais vacant, puisque j'venais pour travailler l'après-midi mais j'ai travaillé à vingt-et-une heures là-bas, j'étais au vin d'honneur jusqu'à dix-huit heures, je suis rentré chez nous, Monique je l'ai conduit à la fête, mon costard j'étais toujours beau le costard trois pièces tu vois il est beau hein on a pris

des photos hein et puis à vingt-et-u- ... vingt heures
quinze je me suis barré en costard à Bougainville, j'ai
fait mon rafiot jusqu'à deux heures du matin et puis
euh arrivé là-bas j'ai défait mon costard je me suis
mis en troufion, y a un mec qui m'dit bon ben, Gérard,
barre-toi t'es du ... de ... t'es de la noce casse-toi.
A une heure et demie je m'suis barré. Je suis revenu
à une heure et demie de Bougainville jusqu'à ... par
la route, par Beaulieu puis la route de Rouelles,
qu'est-ce que j'vois là-bas? même pas arrivé à deux
kilomètres, où c'est qu' t'sais qu'y a des bourrins
là ...

B: Oui, oui, oui.

A: ... j'vois un mec affalé dans la rue, la vache, la
gueule en sang, j'avais dit à Monique euh j'vais venir
à midi à tout ... à minuit à tout casser euh ...

B: Oui et alors ce mec?

A: ... vingt-et-une heures jusqu'à trois heures euh j'irai
pas au-delà d'trois heures, donc à ... à une heure et
demie du matin j'me trouvais aux bourrins là-bas, j'ai
relevé le mec la gueule en sang et, c'était un samedi
soir, et puis j'étais plutôt comme un gland [*imbécile*] là
hein [ ... ] (FH)

8  Insert punctuation into the following, in such a way as to clarify
the structure:

An eleven-year-old talks about his recent judo accident.

A: Pendant la croissance c'est dangereux.

B: à quatorze ans j'pourrai recommencer parce que comme
moi une fois on avait fait une compétition et puis j'étais
contre une ceinture verte et j'ai et j'pouvais pas m'défendre
puisque moi j'étais déjà ceinture jaune et puis quand on est
vert y a déjà deux ceintures de et puis i' m'avait fait une
prise moi j'suis tombé par terre et j'ai et j'ai pas pu mettre
ma main ben j'me suis fait j'me suis très fait j'me suis fait
mal à la colonne vertébrale (CR15)

9  The following expresses a common normative view of the kind
of colloquial discourse discussed above. Summarize the writer's

evaluation of the utterance which he quotes. Then ascertain whether the latter lends itself to a macro-syntactic analysis.

Par malheur, il arrive souvent que toute une phrase, tout un récit, restent enveloppés dans [une] forme embryonnaire. L'auteur est incapable d'aller au-delà de l'ébauche de sa pensée. Les éléments de celle-ci sont énumérés dans l'ordre où les images se présentent à l'esprit, cahin-caha, avec volubilité et essoufflement, car l'infortuné n'en veut pas manquer un. Dans un restaurant, au cours d'une conversation gastronomique, j'ai noté la déclaration suivante, dont je sépare intentionnellement les parties successives, pour bien traduire le travail qui se poursuivait dans l'esprit de l'auteur:

1) Le gibier,
2) moi,
3) ce que je préfère
4) c'est la perdrix;
5) et, comme poil,
6) le lièvre.
7) Pas vous?            (Moufflet 1935: 194–5)

# 7 Grammatical Effects of an Unreformed Spelling System

## 7.1 Background: *orthographe d'usage* and *orthographe grammaticale*

The conservatism and 'irregularity' of French spelling is notorious: in a great many respects it still reflects the way the language was pronounced in the Middle Ages. Particularly important for this chapter is the fact that, in writing, grammatical information about number, gender or person is conveyed by letters which no longer correspond to audible speech sounds.

It is in fact customary, when discussing French spelling, to distinguish between *orthographe d'usage* and *orthographe grammaticale*. The former category relates to those numerous aspects of spelling which are not grammar-related. Its conventions account for mismatches like **eau** (three vowel letters) for the single vowel [o], and innumerable anomalies: **poids** has a silent *d*; **rognon** and **oignon** are identical in pronunciation (apart from the *r*), but are spelt with *-o-* and *oi-* respectively; **imbécile** has one *l*, whereas **imbecillité** has two. And so on.

Relevant to *orthographe grammaticale* is the fact that the *s* of **dois** and the *t* of **doit** indicate first/second person and third person, respectively, or that *-e* marks the feminine of adjectives and *-s* the plural of nouns. The elaborate rules about the agreement of the past participle are another aspect (see 4.2). Grammatical information of this sort is important in the spoken language, too. But how is it conveyed, in the absence of any spoken counterparts of the 'silent' letters of the written code?

---

**EXERCISE**

1  In the following (not untypical) excerpt from a letter, various
   spelling errors are underlined. Say whether they are
   infringements of *orthographe d'usage* or *orthographe
   grammaticale*.

   Je comprend très bien que votre fillette ne peut pas avoir
   plusieurs corespondantes mais si elle avait une petite
   camarade qui voudrais corespondre avec notre petite fille
   Marleine, elle est de l'age d'Isabelle. Nos enfants travaille
   a l'usine Peugeot, comme nous vous lavions déjà dis l'ors
   de votre visite chez nous [ . . . ] Je pense que votre séjour
   en France vous à pleus, et que vous reviendrez nous voir.
   Recever de nous deux toutes nos amitiés. (RB)

---

## 7.2  Singular and plural (especially nouns)

In spoken French, information about number is normally provided at the
beginning, not at the end of nouns. A similar pattern of 'prefixation' will be
encountered again later in connection with verbs (7.4).

### 7.2.1  Basic patterns in writing and speech

The rule about forming the plural of nouns in written French runs somewhat as follows:

Add -*s* to the noun unless an -*s*, -*z* or -*x* is already present in the singular:
**la femme . . . les femmes, le cas . . . les cas, le nez . . . les nez, la noix . . . les
noix**.

This applies to virtually all the nouns in the language. There are a small
number of special cases: nouns ending in -*eau* take -*x*, not -*s* in the plural
(**ce seau . . . ces seaux**); half a dozen nouns ending in -*ou* also (exceptionally)
take -*x* (**un chou . . . des choux**); nouns ending in -*al* or -*ail* mostly have a
plural in -*aux* (**leur cheval . . . leurs chevaux, mon travail . . . mes travaux**).
And there are one or two oddities like **l'ail . . . les aulx, l'oeil . . . les yeux**.
   The first six of these nouns are pronounced as follows:

| Singular | | Plural | |
|----------|---|--------|---|
| [la fam] | . . . | [le fam] | **(femme)** |
| [lə ka] | . . . | [le ka] | **(cas)** |

| | | |
|---|---|---|
| [lə ne] | ... [le ne] | (**nez**) |
| [la nwa] | ... [le nwa] | (**noix**) |
| [sə so] | ... [se so] | (**seau**) |
| [œ̃ ʃu] | ... [de ʃu] | (**chou**) |

There is of course no sign of -*s* or -*x* here. In pronunciation, singular and plural are identical. The difference between them is indicated only by the determiner which precedes the noun.

Number is shown by the form of the determiner in written French too, of course. But in the spoken language, this is the *only* indication of number for these nouns. To put it another way, the written language marks the plural twice in **les femmes**, but the spoken language only once: [le fam].

One indication is usually sufficient. However, in a few cases potential ambiguity does arise. Thus [ɔ̃n a ete o magazɛ̃] contains no plural markers at all, and could therefore correspond either to **on a été au magasin** or to **on a été aux magasins**. In a specific context, however, this is unlikely to be a serious problem, and even out of context, many nouns invite one interpretation rather than the other: in [ɔ̃n a ete o paʀk], **parc** is most likely to be singular. Overall, in any case, there are not enough invariable determiners like [o] to jeopardize the general trend towards invariability of French nouns.

Note, finally, that adjectives follow the same pattern of invariability (see also 7.2.2):

| | | | |
|---|---|---|---|
| [pti] | **petit** | [pti] | **petits** |
| [gʀɑ̃d] | **grande** | [gʀɑ̃d] | **grandes** |

## EXERCISES

1† Using the phonetic alphabet, give the singular and plural forms of the following 'determiner + noun' units:

For example: **mon frère** → [mɔ̃ fʀɛʀ, me fʀɛʀ]

| | | | |
|---|---|---|---|
| (a) | le père | (e) | ce bonhomme |
| (b) | la mère | (f) | son mec |
| (c) | une dame | (g) | not' soeur |
| (d) | un type | (h) | mon neveu |

2† Transcribe the following phrases or sentences phonetically. Then state the number of times 'plural' is indicated in each: (i) by the written language; (ii) by the spoken language.

> (a) ces petites tâches faciles
> (b) je vais aux grands magasins
> (c) ces détestables bâtiments noirs, laids et enfumés
> (d) leurs satellites scrutent le territoire
>
> 3   Comment on the following:
>
> (a) Je m'adresse aux peuples, aux peuples au pluriel [*from a speech by de Gaulle*].
>
> (b) Le livre [ . . . ] est en vente dans les librairie [*from a school essay*]. (RB)

### 7.2.2 A plural prefix, and some irregularities

The nouns considered so far all began with a consonant. The pattern for nouns beginning with vowels is indicated by the following transcriptions of **l'auto . . . les autos** and **l'oiseau . . . les oiseaux** (in pronunciation, the latter in fact begins with the semi-vowel [w]).

[loto]    . . .   [lezoto]
[lwazo]   . . .   [lezwazo]

As before, the definite article changes: [l] to [le]. But this time a liaison [z] is present as well, corresponding to the orthographic -*s* of **les**. In spelling, this -*s* is an integral part of the definite article, of course. However, the corresponding [z] in the pronunciation has 'floated away' from the article and attached itself to the noun. This becomes evident if a pause, or 'hesitation noise' (**euh**: [ø]), is inserted between article and noun. Orthographically, this would be **les . . . euh . . . autos**, but phonetically it would normally be [le . . . ø . . . zoto].

The transcription [lezoto] is something of a compromise, since it is uncommitted as to which word [z] 'really belongs to'. If, instead, a transcription like the following is employed:

[loto]    . . .   [le zoto]
[lwazo]   . . .   [le zwazo]

then it emerges that the form of the article is the same whether or not the plural noun begins with a vowel (or semi-vowel) – it is [le] in all cases:

[le fam]
[le zoto]

What does vary is the noun: [oto], in the singular, but [zoto] in the plural. Once again, nothing is added at the end: instead [z] is prefixed at the beginning. Similarly if there is an adjective before the noun:

[se gʀɑ̃ zɑ̃sɑ̃bl]    **ces grands ensembles**

Usually [z] is redundant, as it merely duplicates the information about number already contained in the determiner. However, there are cases where only the presence or absence of [z] enables singular and plural noun phrases to be differentiated:

[vuz ɛt alʒeʀjɛ̃]    **vous êtes Algérien?**
[vuz ɛt zalʒeʀjɛ̃]    **vous êtes Algériens?**

The general rule for noun plurals in spoken French might, then, be formulated as follows:

Leave the noun unchanged, unless it begins with a vowel (or semi-vowel) – in which case, add the prefix [z].

This is obviously a very different matter from adding -*s* or -*x*.

There are a few untypical nouns which do change in speech as well as in writing. They include [œj] (**oeil**) . . . [ jø] (**yeux**), [məsjø] (**monsieur**) . . . [mɛsjø] (**messieurs**), and nouns ending in [al] or [aj] which have a plural in [o]:

[lə ʃəval]    (**cheval**)   . . .   [le ʃəvo]   (**chevaux**)
[lə tʀavaj]   (**travail**)   . . .   [le tʀavo]   (**travaux**)

Even so, if such a noun begins with a vowel or semi-vowel, it follows the general pattern as far as [z] is concerned:

[lœj]    (**oeil**)    . . .   [le zjø]   (**yeux**)
[lemaj]  (**émail**)   . . .   [le zemo]  (**émaux**)

Such cases are remnants of various historical irregularities, and there are some signs of a tendency to level out the anomalies: nouns in -*al* which have entered the language more recently than those just listed follow the general pattern, even in standard usage:

**le festival**  . . .  **les festivals**
**le récital**   . . .  **les récitals**

So, colloquially, do many adjectives in **-al**, including some that are not so recent: **les résultats finals** for standard **finaux**, etc.

Longer-established nouns like **cheval** and **travail** are more resistant, but the fact that young children sometimes treat them as invariable suggests that they are indeed 'the exception that proves the rule'. And many speakers pronounce **os** ('bone') the same way in **un os** and **des os** (i.e. [ɔs] in both cases), though the norm requires the *s* to be pronounced only in the singular.

## EXERCISES

4†   Use phonetic transcription to indicate the spoken plural forms of the following:

(a)   cette entreprise        (d)   son élève
(b)   l'eau                   (e)   mon ouvrage
(c)   un animal

5†   Which of the following are potentially ambiguous, which are not, and why?

(a)   [iz ɔ̃ vizite lœʀ ɑ̃fɑ̃]        (c)   [iz ɔ̃ vizite lœʀ zɑ̃fɑ̃]
(b)   [iz ɔ̃ vizite lœʀ fis]         (d)   [iz ɔ̃ vizite lœʀ fij]

6†   The plurals of **oeuf** and **boeuf** are regular in the written code but irregular in speech, though sometimes regularized in a parallel way to **os** (see above). Specify these various patterns.

7    Comment on the following anecdote (told by Madeleine Csécsy):

> Un petit garçon se promène avec sa maman dans les rues de Paris (où, à notre époque, on n'a pas souvent l'occasion de voir les quadrupèdes en question):
> – Regarde, maman, des cheval!
> – Non, mon petit, des chevaux.
> Le petit, après un instant de réflexion:
> – Et pourtant, ils ressemblent drôlement aux autres.
> (Rigault 1971: 100)

### 7.2.3   'Intrusive' -z-

It is not just the evidence of hesitation noises and pauses that suggests that [z] is a plural 'prefix' attached in spoken French to nouns that start with vowels. There is a strong tendency to insert [z] even when the written form gives no justification for doing so. This can be illustrated by the phrase **entre quatre yeux** ('between you and me', 'confidentially'). The standard pronunciation of this sounds somewhat odd: [ɑ̃tʀə katʀə jø].

The reason for the oddness is that this is one of the rare occurrences of **yeux** without any preceding determiner or plural adjective, and consequently without a [z] before the semi-vowel [j]. So there is a strong pressure to insert [z] regardless, and most people (at least when not monitoring themselves) would pronounce the phrase: [ɑ̃tRə katRə zjø], or, to use non-standard orthography, *entre quatre-z-yeux*. This is fully in conformity with the spoken French plural rule: 'add the [z] prefix to plural nouns beginning with a vowel or semi-vowel'.

Other such 'errors' show the prevalence of the pattern even more strikingly. For example, Morin and Kaye (1982) report: **ils sont presque-z-amis** and **qu'est-ce que vous avez comme-z-arbres?**. Blanche-Benveniste (1997) quotes: **des tas de-z-hommes** and **les ex-z-otages**.

It is also relevant that, in the Creole French languages spoken in, for example, Haiti, Mauritius and Martinique, there are large numbers of vocabulary items like **un zom** 'a man', or **un zozo** 'a bird'. These derive from **(les) hommes** and **(les) oiseaux**, respectively. The -*s* of **les** is reanalysed as an integral part of the noun and permanently attached to it – to the extent that **zom** and **zozo** have come to be the usual singular as well as plural forms. In French too, **un zozo** (or **un zozio**) is sometimes used by children, while **un z'oeil** (parodying **z'yeux**) is a jocular form affected by some adult speakers (see p. 199 for an example).

## EXERCISES

8†   The following remark was made by a parent commenting on teacher absenteeism and was pronounced according to the rule for spoken plurals given above:

Ce trimestre on a eu vingt absences de prof. (FI)

Specify this speaker's pronunciation of **vingt absences** and compare it with the standard pronunciation.

9†   Bearing in mind the rules of spoken French plural formation, identify the origin of (a) the slang verb **zyeuter** ('to look at'), and (b) the somewhat jocular noun **un zinzin** ('institutional investor').

10†   Reconstruct the French originals of the following Creole nouns:

(a)   **zanimo** 'animal'; **zapot** 'apostle'; **zistwar** 'story' (Seychelles Islands)

(b)   **zepol** 'shoulder'; **zasyet** 'plate'; **zorey** 'ear'; **zo** 'bone' (Martinique)

## 7.3  Masculine and feminine (especially adjectives)

Written French often marks gender agreement in adjectives by adding a vowel. Spoken French, on the other hand, often removes a consonant.

### 7.3.1  Written and spoken patterns

The basic written rule is: to form the feminine, add -e to the masculine, unless the adjective already ends in -e. A small number of adjectives also change their final consonant, or in one or two cases add a consonant. An even smaller group undergo a change of vowel as well.

The following table resumes these categories:

WRITTEN FRENCH

I (invariable)
**aimable**
**jeune**

II (add -e for feminine)
**clair/claire**
**froid/froide**
**apparent/apparente**

III (change consonant and add -e)
**public/publique**
**vif/vive**
**doux/douce**

IV (add consonant and -e)
**favori/favorite**

V (various other changes, including change of vowel)
**beau/belle**
**vieux/vieille**

In spoken French too there is a large group of invariable adjectives, though its membership is not quite the same: the spoken counterparts of **clair/claire** and **public/publique**, for instance, are just as invariable as **aimable** and **jeune**, and therefore have to be grouped with them.

Moreover, a different process comes into play in those cases where masculine and feminine are different. Most accents of French have no audible

counterpart of -*e*: in the large group of adjectives like [fʀwa]/[fʀwad], esti-
mated at 40 per cent of the total, what distinguishes the feminine from the
masculine is the presence of a final consonant.

Here are the groups for the spoken code. Notice that **doux**, **public** and **vif**
differ from one another in the way they mark gender, and are therefore not
grouped together. The same applies to **clair** and **froid**. Conversely, **favori**
assimilates to the Group II pattern and no longer needs to be in a separate
category.

SPOKEN FRENCH

  I   (invariable)
    [ɛmabl]
    [ʒœn]
    [klɛʀ]
    [pyblik]

  II  (no final consonant in masculine)
    [du/dus]
    [fʀwa/fʀwad]
    [apaʀɑ̃/apaʀɑ̃t]
    [favɔʀi/favɔʀit]

  III (change of consonant)
    [vif/viv]

  IV (various other changes, including change of vowel)
    [bo/bɛl]
    [vjø/vjɛj]

A number of nouns referring to male/female pairs also fit one or other of the
above groups. The Group II pattern applies to:

[epuz/epu]  (**épouse**, **époux**)
[luv/lu]  (**louve**, **loup**)
[peizan/peizɑ̃]  (**paysanne**, **paysan**)
[episjɛʀ/episje]  (**épicière**, **épicier**)
[kuzin/kuzɛ̃]  (**cousine**, **cousin**)

(See 7.3.2 for the vowel changes occurring in the last three of these.)

Pairs like [sɛʀvøz/sɛʀvœʀ] (**serveuse**, **serveur**) belong to Group III (change
of consonant). Many other nouns (and a few adjectives derived from nouns)
follow entirely different patterns, of course. However, in these cases there
are no written/spoken divergencies: **prince**, **princesse**; **directeur**, **directrice**, etc.

Past participles of verbs also follow the same patterns as adjectives. Most are Group I invariables in spoken usage: [eme] (**aimée/aimé**); [Rəsy] (**reçue/reçu**). But a few belong to Group II: [pRiz/pRi] (**prise/pris**), [kɥit/kɥi] (**cuite/cuit**).

---

### EXERCISES

1† The following adjectives belong to *orthographic* Group III. Specify the consonant changes involved in each case.

   Example: **faux**, -*x* changes to -*ss*-.

   **doux, tiers, épais, sot, blanc, frais, actif, culturel, sec, neuf, bas, muet, gentil, nul.**

2† Are the following invariable (i) in the written code only, (ii) in the spoken code only, (iii) in both?

   **fragile, social, rationnel, aigu, intense, fini, compliqué, possible, vrai, supérieur, rapide, magique.**

---

### 7.3.2 Adding [ə] and deleting a consonant

Here are some more Group II adjectives:

   [luR/luRd], [gRa/gRas], [pla/plat], [blã/blãʃ], [gRã/gRãd], [lã/lãt].

Starting from the masculine form, there is no way of predicting, in any particular case, what the final consonant will be in the feminine: sometimes it is [d], sometimes [s], sometimes [t], sometimes [ʃ]. However, if the feminine is taken as the starting point, then in all these cases the masculine can be obtained by a simple process of 'deleting the final consonant'. This, of course, is a very different matter from the written rule 'add feminine -*e*', even though the two processes are linked by the reading convention according to which final -*e* is not itself pronounced, but serves as an instruction to articulate the consonant preceding it.

However, final consonants do occur in the masculine when there is a liaison: **il est petit** [il e pti], but **un petit ami** [œ̃ pti t ami]; **il est gros** [il e gRo], but **un gros ennui** [œ̃ gRo z ãnɥi] (liaison -*s* is pronounced [z]). So a more accurate approach would be to say that the basic Group II forms [fRwad, pətit, gʀos], etc. are inherently 'gender-neutral', and can be used for either masculine or feminine. However, the final consonant is omitted in the masculine unless the following noun begins with a vowel.

One further point concerning Group II adjectives (and nouns) relates to various automatic vowel changes occurring when a consonant is deleted.

(a)   If the deletion leaves [ɛ] at the end of the masculine adjective, this mid-low vowel is 'raised' to a mid-high [e]: [pʀəmjɛr/pʀəmje] (**première**, **premier**).

(b)   Similarly, mid-low [œ] becomes mid-high [ø]: [œʀœz/œʀø] (**heureuse**, **heureux**).

(c)   If the deleted consonant is a nasal [n] or [ɲ], then a trace of it is preserved by the nasalization of what becomes the final vowel:

[ɛn] and [in] and [iɲ] all end up as [ɛ̃]: [sɛn/sɛ̃] (**saine**, **sain**), [fin/fɛ̃] (**fine**, **fin**), [maliɲ/malɛ̃] (**maligne**, **malin**);

[an] becomes [ɑ̃]: [paʀtizan/paʀtizɑ̃] (**partisane**, **partisan**);

[ɔn] becomes [ɔ̃]: [bon/bɔ̃] (**bonne**, **bon**);

[yn] becomes [œ̃], or [ɛ̃] in accents which lack [œ̃] (see Appendix 3): [bʀyn]/[bʀœ̃ (bʀɛ̃)] (**brune**, **brun**).

All these changes apply to any Group II adjective with the relevant configuration. So they are different in nature from the idiosyncratic changes characteristic of Group IV adjectives.

## EXERCISES

3†   What, in pronunciation, are the masculine (non-liaison) and feminine forms corresponding to:

**différent, humain, français, saint, successif, précis, enfantin, religieux, commun, second, content.**

4†   To which of (a) the written and (b) the spoken adjective groups do the following belong?

**protestant, musulman, catholique, hindou, juif, allemand, corse, espagnol, andalou, anglais, belge.**

5† In pronunciation, which of these adjectives belong to Group I ('invariable'), which to Group II ('delete consonant') and which to Group III ('change consonant')? This list gives the basic forms; specify the 'non-liaison' form of the masculine in the case of Group II adjectives.

[dus]  [tjɛʀs]  [epɛs]  [sɔt]  [blɑ̃ʃ]  [fʀɛʃ]  [aktiv]  [kʀyɛl]
[sɛʃ]  [nœv]  [bas]  [myɛt]  [ʒɑ̃tij]  [nyl]  [kɔʀɛkt]  [lɔ̃g]

6   If French had no writing system (other than the IPA), how would one go about learning gender marking in adjectives?

### 7.3.3 *Varieties of French with 'non-mute' -e*

There are a number of varieties of French in which the 'mute' -*e* of the orthography does in fact correspond to an audible [ə] in the pronunciation (and not just in feminine adjectives). This applies to the regional accents of southern France; and also to Parisian and other northern pronunciations in 'declamatory' style. Thus in poetry, a phrase like **à la claire fontaine** counts as seven syllables, not five: there is a [ə] at the end of **claire** and another at the end of **fontaine**.

Pronunciations of this sort have remained closer to the earlier stages of the language in which 'mute -*e*' was not in fact mute. In such varieties, Group II feminine adjectives add an [ə] suffix, rather than just using the basic form by default. The patterns in 7.3.2 will therefore need some adjustment if they are to be applicable to these cases.

Invariable Group I adjectives like **aimable** have to be represented as [ɛmablə]. As for adjectives like **clair/claire**, they have a [ə] in the feminine ([klɛʀə]), but not in the masculine (unlike Group I). But the masculine retains the final [ʀ] ([klɛʀ]), unlike Group II adjectives. So a separate category needs to be set up for them. Lastly, the Group III description needs modifying: these adjectives not only change their final consonant, they also add the feminine [ə]: [vif/vivə]. Even so, the northern and southern systems are still basically quite similar, as the following summary suggests:

NORTHERN (standard)
Group I     Invariable
Group II    Basic form ends in consonant, masculine deletes consonant (except liaison)
Group III   Consonant change
Group IV    Irregular changes

SOUTHERN (and 'declamatory' standard)
Group I     Invariable: [ɛmablə]
Group II    Basic form ends in consonant: [fʀwad]; feminine adds [ə]: [fʀwadə]; masculine deletes consonant (except liaison): [fʀwa]
Group III   Basic form ends in consonant: [vif]; feminine adds [ə] with change of consonant: [vivə]
Group IV   Basic form ends in consonant: [klɛʀ]; feminine adds [ə]: [klɛʀə]; masculine retains consonant: [klɛʀ]
Group V    Irregular changes: [bo/bɛlə]

---

## EXERCISES

7†  Allocate the following to appropriate groups according to southern pronunciation:

> **doux, tiers, épais, sot, blanc, frais, actif, cruel, sec, neuf, bas, muet, gentil, nul, correct, long, public, tendre.**

8   How does gender marking in southern French pronunciation combine features both of standard orthographic practice and of standard (northern) pronunciation?

---

## 7.4 Conjugating verbs

Number and person markers in written French usually take the form of suffixes, which also contain information about tense. In speech, tense is still shown by suffixes, but number and person are indicated at the beginning of the verb.

### 7.4.1 The absence of number and person endings

Here is the present tense of a regular -er verb, first in standard spelling and then in phonetic transcription:

| | |
|---|---|
| **j'arrive** | ʒaʀiv |
| **tu arrives** | ty aʀiv |
| **il/elle arrive** | il/ɛl aʀiv |
| **nous arrivons** | nu zaʀivɔ̃ |
| **vous arrivez** | vu zaʀive |
| **ils/elles arrivent** | il/ɛl zaʀiv |

In the written version, this verb has five different forms, with five different suffixes; only the first- and third-persons singular are the same. In the spoken version, there are just three different forms: moreover, one of these is the 'bare stem' [ariv], so there are only two distinct endings: [ʒ] and [e].

In fact, this phonetic transcription represents a rather formal style. As was explained in 3.2, more familiar registers systematically replace **nous** by **on**. Furthermore, the standard elision of **je** to **j'** before a vowel is, in colloquial speech, extended to **tu**, which is reduced to **t'**. Conversely, the [l] of **il**, and sometimes even **elle**, is elided before a consonant.

These factors mean that the conjugation of the present tense of **arriver** is as follows in more colloquial style (a 'popularizing' orthographic version is used here):

| | |
|---|---|
| ʒaʀiv | **j'arrive** |
| taʀiv | **t'arrives** |
| ilaʀiv/ɛlaʀiv | **il/elle arrive** |
| ɔ̃naʀiv | **on arrive** |
| vuzaʀive | vous arrivez |
| izaʀiv/ɛzaʀiv | **i'z arrivent/e'z arrivent** |

In the left-hand column, the **vous** form is now the only one where there is any change in the verb itself. Otherwise, the bare stem occurs throughout: number and person are not indicated by endings, but solely by the pronouns that precede it. The consequence is that number and person are often marked twice over in the written code (**t(u) arrives**), but only once in the spoken ([taʀiv]). This is similar to the state of affairs with nouns, where there are also fewer plural markers in speech (see 7.2.1).

One of the main functions of the **vous** form is to serve as a polite, formal equivalent of **tu**. So it is probably no coincidence that the **vous** form should remain the 'odd one out', resisting the levelling that has affected all the other forms. So far anyway: some kinds of French used in North America have gone further than other varieties in this respect, even abandoning the -*ez*/[e] ending. Thus **vous parl'** and **vous gagne** are reported by field workers investigating dialects still surviving in Missouri and Louisiana (Lambrecht 1981: 47).

---

### EXERCISE

1† Transcribe phonetically the present tenses of **donner**, **envoyer**, **jouer** and **travailler**, assuming as colloquial a level of language as possible.

## 7.4.2 *Pronouns, prefixes and clitics*

The 'pronouns' which carry the crucial information about number and person turn out, on closer inspection, to be not quite what they seem. For one thing (with the exception of **vous** and, in those registers that use it, **nous**), they have to be accompanied by a verb. 'Oui, je!' is not an acceptable answer to the question 'Y a-t-il quelqu'un dans la salle qui parle français?': the disjunctive pronoun **moi** is required. And when a verb *is* present, there are severe restrictions on the material that can intervene between pronoun and verb. This is why the set formula **Je soussigné déclare que . . .** ('I the undersigned declare that . . .') sounds archaic: in spoken and in most written usage, only the negative **ne** or other pronouns can stand between **je, tu, il(s)** and the verb (**je ne le fais pas**). Moreover, the elision undergone by some pronouns makes further inroads into their separate identity.

So the tendency in all spoken registers is for the unemphatic pronouns to be, as it were, 'demoted' or 'eroded' to the status of mere prefixes – for prefixes are, by definition, bound to a following word and cannot be used in isolation. This is why [tariv] and the other forms were 'written in one word' in 7.4.1. The more informal the register, the stronger this tendency. Before 'voiceless' consonants like [p, t, k, f, s], [ʒə] ( **je**) is often reduced to [ʃ] (**ch'travaille**). And in cases like **ch'rais** ('je serais') or **ché pas** ('je ne sais pas'), **je** has been completely absorbed into the verb, via stages like **je n'sais pas**, **je sais pas** and **ch'sais pas**.

Rather than refer to **je, tu, il**, etc. as 'prefixes', linguists usually call them 'bound pronouns', 'clitic pronouns' or simply 'clitics'. This process of 'cliticization' has had far-reaching effects on various areas of grammar: see 8.1.

In short, written French indicates number and person by means of a variety of verb endings, as well as by (compulsory) pronouns which have the status of independent words in the orthography. Spoken French, especially in its more colloquial varieties, has gone a long way towards abandoning verb endings, and relies on 'bound' or 'cliticized' pronouns to convey the relevant information.

If modern French is compared in this connection with medieval French or with Italian or Spanish, its written code turns out to be located halfway along an evolutionary path comprising the following stages:

(a)  Optional (emphatic) pronouns and compulsory verb endings: i.e. the Latin system, which is preserved in Spanish *(yo) trabajo, (tu) trabajas, (ellos) trabajan.*

(b)  Compulsory pronouns *and* compulsory verb endings: standard written French **je travaille, tu travailles, ils travaillent**.

(c)  Compulsory (clitic) pronouns and no verb endings: colloquial French [ʃtʀavaj], [tytʀavaj] [itʀavaj].

As system (b) contains more redundancy than the other two (number and person are indicated twice), it is perhaps not surprising that it has turned out to be a relatively transient phase in terms of language evolution, though carefully preserved in written usage.

---

## *EXERCISES*

2†   Give standard orthographic equivalents of the following spoken forms:

    (a)   [ʃe pa]
    (b)   [ʃe bjɛ]
    (c)   [ʃɥi fatige]

3†   Here are some verb forms containing elided pronouns. Rewrite them in standard orthography (with **ne** when appropriate).

    (a)   [ʒvwa]        (e)   [tatɑ̃]
    (b)   [ʃkʀwapa]    (f)   [ʃpøpa]
    (c)   [tapɛl]       (g)   [isɛpa]
    (d)   [ivø]

---

### *7.4.3   Suffixes indicating tense*

Only the present indicative has been considered so far, but similar patterns are found in other tenses and moods.

Even in the written language, the present subjunctive of **-er** verbs is to a large extent identical to the indicative: only **que nous arrivions** and **que vous arriviez** have separate subjunctive endings. In those spoken varieties in which **on** replaces **nous**, the overlap with the indicative is complete, apart, once again, from the **vous** form:

kəʒaʀiv          **que j'arrive**
kətaʀiv          etc.
kilaʀiv
kɔ̃naʀiv
(kəvuzaʀivje)
kizaʀiv/kɛzaʀiv

The imperfect indicative and the conditional are conjugated as follows:

| ʒaʀive | **j'arrivais** |
| taʀive | etc. |
| ilaʀive | |
| ɔ̃naʀive | |
| (vuzaʀivje) | |
| i/ɛzaʀive | |

| ʒaʀivʀɛ | **j'arriverais** |
| taʀivʀɛ | etc. |
| ilaʀivʀɛ | |
| ɔ̃naʀivʀɛ | |
| (vuzaʀivʀje) | |
| i/ɛzaʀivʀɛ | |

In these cases, endings *are* present: [ɛ] throughout the imperfect, and [ʀɛ] throughout the conditional: [ʒaʀiv + ɛ], [ʒaʀiv + ʀɛ], etc. (In the colloquial French of Paris and other northern centres, [e] and [ʀe] are often used instead of [ɛ] and [ʀɛ], so that **j'arriverais** is indistinguishable from **j'arriverai**.)

Now as [ɛ] and [ʀɛ] do not vary according to number or person, they are best analysed as relating solely to tense: [ɛ] is added to the stem [aʀiv] for the imperfect, and [ʀɛ] for the conditional, with number and person catered for by the 'bound pronouns', as before. If there is no ending, the verb is in the present tense. The structure of the spoken form of **j'arriverais** may therefore be represented as follows:

person/number + stem + tense: ʒ + aʀiv + ʀɛ

The absence of a suffix in the present can be indicated by the symbol Ø ('zero'):

**j'arrive**: ʒ + aʀiv + Ø

Again, this is very different from the written system, where endings like **-ais**, **-ait**, **-aient** convey information about number and person as well as tense. A vestige of the *-s* and *-t* of the written form is of course preserved in the liaison consonant heard in more formal style (**il attendait-encore**). But, in conformity with the tendency for number and person endings to disappear, such liaisons are increasingly rare in colloquial French (unlike those between an adjective and a noun: cf. 7.3.2). What is more, in written French the conditional endings are added to the infinitive **arriver** (**arriver + ais**). This is not the case in the spoken code, where [ʀɛ] is added directly to the stem [aʀiv].

The future, unlike the tenses considered so far, includes endings that do change according to number and person, so it fits the pattern less neatly, with three different suffixes, [ʀe], [ʀa] and [ʀɔ̃]:

| ʒaʀivʀe | **j'arriverai** |
|---|---|
| taʀivʀa | etc. |
| ilaʀivʀa | |
| õnaʀivʀa | |
| vuzaʀivʀe | |
| izaʀivʀõ | |

But, as was pointed out in 4.1.3, the simple future has lost ground in collo-quial speech, and is more marginal to the spoken code than the other tenses considered so far. Indeed, young children sometimes partly 'regularize' it by replacing **j'arriverai** with **j'arrivera**, though the influence of the norm makes such levelling unusual with older speakers.

As for the past historic and imperfect subjunctive, they certainly show a range of first-, second- and third-person endings, whether orally or in writing. But the imperfect subjunctive is not used in conversation, and the past historic is quite restricted in its occurrence (see 4.1.1). Indeed, speakers are sometimes hesitant about what the appropriate forms are. So these tenses are very marginal to the colloquial system.

Note that the infinitive and the participles are marked by suffixes in both the written and the spoken codes: [aʀiv + e] **arriver**, [aʀiv + e] **arrivé**, [aʀiv + ã] **arrivant**. This is as far as the parallelism extends: as the transcription shows, infinitive and past participle are identical in pronunciation: [e]. More-over, for large numbers of speakers there is no longer any difference between either of them and the various forms of the imperfect: **-er, -é, -ée, -és, -ées, -ais, -ait, -aient** are all [e].

---

## *EXERCISES*

4† Analyse the verb forms below into their component parts (clitic pronoun + stem + tense suffix), and give their written equivalents. If there is no tense suffix (i.e. if the verb is in the present), indicate this with Ø ('zero').

Examples:

[õnaʀiv]: õ + aʀiv + Ø (**on arrive**)
[taʀivʀɛ]: t + aʀiv + ʀɛ (**t(u) arriverais**)

(N.B. The [n] in [õnaʀiv] is a liaison consonant linking [õ] with the following [a]. Such consonants can be disregarded in your analysis.)

|     |             |     |             |
| --- | ----------- | --- | ----------- |
| (a) | [ɛlpaʀlɛ]   | (f) | [õdin]      |
| (b) | [ʒəmɑ̃ʒ]     | (g) | [ʒapɛlʀɛ]   |
| (c) | [tavɑ̃sɛ]    | (h) | [tyfymɛ]    |
| (d) | [ipusʀɛ]    | (i) | [izɛmɛ]     |
| (e) | [kəʒʀgaʀd]  | (j) | [õnetydjɛ]  |

5†   Now proceed in the opposite direction, by transcribing the following. Then analyse the spoken forms as in the previous exercise.

|     |                  |     |                |
| --- | ---------------- | --- | -------------- |
| (a) | je pensais       | (e) | tu étudies     |
| (b) | tu travaillerais | (f) | j'arrête       |
| (c) | on déjeune       | (g) | elles toussaient |
| (d) | il voyageait     | (h) | ils tomberaient |

6   Identify and account for the errors of *orthographe grammaticale* in the following sentences written by French schoolchildren:

(a)   M. Durant a été interrogait par M. Dupont. (RB)
(b)   Je vois le facteur monté. (RB)
(c)   La rue où les gens danses tout l'été. (RB)
(d)   La rue que l'ont vient de passaient, mon oncle y abittera. (RB)
(e)   Dans le livre dont je t'est parlais [ . . . ] (RB)

### 7.4.4   *Verbs with two stems*

Only regular **-er** verbs have been considered so far, but this is the type to which the great majority of the verbs in the language belong. In particular, all newly coined verbs have an **-er** infinitive (**déboguer** 'debug', etc.).

However, the 'clitic + stem + tense suffix' pattern applies also to the **-ir**, **-oir** and **-re** verbs, including those traditionally classified as irregular. There are many irregularities in the spoken code too, of course, but they are probably fewer in number.

There is, for example, much overlapping of endings and stems in written French: the **-s** of (**je**) **lis** is a first-person singular ending, whereas the **-s** of (**ils**) **lisent** is part of the stem, and number and person are conveyed by the **-ent** suffix. If silent letters are eliminated, stems and endings can be differentiated more clearly. Take the present tense of **perdre**:

ʒəpɛʀ    **je perds**
typɛʀ    etc.
ipɛʀ
ɔ̃pɛʀ
vupɛʀde
ipɛʀd

As before, there are no endings except for the second-person plural. This time, however, the stem has *two* forms: [pɛʀd] (used for the second- and third-persons plural) and [pɛʀ] (used for all the other persons). So with verbs like these, the third singular/third plural distinction is retained: [ipɛʀ/ ipɛʀd] **il perd/ils perdent**, unlike [idɔn], which corresponds both to **il donne** and to **ils donnent**.

In the case of **perdre**, tense and other suffixes are added to the 'long' stem [pɛʀd]:

[ʒə + pɛʀd + ʀɛ]    **je perdrais**
[ʒə + pɛʀd + ɛ]    **je perdais**
[pɛʀd + ã]    **perdant**

Noteworthy differences between two-stem verbs like **perdre** and single-stem verbs like **arriver** are, firstly, the existence of a distinctive subjunctive form:

[kə + ʒə + pɛʀd + Ø]    **que je perde**

and, secondly, the fact that the infinitive is marked by [ʀ]:

[pɛʀd + ʀ]    **perdre**

Most other **-ir** and **-re** verbs also have two stems, differentiated by the presence or absence of a final consonant. For example:

[fini] and [finis]    **(finir)**
[vã] and [vãd]    **(vendre)**
[li] and [liz]    **(lire)**
[plɛ] and [plɛz]    **(plaire)**

In the present tense these alternate like the two stems of **perdre**:

[ty + vã], [i + vãd]: **tu vends, ils vendent**
[i + li], [i + liz]: **i(l) lit, i(l)s lisent**
[ʒə + dɔʀ], [i + dɔʀm]: **je dors, ils dorment**
[i + fini], [i + finis]: **i(l) finit, i(l)s finissent**

And again, the long stem is the basis for certain other forms:

imperfect: [ʒə + vãd + ɛ]: **je vendais**
pres subjunctive: [kə + ʒə + liz + Ø]: **que je lise**
pres participle: [finis + ã]: **finissant**

In the written code, by contrast, things are more complicated, with certain verbs losing their final stem consonant in the singular present, and others retaining it: **je dors/ils dor<u>m</u>ent** but **je per<u>ds</u>/ils per<u>d</u>ent**.

---

## EXERCISES

7† Using the phonetic alphabet, indicate the two stems of each of the following verbs:

  **écrire, mettre, mordre, nuire, suivre, vaincre.**

In which cases does the written code retain a final stem consonant throughout? And what (in the written code only) is distinctive about **vaincre**?

8 Insert + at appropriate points in order to show each occurrence of number and person marking in the spoken code as compared to the written code.
  Examples:

  [izaʀiv] (third person and plural number each marked once)
  ++

  **ils arrivent** (person and number each marked twice)
  ++       ++

(a)  [iʃɑ̃tɛ]        **ils chantaient**
(b)  [izɔ̃ʃɑ̃te]      **ils ont chanté**
(c)  [iʃɑ̃tʀɔ̃]       **ils chanteront**
(d)  [ivɔ̃ʃɑ̃te]      **ils vont chanter**
(e)  [iʃɑ̃tʀɛ]       **ils chanteraient**
(f)  [ifinis]        **ils finissent**
(g)  [idɔʀm]         **ils dorment**
(h)  [izapaʀɛs]      **ils apparaissent**
(i)  [izekut]        **ils écoutent**

What general characteristic of the written code is revealed by such data?

In the spoken code, which verbs have the largest number of + signs, and why?

### 7.4.5  Some anomalies

The examples considered so far suggest that the majority of verbs in spoken French belong either to a 'one-stem type' (**arriver**) or a 'two-stem type' (**lire**). And indeed, many commentators have proposed replacing the traditional **-er**, **-ir**, **-re** classification by a grouping based on the number of stems. But whatever system is adopted, many of the irregularities of the written code continue to be encountered in the spoken code. Here are just a few examples (see Dubois 1967, Martinet 1969 and Rigault 1971 for more detailed analysis).

The category of 'two-stem' verbs falls into two sub-groups, depending on the way the future, conditional and infinitive are formed. The suffixes are added to the 'long' stem of **perdre** (see 7.4.4) and various other verbs:

[i + vãd + ʀɛ]        (**il vendrait/ils vendraient**)
[ʒə + viv + ʀɛ]        (**je vivrais**)
[viv + ʀ]        (**vivre**)

But there is a second group in which they are added to the 'short' stem:

[ty + li + ʀɛ]        (**tu lirais**)
[ɔ̃ + fini + ʀɛ]        (**on finirait**)
[fini + ʀ]        (**finir**)

There are also many idiosyncracies affecting the past participle: [fini] but [vãdy], [veky], [etɛ̃], etc. Moreover, a few verbs have more than two stems. **Craindre** has three, [kʀɛ̃, kʀɛɲ, kʀɛ̃d] as in **je crains, je craignais, je craindrai**; **venir** has four, [vjɛ̃, vjɛn, vən, vjɛ̃d] as in **je viens, ils viennent, je venais, je viendrai**.

The important point, however, is that the 'clitic + stem + tense' pattern applies to these verbs, too. The irregularities relate essentially to the multiplicity of stems.

[ʃ + kʀɛ̃ + Ø]        (**je (ch') crains**)
[i + kʀɛɲ + Ø]        (**ils craignent**)
[ʒə + vən + ɛ]        (**je venais**)
[ʒə + vjɛ̃d + ʀɛ]        (**je viendrais**)

Such complexities are sometimes levelled out in colloquial usage. This typically happens with 'multi-stem' verbs (particularly, but not exclusively, the less common ones), which are assimilated to the 'two-stem' type:

| STANDARD | COLLOQUIAL |
|----------|-----------|
| ils éteindront | [izeteɲʀɔ̃] (*ils éteigneront) |
| ils peignent | [ipɛ̃d] (*ils peindent) |
| elles cousent | [ɛlkud] (*elles coudent) |
| il vêt | [ivɛti] (*il vêtit) |
| elles moulent | [ɛlmud] (*elles moudent) |

In the last case, the infinitive **moudre** may, alternatively, be replaced by [mule] (**\*mouler**), and the other forms in **moul-** retained.

The highly irregular **s'asseoir** is also often extensively remodelled. Forms like **je m'assois, ils s'assoient, on s'assoira** and (more popular) **assoyez-vous** replace **je m'assieds, ils s'asseyent, nous nous assiérons** and **asseyez-vous**, respectively. But the standard past participle is retained: **je me suis assis**.

Another way of avoiding anomalies is simply not to use the 'difficult' verb at all. Thus **solutionner** and **émotionner** often replace **résoudre** and **émouvoir** – much to the disapproval of normative grammarians. An example is the following statement by a prominent politician:

(1)    Monsieur Chirac refuse de solutionner la crise nationale [A. Lajoinie].
       (FI)

## EXERCISES

9†    The following verbs all have two stems (like **perdre**).
      Transcribe the stems phonetically.

   **battre, conduire, dire, rompre, suffire.**

   Which stem is the base for (a) the imperfect and
   present participle, (b) the future and conditional, (c) the
   infinitive? In written French, which of these verbs keep their
   final stem consonant throughout the present tense?

10†   The following also have two stems. Again, transcribe them.
      Then say in what respect the verbs in this group differ from
      those in Exercise 9:

   **dormir, mentir, partir, servir, sortir, vêtir.**

11†   The following are single-stem verbs, but their pattern is not
      quite the same as that of **arriver** or **donner**. Specify the
      resemblances and differences.

**croire, cueillir, extraire, fuir, rire.**

12† Transcribe and analyse the following (as in Exercise 4).

Example: **je bats**: [ʒə + ba + Ø]

**tu mens, ça suffira, elle conduisait, on sort, ils mordraient, elles suivent.**

13† Match the irregular verbs in list A with the regular verbs (or verbal expressions) in list B, which often replace them in everyday usage:

| A | B |
|---|---|
| **mouvoir** | **faire semblant de** |
| **acquérir** | **avoir peur de** |
| **haïr** | **diminuer** |
| **contraindre** | **pousser** |
| **craindre** | **bouger** |
| **croître** | **donner l'absolution** |
| **absoudre** | **détester** |
| **feindre** | **forcer** |
| **décroître** | **se procurer** |

14 Account for the following slip of the tongue by former Prime Minister Laurent Fabius during a political debate:

Disez simplement . . . euh . . . dites simplement que [ . . . ]
(FI)

# 8 Conclusions

## 8.1 Interconnections: verb structure and other areas of grammar

The various aspects of informal French presented so far are not necessarily isolated features. Several of them are interconnected in ways that make the grammar of the colloquial language more coherent than might be supposed: not so much a set of random deviations from the norm as an alternative system with its own characteristic patterns. Central to this system is the tendency for pronouns to be more and more closely bound to a following verb – to pattern more like prefixes than like independent elements.

### 8.1.1 Verb units

Let us recapitulate and enlarge on some of the points made earlier about bound pronouns or 'clitics' (see 7.4.2). They cannot stand on their own. They cannot be separated from the verb except by other clitics ('object pronouns') or by **ne**. They undergo various processes of elision: in standard usage **je** to **j'**; more colloquially, **tu** to **t'** (**t'as**) or **il(s)** to **i'** (**i'fait, i'font**); in popular usage **elle(s)** is sometimes reduced to **e'**. Even **vous** can undergo elision: [vzɛt], [vzave] for **vous êtes, vous avez**, for instance. All these truncations have the effect of fusing subject clitics more closely with the following verb; in extreme cases they lose their separate phonetic identity altogether (**ché bien** for **je sais bien**).

Object clitics are also elided before vowels in standard French, of course: **m'** for **me**, **t'** for **te** or **l'** for **le/la**. Colloquial usage again goes further, and often contracts them before consonants. Thus **je te le donne** is commonly pronounced [ʃtəldɔn] or [ʃtlədɔn] rather than [ʒətələdɔn] (though not in southern France, admittedly). The elision process is subject to various rather

complex phonetic constraints about possible or impossible consonant sequences: *[ʃtldɔn], for example, is ruled out.

Truncation 'in the opposite direction' occurs with **lui**. Just as **celui-là** is
often reduced colloquially to **c'ui-là**, so **lui** can become **'ui**, or even **'i** (**je lui
parle**, **j'ui parle**, **j'i parle**). At this point it coalesces with **y**, giving rise to a
pronoun [i] meaning not only 'to it' but also 'to him' or 'to her':

(1)   On . . . on arrive à la Gare du Nord tous les deux, alors, j'y dis, tu
      viens boire, y a une demi-heure à attendre. (JE38)

(2)   Tordez-y les parties viriles. (RQ177)

Now the patterns of liaison and elision affecting **il(s)** and **elle(s)** differ
significantly from those found with nouns. For one thing, final [l] is never
elided in the case of a noun: **il compte** can become [ikɔ̃t] (**i' compte**), but **la
ville compte un million d'habitants** would never be pronounced *[la vi kɔ̃t . . . ]
(**la vi' compte** . . . ). And, though normal between a subject pronoun and a
following verb (in standard as well as in colloquial usage), liaison is not
possible between a subject noun and a verb: **ils attirent** is [i(l) zatir], but
**ces villes attirent beaucoup de visiteurs** is [sevil atir] without liaison – not
*[sevil zatir].

This is further evidence that the status of **il(s)** and **elle(s)** (and by extension **je**, **tu**, **le**, **lui** and other clitics) is different from that of genuinely independent units: there is a major grammatical barrier between subject nouns
and verbs, across which liaison is 'prohibited'. By contrast, the barriers
between the elements within sequences like [ʃe] or [ʃtəldɔn] have become
highly permeable – so much so that they disappear altogether in **ché
bien/pas**.

Consequently, it makes sense to consider [ʃe] or [ʃtəldɔn] as self-contained
units which have a closer resemblance to single words than to the multi-
word phrases corresponding to them in the written code (**je sais**, **je te le
donne**). At the same time, there is a tendency (mentioned in 3.3.2) to sim-
plify their structure in some cases by reducing the number of object clitics
occurring before the verb: instead of standard **je le lui dirai**, familiar usage
often has **je lui dirai ça** (with the direct object after the verb), **je lui dirai** or
**j'ui dirai** (with no direct object at all). F. Gadet gives popular examples like:
**On lui a demandé ses papiers: elle avait pas sur elle** (1992: 65); however,
omission of **le/la/les** is less usual in the absence of an indirect object, the
structure of the verb unit here being comparatively simple already.

**EXERCISES**

1† Give standard written equivalents of the following:

| | | | |
|---|---|---|---|
| (a) | [ʃpaʀ] | (l) | [samplɛ pa] |
| (b) | [ipaʀ] | (m) | [ɔ̃spaʀl ʒamɛ] |
| (c) | [ipaʀt] | (n) | [fo ktytsov] |
| (d) | [tatɔ̃] | (o) | [ʒɥiɑ̃nedɔne] |
| (e) | [izɑ̃tʀɛ] | (p) | [iməlpʀɛt] |
| (f) | [tenɛʀv pa] | (q) | [ʒipaʀlpa] |
| (g) | [ispoʀt bjɛ̃] | (r) | [ɛmlapas] |
| (h) | [ɛmdi bɔ̃ʒuʀ] | (s) | [imleʀɔ̃] |
| (i) | [ʒəlvø] | (t) | [ʒlafɛvniʀ] |
| (j) | [imladɔn] | (u) | [ʒvø ktaʀɛt] |
| (k) | [tɥidɔn sa] | (v) | [ʒlezɛm] |

2† Use phonetic script to represent colloquial equivalents of:

| | | | |
|---|---|---|---|
| (a) | j'entends | (j) | tu me l'as emprunté |
| (b) | je cherche | (k) | ils en ont assez |
| (c) | je travaille | (l) | il me l'a promis |
| (d) | je désire | (m) | il le leur a présenté |
| (e) | je préfère | (n) | il faut qu'on se tire |
| (f) | je le veux | (o) | on te pardonne |
| (g) | je les ai vus | (p) | on te le montre |
| (h) | je ne lui dis pas merci | (q) | on va te la présenter |
| (i) | tu n'y vas pas | (r) | qu'on se le dise |

### 8.1.2  Links with interrogatives, negatives and noun structure

The 'demotion' of pronouns to clitic status and the emergence of word-like verb units have had repercussions on several of the areas of grammar considered in previous chapters. As suggested in 2.1, the absence of **ne** from colloquial French negatives may be attributable to such factors as the lack of phonetic substance of **ne**, or its semantic redundancy (the negative meaning being adequately conveyed by **pas**, **jamais**, etc.). But it is also true that **ne** is not a clitic or bound pronoun. So when it is included in a phrase like **je ne le fais pas**, the word-like verb unit je-le-fais ([ʒəlfɛ] or [ʒləfɛ]) is broken up by a piece of 'extraneous' material in a way which is inappropriate, even unnatural, in terms of the patterns of colloquial grammar. Words are resistant to interruption: within a word, the only item which can come between a prefix and the stem is another prefix: **placement** – **déplacement** – **anti-déplacement**. The same evidently applies to a French 'clitic + clitic + verb' unit like [ʒəlfɛ]: it does not lend itself to being turned into, say, a 'clitic + negative + clitic + verb' unit. So the colloquial '**pas** only' negative pattern is well motivated in the light of these more general characteristics of verb structure.

Inversion (as in **suis-je?**) is another potential source of disruption of 'clitic + verb' units: it removes one of the elements making up the [ʒəsɥi] complex and relocates it. Prefixes are not moveable in this way: they occupy a fixed position within a word and cannot be interchanged or, still less, treated as though they were suffixes (**\*déantiplacement** or **\*déplacementanti**). To the extent that clitics resemble prefixes, they are similarly resistant to being 'uprooted'. So the avoidance of inversion, like the omission of **ne**, is compatible with the 'non-interruptibility' principle governing 'clitic + verb' units. As with the negatives, alternative ways of expressing the notion 'interrogative' are brought into use (see 2.2).

Other inversions too are avoided in colloquial usage, and for the same reasons. The result is that constructions like **ainsi sont-elles parties** or **peut-être est-il arrivé** have literary or rhetorical overtones, and sound pretentious and out of place in everyday conversation. Instead, formulations without inversion such as **alors elles sont parties**, **il est peut-être arrivé** or **peut-être (qu') il est arrivé** are used.

The distinctive structure of the verb in spoken and particularly in colloquial French, with its tendency to maximize the use of prefixes at the expense of suffixes, echoes the structure of that other major word category, the noun (see 6.2). As with verbs, information about the number of a noun is conveyed, not by an ending, but sometimes by the plural prefix [z], and almost always by a prefix-like determiner. Whatever the register, there are very few instances where a 'bare' noun can occur without any prefixed elements. So a noun phrase like **les mains** could be described as a 'prefix + stem' unit [le + mɛ̃], parallel to 'clitic + stem' units like [ʒ + aʀiv] (**j'arrive**).

## EXERCISES

3† Arrange the sentences in each of the following groups in descending order of formality:

  (a) je vais peut-être sortir
  (b) peut-être vais-je sortir
  (c) peut-être que je vais sortir
  (d) peut-être je vais sortir

>     (e)  alors on est partis
>     (f)  on est donc partis
>     (g)  ainsi sommes-nous partis
>     (h)  nous sommes donc partis
>
> 4†  Say whether the following are noun or verb units, and divide
> each into its 'prefix + stem' components:
>
>     (a)  [œ̃nivɛʀ]
>     (b)  [ɔ̃niva]
>     (c)  [idiz]
>     (d)  [dezil]
>
> 5†  Each of the following can be interpreted as either a noun or a
> verb unit. Use traditional spelling to distinguish between the
> possibilities.
>
>     (a)  [saʒu]
>     (b)  [tebɛt]
>     (c)  [seʒɑ̃]
>     (d)  [ʒɑ̃se]

### 8.1.3   Links with imperatives, co-ordination, relatives and topicalization

It is possible to take this approach somewhat further and to speculate, for example, that the trend towards fused 'clitic + verb' units may not be unconnected with the tendency to express commands as declaratives rather than as imperatives: **tu jettes ces papiers!** or **tu les jettes!** in preference to **jette ces papiers!**, **jette-les!**. In the last two cases, the subject clitic **tu** is absent altogether and in **jette-les!** the object **les** is not in its usual position before the verb: all of which again conflicts with the verb-unit pattern described above. (An intermediate possibility is to retain the imperative but to substitute **ça** for post-verbal **le/la/les**: **jette ça!**.) Here are some further examples of alternatives to the imperative in commands (see also 4.1.3):

(3)   Tu me passes un mouchoir, s'il te plaît. (RL28)

(4)   –  Tu fais quoi ce soir? – Ben, j'ai le taxi. Et . . .
       –  Tu te pointes vers sept heures chez Francis. Tu t'installes. Tu te bois une bière. Tu mates [*regardes*] les femmes. Et quand ton pote arrive, tu lui dis bonjour. (IZ158)

It is also the case that standard co-ordinations like **je mange du pain et bois du vin** (where **bois** occurs without a clitic) would, in colloquial usage, be likely instead to take the form **je mange du pain et je bois du vin**, with a first-person clitic attached to each of the verbs, thus avoiding the bare form **bois**.

In standard French, relative clauses are a conspicuous instance of verbs occurring without accompanying personal pronouns: **l'homme qui est là**, **c'est moi qui conduis**. The replacement of these structures in colloquial speech by **l'homme qu'il est là** or **c'est moi que je conduis** restores the missing clitics (underlined), and this fits the overall pattern of verb units better.

However, the formulation **l'homme qu'est là**, without a clitic, occurs very frequently, so other factors may be involved. One relevant point is that languages which make use of 'resumptive' relative clauses (see 2.3.4) often do not include third-person *subject* resumptive pronouns in the relative clause. That is to say, a sentence which might be translated word-for-word as 'the friend what he came to tea' (with subject 'he') would be avoided and 'he' omitted, whereas 'the friend what I visited him' (with object 'him') is normal: 'him' *must* be present. Colloquial French may simply be following this universal pattern.

The preferred 'clitic + verb' pattern may have ramifications in one further area: topicalization (see 6.1). If a noun subject is present in a sentence, then a *reprise* clitic can accompany the verb only if the noun is a topic fulfilling the criteria of 'previous mention' (**Jean il est parti**). Otherwise there is no clitic (**Jean est parti**), and therefore once again a conflict with the pattern for colloquial verb units. But recently there has been a good deal of debate among commentators as to whether this is merely a stage in a longer-term trend in colloquial French towards the obligatory presence of a subject clitic in all circumstances, whether the corresponding NP is a topic or not.

In other words, the prediction is that **Jean est parti**, without **il**, will eventually become ungrammatical in colloquial usage. This kind of development has certainly occurred elsewhere: in many languages of Africa, the equivalent of 'John he went away' is grammatically correct, whereas 'John went away', without a pronoun, is unacceptable.

At present, the topic/non-topic distinction is well established in colloquial, though not in standard, French, as the discussion in 6.1 has suggested. But, as was also suggested, there is a strong tendency to avoid placing non-topic NPs at the beginning of sentences with a 'clitic-less' verb following. Instead, a presentative is used (see 6.1.7), and the noun moved into a relative clause. Not **Jean est parti**, but **Y'a Jean qu'est parti** (or **Y'a Jean qu'il est parti**, or even **Y'a Jean, il est parti**). This enables subjects that are topics to be distinguished from those that are not. At the same time, noun phrases without *reprise* can be avoided at the beginning of sentences – in accordance with the predicted development. In other words, structures like **Jean est parti** are indeed becoming less typical of spoken usage.

**EXERCISES**

6† Why are the following standard French phrases or sentences not in conformity with the prevailing structural tendencies of colloquial French?

(a) je ne sais pas
(b) maman est arrivée
(c) que vois-tu?
(d) c'est nous qui sommes là
(e) une bombe a explosé
(f) nous ne sortons pas
(g) il danse et chante
(h) où vais-je?
(i) l'homme qui n'est pas venu
(j) est-ce vrai?

7† Make up colloquial sentences containing the verb units below. Keep the latter intact while incorporating them in the type of structure indicated. Use a 'popularizing' orthography.

Example: [tatɑ̃] (command) → **t'attends un p'tit peu**.

(a) [ʒəlvø] (relative clause)
(b) [tyʒɛt] (command)
(c) [idɑ̃s] (second element of co-ordinated sentence)
(d) [isamyz] (with non-topic subject)
(e) [taʀɛtpa] (command)
(f) [ʃym] (second element of co-ordinated sentence)
(g) [ɛlaʀiv] (with non-topic subject)
(h) [savapaʀtiʀ] (relative clause)

8 Explain the following statement: 'La tendance à renforcer l'intégrité de l'unité verbale a des retombées dans de nombreux domaines de la grammaire du français relâché.'

## 8.2 Colloquial French in various guises

So far the exemplification of familiar and popular grammatical patterns has, inevitably, been in the form of isolated sentences – apart from a few longer passages in 6.2.4. Some further extended excerpts will now be given in order to show how the same text can contain a variety of colloquial features. These passages will also illustrate the way in which *français relâché*, though essentially a spoken phenomenon (excerpt 1), is making inroads into written usage, where it performs a variety of functions (excerpts 2–8 and 10–14).

### 8.2.1 Everyday discourse

In the following characteristic monologue, a working-class woman from a Paris suburb describes how she was once proposed to. (The spelling reflects the numerous elisions characteristic of northern French pronunciation.)

(1) Alors j'dis, dis donc j'dis, c'est justement lui, j'dis, qui m'a d'mandée en mariage. Y veut, j'dis, qu'j'aille chez lui, y voulait s'mett' en ménage avec moi pis plaquer mon logement! Et pis l'jour qu'ça va pas, y m'fout dehors, hein! J'suis pas si bête que ça! Y m'dit: dites Madame Angèle, ah oui, parce qu'il sait mon nom, j'dis oui? Qu'est-ce qu'y a? Y s'appelle . . . Comment qu'y s'appelle? Ah ben, j'm'rappelle plus d'son nom! C'est un tout p'tit bonhomme, moi qu'aime pas les p'tits, alors y tombe mal! Il est pas plus grand qu'moi! Oh! J'aime pas les p'tits bonhommes comme ça! Même que j'suis vieille, j'en voudrais pas hein! Ah non, même un grand d'abord, j'veux pas m'emmerder avec! Non, j'suis trop habituée toute seule. Vous savez, quand on est habitué tout seul, hein, on a du mal à s'y faire. Alors v'la qu'y m'dit: Madame Angèle, vous savez pas, qu'y m'dit, j'voudrais vous d'mander quelque chose. J'dis: quoi, j'dis? Y dit: assoyez-vous, prenez quelque chose. Alors bon, j'ai pris un diabolo-citron, j'adore ça. (IVR)

---

**EXERCISE**

1   Identify familiar and popular grammatical features in this passage, and comment on the general organization of the text.

---

### 8.2.2 Journalists' colloquial

Some newspaper or magazine columnists, like Claude Sarraute (until recently in *Le Monde*) or Delfeil de Ton (in *Le Nouvel Observateur*), make extensive use of familiar and popular French – creating humorous effects, enlivening unpromising subject matter, or highlighting a telling point ('the voice of plain common sense'). But striking though the effects may be, the language itself can seem rather contrived and unnatural: too many standard forms may be used alongside the colloquialisms, or the general organization of the text may be too smooth and sophisticated (cf. excerpt 4, with its triple repetitions, mini-climaxes and rhetorical questions).

(2)  Vaut-il mieux vivre en France et y être un chômeur secouru, ou vivre en Hollande ou en Grande-Bretagne et y être un chômeur enfin pourvu d'un travail mal payé? Les statisticiens se disputent sur le point de savoir quelles conclusions tirer de leurs savants calculs. Les sociologues, eux, se demandent plutôt où c'est-y que les pauvres ils sont le moins malheureux. Quant au penseur, il s'interroge: qu'est-ce qui est le plus sage, travailler pour des clopinettes ou toucher des clopinettes en restant à la maison? On atteint là à la morale, stade ultime de la réflexion philosophique. Marcel, t'as pensé à rapporter de la bière? (Delfeil de Ton, *Le Nouvel Observateur*, 9 April 1998)

(3)  Sa ferme est démolie. Ses vaches sont éventrées. C'est au Monténégro. Des dizaines de petites bombes jaunes, celles-ci non explosées, jonchent sa cour et son champ. Il dit: «*Ce sont des mines antipersonnelles interdites par les conventions internationales.*» L'Otan le reprend: «*Ce sont des mines anti-matériel.*» Ses vaches avaient qu'à être moins cons. Les petites filles aussi, sur la route. Pas savoir qu'on n'est pas du matériel! (Delfeil de Ton, *Le Nouvel Observateur*, 6 May 1999)

(4)  J'ai une copine au journal, ça va pas, ça va pas bien du tout. Tragique! Une crème, cette fille, douce, indulgente, gentille. Très cool, très relax, très calme. Un lac, une mer étale, jamais de vagues. Oui et alors? Qu'est-ce qu'elle a? Ben, elle a ça, bon caractère, et ça ne se pardonne pas. Non, sérieux, contrairement à ce qu'on croit, c'est pas le stress qui est fatal, c'est la sérénité. Bonne humeur égale mauvaise santé. Pour les femmes, attention! Les hommes, eux, plus ils se contrôlent, mieux ils se portent. D'où je le tire? D'une étude menée pendant onze ans à l'université du Michigan. Il en ressort que sa colère faut la piquer, pas la rentrer, si on veut couper à une mort prématurée. (Claude Sarraute, *Le Monde*, 22 November 1990)

## EXERCISES

2  At what points and for what reasons does the author of (2) and (3) shift from standard into colloquial French?

3  In (4), identify conversational features of grammar, and not-so-conversational features of structure and organization.

### 8.2.3 *Populist fiction*

An increasing number of novelists these days attempt to reinforce their evocation of working-class or otherwise underprivileged surroundings by using an appropriate variety of French – in narrative as well as in dialogue. In (5) the author is describing the immigrant district of Paris in which he grew up. There are two uses of 'universal **que**' here which are particularly worthy of note (and so, in a different way, is a rather out-of-place **ne**).

(5)  A droite en montant, il y a la porte du bistrot à Mme Pellicia, une petite porte avec une petite fenêtre que tu devinerais jamais que c'est un bistrot s'il n'y avait pas écrit sur la vitre: «Au Petit Cavanna». Parce qu'avant c'était le bistrot à Grand-mère, la grand-mère Cavanna, la mère du grand Dominique, le Patron. Ça s'appelait «Au Petit Cavanna» pour pas que les gens confondent avec l'autre Cavanna, le grand beau restaurant juste en face du commissariat qu'il y en a qui viennent de loin et même de Paris, des fois, par l'autobus, pour y faire la noce tellement que la cuisine est bonne. (FCT18)

The following, from a rather sordid novel about poverty, drink, abortion and murder, is a further example of an attempt to make the grammar fit the *milieu* of the characters. The narrator is a single mother-of-three turned lesbian.

(6)  Y a qu'Olivier qui pourrait dire mais je veux pas l'emmerder avec ça. Et puis ils posent pas de questions, sauf Quentin, un jour, en plein Prisunic: Dis maman, tu l'aimes Thérèse? – Ben, oui. – Tu fais l'amour avec elle? Je savais plus où me mettre, j'ai dit: Chut Quentin, chut! Il devait avoir sept ans. Un jour il m'a demandé: Et si papa il buvait plus [ . . . ] est-ce que tu retournerais avec lui? Je lui ai répondu que non: Parce que quand on aime plus quelqu'un on retourne plus avec. – Alors tu l'aimes plus? J'ai dit: Non. Il a dit: Ça fait rien, même si c'est pas l'même, moi j'voudrais bien un papa. (DB128)

In (7), from yet another novel, the unemployed narrator is speaking to herself after being deserted by her lover, Mehdi:

(7)  Merde j'ai perdu la formule magique. Abra ca da bra je veux qu'il revienne. Tu dérailles ma vieille tu yoyotes de la touffe. Bouche bée t'es prête à croire au miracle. Le lapin sortant du chapeau du prestidigitateur tu l'as bouffé un certain dimanche ça te suffit pas pauv' niace. T'aimes ça vraiment le mélo-mélasse. Mehdi si tu revenais

on chialerait comme deux veaux et on se dirait qu'on s'est aimés comme personne. Que vraiment finir comme ça aussi connement avec autant d'amour dans le coeur . . . Allez. Arrête. Souviens-toi. La lettre. Tu l'as perdue rapide hein. La preuve d'une telle glauquerie. La fuite de Valentino se regardant en train d'être aimé à la folie. Prends ça dans la tronche Lucette. Remets tes patins à roulettes on s'en va. Mouche ton nez et dis au revoir à la dame. Et toujours les potes et les potines. Y t'aime plus. De toute façon depuis six mois faut reconnaître t'es pas brillante y t'démolit. (EHA78–9)

---

### EXERCISE

4 Identify colloquial features in (5), (6) and (7), and suggest one or two ways in which the colloquial effect could be enhanced even further.

---

### 8.2.4  Pastiche

In the early twentieth century, the literary critic Emile Faguet composed the following celebrated verse, enshrining the half dozen *fautes de français* of which he most disapproved. (Curiously, he misses the opportunity to satirize negation without **ne**.)

(8)  Malgré qu'il pleut, on part à Gif, nous deux mon chien.
     C'est pour sortir Azor, surtout qu'il n'est pas bien.

   [**Gif-sur-Yvette**: a village south of Paris. **Azor**: an equivalent of 'Fido'.]

The purist André Moufflet, whose views have often been quoted in the preceding chapters, claims that he once came across the following newspaper version of an eye-witness account of an accident (written in impeccable *français soigné*):

(9)  Huit heures venaient de sonner. Ma femme et moi étions en train de dîner, lorsque nous entendîmes des cris affreux partant de la cour. Nous sortîmes en hâte et, là, nous aperçûmes sur le sol le corps de la locataire du troisième étage, horriblement défigurée et baignant dans une mare de sang. La malheureuse, qui s'adonnait, dit-on, à la pratique des stupéfiants, avait mis fin à ses jours en se précipitant dans le vide.

He provides his own reconstruction of the speaker's original words, using a number of popular vocabulary items, grammatical features and (occasionally) pronunciations. Notice also how the hypotactic structures of the above paragraph are astutely replaced by a paratactic arrangement (see 6.2.4).

(10)  Il était quéque chose comme huit heures. Nous deux ma bourgeoise on mangeait. Même qu'on avait ce soir-là des z'haricots verts. Puis, voilà qu'on entend gueuler dans la cour; mais alors, ça, vous parlez d'un boucan! Vivement on se trotte pour voir qu'est-ce que c'est. Y avait la môme du troisième qui s'avait f . . . par la fenêtre. Qu'est-ce qu'on a trouvé comme mélasse. Pour moi, voulez-vous que je vous dise, elle en tenait une muffée de première; c'est encore un de leurs trucs de coco. (AM256–7)

[**des z'haricots** [dezaʀiko]: a much-mocked 'mispronunciation' of **des haricots** [deaʀiko], which has become one of the stereotypes of *français populaire*; **muffée**: intoxication; **coco**: cocaine.]

---

### EXERCISES

5  Give a standard (prose) version of (8) and list the non-standard forms to which Faguet took exception.

6  Comment on the differences between (9) and (10).

---

### 8.2.5  Language games

Many authors obtain ironic or other effects by switching backwards and forwards between language levels. Indeed, language play is sometimes the salient feature of their writing. A case in point is Commissaire San-Antonio, whose fast-moving and far-fetched thrillers are the pretext for some spectacular grammatical and lexical virtuosity.

Characteristic examples of 'register shift' occur in the following reflection on the nature of life:

(11)  Je pige. Combien forte est la vie! Quelle belle sève vivace! Comme c'est dru, impétueux! Ça me fait penser à la frêle pousse de lierre qui finit par étrangler l'orgueilleux sapin. Vous avez jamais vu grimper du lierre après un sapin? Au début c'est joli. Ça pare le tronc. Ça lui ôte son côté futur poteau télégraphique. Et puis, quand le lierre est bien haut, bien fourni, bien luisant, on s'aperçoit

que les branches basses de l'arbre jaunissent. C'est irréversible chez le sapin. C'est comme les tifs des bonshommes. Quand ça crève, ça repousse plus. Un jour, le sapin, il lui reste plus que son cône, tout là-haut. Il est clamsé dans la verdure. (SAB301)

This writer's predilection for play on words and self-parody, as well as for various colloquial effects of grammar and lexis, is illustrated in the following description of a hand grenade attack:

(12)   Mort de mes os! Je reconnais une grenade. Une main on ne peut plus criminelle vient de la jeter par l'entrebâillement de la lourde. Je fonce comme un fou dans le couloir en entraînant Béru. On vient à peine de débouler dans l'entrée qu'une explosion formidable retentit. Je pourrais essayer de vous l'exprimer avec des «rrraôum!» des «vlangggg» et des «tziboum-badaboum» (les meilleurs), mais à quoi bon? Et surtout à quoi bonds? Et même, à quoi James Bond? Ça plâtrarde partout. Y a une brèche dans la cloison. Par icelle, je coule un z'oeil dans la cuisine. J'aimerais bien savoir ce qu'il est advenu (des Champs-Elysées) d'Alfred. Au milieu de ce bigntz il a dû être décoiffé, le coquet. Je le vois pas, biscotte la fumaga. Le plaftard continue de faire des petits. Ça remue-ménage dans l'immeuble. Ça déménage! Ça change de rue! Les bouillaveurs changent de rut! Les marchands de bagnoles changent de ruses! (Je peux vous en pondre commak à la pelle, ça ne me fatigue pas.) (SAB311)

Note the puns (often in series) triggered off by **bon**, **advenu** ('avenue') and **remue-ménage**. **Une main on ne peut plus criminelle** is a literary expression; **icelle** ('celle-ci') is archaic; **un z'oeil** is a jocular allusion to plurals like **entre quatre z'yeux** (see 7.2.3). Slang vocabulary elements include **lourde** ('porte'), **débouler** ('arriver'), **biscotte** (a jocular variant of the already jocular **because**: 'parce que', 'à cause de'), **bigntz** ('business'), **fumaga** ('fumée'), **plaftard** ('plafond'), **commak** ('comme ça').

The humorist Raymond Queneau, another experimenter with language, did much to make colloquial French acceptable as a written medium. He is celebrated, among other things, for his phonetic representations of spoken utterances, notably the opening 'word' of his best-known novel, *Zazie dans le métro* (Gabriel in this scene is meeting his young niece, Zazie, at a Paris railway station):

(13)   Doukipudonktan, se demanda Gabriel, excédé. Pas possible, ils se nettoient jamais. Dans le journal, on dit qu'il y a pas onze pour cent des appartements à Paris qui ont des salles de bains, ça m'étonne

pas, mais on peut se laver sans. Tous ceux-là qui m'entourent, ils doivent pas faire de grands efforts. D'un autre côté, c'est tout de même pas un choix parmi les plus crasseux de Paris. Y a pas de raison. C'est le hasard qui les a réunis. On peut pas supposer que les gens qu'attendent à la gare d'Austerlitz sentent plus mauvais que ceux qu'attendent à la gare de Lyon. Non vraiment, y a pas de raison. Tout de même quelle odeur. (RQ11)

---

## EXERCISES

7  Identify and comment on colloquial aspects of the grammar of (11) and (12).

8  Write **doukipudonktan** in standard orthography, comment on its grammatical structure, and identify as many other colloquial grammar features as possible in (13). Comment also on the use of the past historic in the first line.

---

### 8.2.6  Literary use

In his less playful (and less distinguished) works of fiction, Queneau was content to use perfectly standard French. Probably the most accomplished user of popular grammar and lexis in serious novels of outstanding literary merit is his near contemporary, Louis-Ferdinand Céline, who was no less an influence than Queneau on the emergence of a new written style. In Céline's writing, too, there is an intricate alternation of colloquial and standard forms. And at times, the potential of popular French is stretched to the very limit (or possibly beyond it). Here, from *Voyage au bout de la nuit*, first published in 1932, are three examples in which Céline is arguably 'plus populaire que le peuple' ('Robinson' is the name of one of the main characters):

(14)  T'avais ta gueule enfarinée, hein, grand saligaud qu'<u>on l'asticotait nous Robinson</u>, histoire de le faire grimper et de le mettre en boîte. [**asticoter**: 'tease'.] (LFCV143)

(15)  [ . . . ] vous savez Ferdinand qu'ils n'arrêtent même plus la nuit de se forniquer à longueur de rêves ces salauds-là! . . . C'est tout dire. Et je te creuse! Et je te la dilate la jugeote! <u>Et je te me la tyrannise!</u> [*The reference is to those responsible for the latest psychiatric theories*; **jugeote**: 'common sense'.] (LFCV534)

(16)   <u>La sienne Robinson d'enfance</u>, il ne savait plus par où la prendre quand il y pensait tellement qu'elle était pas drôle. (LFCV419)

Elsewhere in Céline's writing, colloquial features of a less eccentric kind contribute to the creation of poetic effects. This is especially true of his favourite device, the dislocated sentence:

(17)   Au bord du quai les pêcheurs ne prenaient rien. Ils n'avaient même pas l'air de tenir beaucoup à en prendre des poissons. Les poissons devaient les connaître. Ils restaient là tous à faire semblant. Un joli dernier soleil tenait encore un peu de chaleur autour de nous, faisant sauter sur l'eau des petits reflets coupés de bleu et d'or. Du vent, il en venait du tout frais d'en face à travers mille feuilles, en rafales douces. On était bien. Deux heures pleines, on est resté ainsi à ne rien prendre, à ne rien faire. Et puis, la Seine est tournée au sombre et le coin du pont est devenu tout rouge du crépuscule. Le monde en passant sur le quai nous avait oubliés là, nous autres, entre la rive et l'eau.

La nuit est sortie de dessous les arches, elle est montée tout le long du château, elle a pris la façade, les fenêtres, l'une après l'autre, qui flambaient devant l'ombre. Et puis, elles se sont éteintes aussi les fenêtres. (LFCV366)

---

## EXERCISES

9   Comment on colloquial features in (14), (15) and (16), especially those underlined.

10   (14)–(17) all contain dislocated sentences. Identify examples and assess the effect of this construction in (17). What other non-standard grammatical patterns occur in (17)?

# Appendix 1: Answers to Selected Exercises

Answers are provided for exercises marked with a dagger (†) in the text.

## 2.1 Forming negatives

1  (a) personne ne l'a vu; (b) avant qu'il ne soit candidat; (c) ils ne voudront plus jamais aller; (d) qui n'a pas de quoi vivre; (e) il ne tuait plus personne; (f) de ne pas se faire plaisir.

2  No **pas** in standard French: on ne va citer ni les films ni les gens.

3  (a) n'ose, n'ose pas, ose pas; (b) ne peux, ne peux pas, peux pas.

4  (a) me casse pas (fam), ne me casse pas (standard); (b) t'énerve pas (fam), ne t'énerve pas (standard); (c) touche pas (fam), ne touche pas (standard).

5  standard: (a), (d), (g), (j); colloquial: (c), (e), (i); unacceptable: (b), (f), (h).

6  (a) is nothing (to shout about); (b) is (quite) something.

7  very likely: (a), (e), (f), (i), (j); fairly likely: (b), (g), (h); less likely: (c), (d).

8  (a)–(d) are somewhat ceremonial: a formal declaration of innocence, the statement of a general truth, a reference to a very important person (the novelist André Malraux), a jocular attempt to be dramatic; (e) is a case where **ne** merges with the liaison *n*. (f)–(j) are much more mundane.

9    (a) ça présente pas de difficulté; (b) pas un seul élève (n') a répondu;
     (c) personne d'entre eux (n') a voulu; (d) sans la moindre intention de;
     (e) j'en ai pas du tout besoin; (f) pas le moindre doute.

10   (a) (i) Friday is the only day they eat fish, (ii) on Friday fish is all they
     eat; (b) (i) it's only a week that I've been working nights, (ii) for a week
     I've been working nights only.

11   (a) ne s'occupe que des vieux: just looks after old people; (b) il n'y a pas
     que ça: that's not all there is in our lives; (c) tu n'avais qu'à ne pas
     signer: you could simply have not signed (i.e. refused to sign); (d) il n'a
     qu'à se cacher: he can just go and hide somewhere; (e) on ne comprend
     que ce qu'on veut: you only understand what you want to understand;
     (f) seuls ces maudits bourgeois peuvent croire que les artistes ne peuvent
     créer que dans le dénuement: those middle-class bastards are the only
     ones who think artists have to be poor to be creative.

12   (a) a real beehive where they're nearly all girls; (b) other friends than
     just French ones; (c) not just in oysters, but in all shellfish; (d) It's a
     good thing they aren't all like that!

13   (a) are operating only 75 per cent  of their flights; (b) promise that
     75 per cent of their flights will operate.

14   (a) he may disagree; (b) he can't possibly agree; (c) I've not done a bad
     job of work; (d) I've worked quite a lot.

15   Asterisks for (c), (e), (h) and (i). **Beaucoup** a possibility in (a), (b),
     (f) and (g); **plein** in (f) and (g). 'Not badly' a possible meaning in (b)
     and the only meaning in (d).

16   (a) [plys]; (b) [plys] . . . [plys]; (c) [ply]; (d) [ply], i.e. 'no more than',
     'only', and *not* 'more than', which would be **plus de**; (e) [ply].

17   **une plus jeune**: comparative; **t'es plus belle, t'es plus jeune**: both 'no
     longer'.

## 2.2  Forming questions

1    (a) Est-ce que vous avez bien dormi? (b) Est-ce que tu reprends . . . ?
     (c) Est-ce que Marie est venue . . . ? (d) Est-ce que Pierre travaille . . . ?
     (e) Est-ce que Georges va . . . ? (f) Quand est-ce qu'il part? (g) Pourquoi
     est-ce que je suis . . . ?

2 (a) courant; (b) soigné; (c) soigné; (d) soigné; (e) courant; (f) courant; (g) ungrammatical; (h) grotesque.

3 (a) sors-tu? est-ce que tu sors? tu sors? (b) Pierre arrive-t-il? est-ce que Pierre arrive? Pierre arrive? (c) Marie connaît-elle Christiane? est-ce que Marie connaît Christiane? Marie connaît Christiane?

4 (a) ment-il? est-ce qu'il ment? il ment? (b) le connaissez-vous? est-ce que vous le connaissez? vous le connaissez? (c) le président a-t-il démissionné? est-ce que le président a démissionné? le président a démissionné? (d) l'Otan va-t-elle déclarer la guerre? est-ce que l'Otan va déclarer la guerre? l'Otan va déclarer la guerre?

7 (a) Quand est-ce qu'il part? Il part quand? Quand c'est qu'il part? Quand est-ce que c'est qu'il part? C'est quand qu'il part? Quand ça qu'il part? Quand qu'il part? (b) same possibilities: Comment est-ce que tu t'appelles? etc., plus Comment tu t'appelles?; (c) same possibilities: Qui est-ce que tu connais? etc.; (d) same possibilities but no variant with **ça**; (e) Quelle heure est-ce qu'il est? Il est quelle heure? Quelle heure il est? Quelle heure qu'il est?

8 (a) Où est le malade? *or* Le malade, où est-il? (b) Qui aimes-tu le mieux? (c) Où danse-t-elle? (d) Comment vois-tu l'an 2000, toi? (e) Pourquoi as-tu fait cela, Catherine? (f) Qui es-tu? (g) Quand va-t-on au cirque?

9 (a) comment vas-tu? comment tu vas? comment que tu vas? (b) qui êtes-vous? vous êtes qui? qui vous êtes? qui que vous êtes? (c) comment ça va? comment que ça va? *comment va ça?

10 (a) (i) Il part quand, le train . . . ? (ii) Quand qu'il part, le train . . . ? (b) (i) Ils étaient déguisés comment, les voleurs? (ii) Comment qu'ils étaient déguisés, les voleurs? (c) (i) Combien il a coûté . . . ? *or* Il a coûté combien, ce repas? (ii) Combien qu'il a coûté, ce repas? (d) (i) Pourquoi tu prends la voiture? (ii) Pourquoi que tu prends la voiture?

12 (a) nous dire où vous vous trouvez; (b) On ne sait pas ce qui se passe là-haut; (c) Tu ne sais pas quand elle me l'a avoué? (d) je ne comprends pas pourquoi tu sortirais; (e) on ne savait plus où on était; (f) fais bien attention où tu mets les pieds; (g) Il ne sait pas pourquoi il mange: comme les jeunes de maintenant sont bêtes!; (h) je ne sais pas qui c'est.

14  (a) est-ce que je sais? (b) où est-ce que vous allez? (c) est-ce qu'elles sont gratuites? (d) est-ce que tu ne me connaîtrais plus? (e) Est-ce qu'il est dans ma tête? Est-ce qu'il y est, dans la vôtre?

## 2.3    Forming relative clauses

1   (a) que: antecedent **soldats** (object); (b) qui: antecedent **soldats** (subject); (c) qui: antecedent **train** (subject); (d) que: antecedent **train** (object); (e) laquelle: antecedent **situation** (object of **dans**); (f) qui: antecedent **étudiants** (object of **avec**); (g) dont: antecedent **enfants** (possessive).

2   (a) à qui j'ai écrit une lettre; (b) dont on est sans nouvelles; (c) dont j'ai aperçu la voiture; (d) dont je vous parlais; (e) avec qui je suis sorti; (f) dont le chien aboyait; (g) dont le chien va mordre Marie.

3   (a) la personne que je lui ai montré votre lettre; (b) l'homme que je vous en ai parlé; (c) l'agent qu'il lui a demandé le chemin; (d) la dame que nous la visitons; (e) un garçon qu'on le connaît pas; (f) les bêtes qu'elle leur a donné à manger; (g) un ami que je partirais pas sans lui; (h) la femme que son mari vient de mourir.

4   (a) 1 qu'a donné un cadeau à sa maman; 2 qu'il a donné un cadeau à sa maman; 3 que sa maman lui a donné un cadeau; *standard equivalents*: 1 qui a donné un cadeau à sa maman; 2 qui a donné un cadeau à sa maman; 3 dont la maman lui a donné un cadeau *or* à qui sa maman a donné un cadeau.

   (b) 1 qu'a dit bonjour au petit garçon; 2 qu'il a dit bonjour au petit garçon; 3 que le petit garçon lui a dit bonjour; *standard equivalents*: 1 qui a dit bonjour au petit garçon; 2 qui a dit bonjour au petit garçon; 3 à qui le petit garçon a dit bonjour.

5   (a) un taxi lequel m'a acheminé à ma destination; le bus qui arrive; le train qu'est parti (pop); l'avion qu'il est tombé en panne (pop).

   (b) le café auquel il se rendait tous les jours; le casino où on a fait banco; l'hôtel où qu'on s'est installés pour un mois (pop); le petit bistrot où c'est qu'on s'est bien amusés (pop).

6   (c); second occurrence of **qui** in (e); both occurrences in (f).

7   (a) colloquial; (b) standard; (c) standard (with inversion: equivalent to **que le passager achète**); (d) colloquial; (e) colloquial; (f) standard (equivalent to **que les enfants écoutent**).

8    (a) *colloquial reading*: le rat qui a chassé le chat; *standard reading*: le rat
      que le chat a chassé (with inversion); (b) *colloquial*: le PSG qui a battu
      l'OM; *standard*: le PSG que l'OM a battu; (c) *colloquial*: les Serbes qui
      ont conquis les Albanais; *standard*: les Serbes que les Albanais ont
      conquis.

9    (a) le fusil avec lequel il a tiré, la canne qu'il sort jamais sans (fam), *le
      couteau qu'elle a commis le meurtre (no **avec**), *l'arme à feu il a utilisé
      (no relative marker); (b) le voyage duquel je me souviens, le voyage
      dont je me souviens, le voyage que je m'en souviens (pop), *le voyage je
      m'en souviens (no relative marker).

10   (a) Mon mari que je suis toujours sans ses nouvelles/sans nouvelles de
      lui (*standard*: mon mari dont je suis toujours sans nouvelles); (b) les
      associés que nous en avons besoin (*standard*: les associés dont nous
      avons besoin); (c) le type que je t'en parle (*standard*: le type dont je te
      parle); (d) Le carambolage qu'on vous en a beaucoup parlé ces derniers
      jours (*standard*: le carambolage dont on vous a beaucoup parlé).

## 3.1   Nouns, articles and modifiers

1    **acné**, **bodega**, **coquecigrue**, **fourmi**, **interview**, **paroi** end in vowels; **écritoire**
      phonetically resembles masculines in **-oir**; **primeur** is assimilated to
      **directeur**, etc.; **campanule** and **molécule** end in **-ule**.

2    **automne**, **emblème**, **haltère**, **indice**, **insigne** are vowel-initial/consonant-
      final; **planisphère** is assimilated to **sphère**, etc.; **globule**, **opuscule**, **tentacule**
      end in **-ule**.

3    Masculine except for **mandibule**, **marge**, **molécule**, **orbite**, **vis**. Sometimes
      recategorized: **armistice**, **effluve**, **exutoire**, **mandibule**, **molécule**, **tubercule**,
      **ustensile**.

4    (a), (c), (d), (f).

5    (a) c'est très amusant comme émission; (b) qu'est-ce que t(u) attends
      comme train? (c) i(l) nous reste plus rien comme argent *or* comme argent
      i(l) nous reste plus rien; (d) comme plaisanterie c'était de fort mauvais
      goût; (e) qu'est-ce que tu préfères comme vacances? (f) ça me semble pas
      très original comme idée; (g) qu'est-ce qu'il te reste comme temps?

7    (a) C'est bien meilleur; (b) C'est bien pire; (c) C'est le pire de tous; (d) A
      cette époque il devrait faire meilleur; (e) Il est aussi mauvais que l'autre;
      (f) C'est pire qu'un enfant.

8    (a) ou; (b) à; (c) ou; (d) ou; (e) à.

## 3.2   **Pronouns:** nous **and** on

1   (a) they're making us pay too much tax; (b) we're paying too much tax.

2   (a) nous avons été; (b) nous sommes fiers; (c) Nous nous regardons et nous nous lisons nos horoscopes [*we read our horoscopes to one another*] en faisant des bêtises.

3   (a) on est allé(s) jusqu'à Paris pour faire nos achats; (b) l'agent nous a dit qu'on (n') avait pas le droit de mettre nos vélos dans le parking; (c) nous on apprend le français, mais vous vous étudiez l'allemand (*or, more familiarly*, vous autres vous étudiez).

4   **nous** in (a), **tous** in (b), **deux** in (c) and **normaux** in (d) all point to a plural interpretation.

5   'you'; 'we'; 'we'; 'they'.

## 3.3   **Other aspects of pronoun use**

1   **est-ce** should be **est-il**; **il est** should be **c'est**.

2   (b), (a), (c).

3   (b).

4   (a), because if it is intended to be colloquial it should be **ça**, not **cela**, and if it is intended to be standard, then it should be **il**, not **cela/ça**.

5   (a) and (e).

6   (a) c'est fini/c'est réussi; (b) est-ce que cela suffira? (c) comme cela; (d) c'est surprenant! (e) est-ce que vous allez bien? (f) est-ce que vous vous sentez mal?

9   'where/why/when/who/how's that?' *or* '... was that?'. 'How come?' is another possibility for (b) and (e).

10   (g) is a celebrated French 'translation' of the English cartoon caption 'Waiter, a crocodile sandwich, please! And make it snappy!'

12    (a) (i) standard; (ii) popular; (iii) popular; (iv) familiar; (b) (i) popular; (ii) standard; (iii) popular; (iv) familiar; (c) (i) popular; (ii) popular; (iii) standard; (iv) familiar.

13    (c), (d) and (g) are ethic.

14    (a) moi et ma femme; (b) moi et mon fils; (c) moi et mon chat.

## 4.1    Tenses and moods

1    Past historic: **enleva**, **prit**, **mit**, **sortit**, **retomba**. Also the ill-formed **\*metta** (for **mit**). These are interspersed seemingly randomly with various perfects. There are also one or two pluperfects.

4    (a) eut bu, appela; (b) a eu bu, a appelé; (c) a bu, a appelé; (d) avait bu, a appelé.

6    In (a) and (c), the event referred to seems imminent (the car crash, the collapse of the house); in (b) and (d) it actually is imminent (crossing the bridge, telling the story).

7    In (a) and (d), the events referred to are possibilities only, so colloquial overtones. In (c) there is more likelihood, but it is still relatively remote. In (b), (e) and (f), the events are on the point of happening, so the compound tense is standard.

8    (a) si on ne l'avait pas dit; (b) si Yves Montand avait été SDF; (c) s'il s'était agi de Karajan; (d) si tu partais une semaine (tu ne manquerais pas); (e) si c'était le droit.

9    (a) J'aurais été seule, ç'aurait pas eu d'importance (FI); (b) Je serais pas chez moi, le logement i's'rait dans son nom à lui (IVR); (c) Moi, je serais président [ . . . ] je serais triste [ . . . ] (LFM141); (d) T'aurais remonté la rue [ . . . ] jusqu'à la grille, arrivé là, t'aurais vu, sur le côté à droite, que la rue continue (FCT17).

10    Standard French requires the subjunctive: in relative clauses following noun phrases with **seul** or an equivalent, as in (a), (b) and (c); following superlatives, as in (d); with antecedents that are hypothetical, as in (e). Also after **bien que**, as in (f) and (g), and after 'negative **croire**', as in (h).

11    (a)–(e) show subjunctives after various colloquial and/or spontaneously coined conjunctions and other expressions (**c'est logique que**, etc.). (f) shows it used to express volition. (g) shows **que** + subj (in fact identical in form with indicative in this instance) used in preference to standard infinitive (**dis-leur de venir**).

## 4.2 Past participles, agreement, auxiliaries

1    (a) reprise; (b) faites; (c) écrite; (d) faites; (e) apprise; (f) dites; (g) séduite.

2    The grammar is colloquial in all other respects: (a) WH-question without inversion; (b) detached NP (see 6.1); (c) **pourquoi** followed by **que**.

3    (a) **fait** not at end of sentence; (b) **dites** at end of sentence; (c) agreement with **faire** + infinitive; (d) **mise** not at end of sentence but agreement favoured by presence of third-person **l'**; (e) **surpris** at end of sentence, but object is **me**; (f) agreement with **faire** + infinitive.

5    (a) clash with non-colloquial **aucun** and **ne**; (b) if spoken, how does one know **observe(nt)** is plural? (c) presence of **ne** again. In both (b) and (c), the vocabulary and idiom are far from colloquial.

6    (a) va, vais; (b) sort, sors; (c) décide, décide; (d) est, suis; (e) finit, finis; (f) met, mets; (g) veut, veux. No audible difference in (b), (e), (f), (g); no audible or visible difference in (c).

7    (a) he didn't return at noon, he hasn't returned yet; (b) he died in 1900, he's been dead for fifty years.

8    (a) implication that the speaker is no longer in Lyon; (b) the speaker is able to emphasize the fact that the visit was short and is now over; (c) not only is the speaker indoors at the time of speaking: he has not been out all year.

## 4.3 Transitive and intransitive; active and passive

1    (a) commencer le travail, débuter le travail; (b) pallier un défaut, pallier à un défaut; (c) promener le chien, sortir le chien; (d) réussir à son baccalauréat, réussir son bac; (e) se rappeler l'adresse de qqn, se rappeler de l'adresse de qqn; (f) invectiver contre un rival, invectiver un rival.

2    Transitive to intransitive: **énerver, dégager, déguster, culpabiliser, assumer, assurer, abuser, assassiner, craindre, activer**. Intransitive to (directly) transitive: **éclater** (normally intransitive or reflexive: **s'éclater**).

4 (a) la souris s'est fait attraper par le chat; (b) il s'est fait marcher dessus; (c) il s'est fait voler son auto-radio; (d) il s'est fait prier de rester; (e) il s'est fait rentrer dedans.

5 (a) causative ('had a tooth out'); (b) passive ('had an arm ripped off'); (c) passive ('wasn't allowed in'); (d) passive ('had his licence withdrawn'); (e) causative ('had breakfast served in his room'); (f) causative ('obtained an extension'); (g) passive ('had his cellar burgled').

## 5.1  Subordinating conjunctions

3 (d), (b), (a), (c).

4 **à cause que**: because; **des fois que**: just in case; **histoire que**: so that, in order to; **malgré que**: although; **même que**: even if, even; **pour pas que**: so that . . . not; **surtout que**: especially as; **vu que**: seeing that (or colloquially 'seeing as how').

6 (22) according to which; (23) showing how; (24) to say that; **un certificat comme quoi**: a certificate stating that; **une pièce d'identité comme quoi**: an identity document proving that; **c'est marqué comme quoi**: it says that.

## 5.2  Extending the role of que

1 (a) pour que; (b) si bête qu'on n'y croit pas, bête au point qu'on n'y croit pas; (c) puisque; (d) pour que, afin que; (e) lui fais-je; (f) te dis-je.

2 (a) ces tilleuls devenus si grands qu'on ne voyait plus rien; (b) j'ai beaucoup de choses à vous signaler dont on n'est pas du tout content; (c) même si je te jetais à terre, on ne le remarquerait pas; (d) elle est difficile et par conséquent je ne sais pas quoi lui donner; (e) veux-tu que je monte quelque chose pour toi?

## 5.3  Prepositions

1 (a) on a vécu avec eux (*or* ça); (b) partie avec elle; (c) me fâcher avec eux; (d) intervenu contre elles/ces mesures; (e) avec ça, avec ce pot d'échappement; (f) avec ça, avec cette eau.

2 (a) lui ont crié après; (b) lui ont sauté dessus; (c) je suis totalement pour; (d) est étudiée pour; (e) n'a pas voulu sortir avec.

3   (10) so as to check, just to check; (11) so (that) we don't lose sight of reality.

5   (a) territorial ('within the city limits'); (b) territorial ('for these constituencies'); (c) directional ('phone (to) Paris'); (d) territorial ('in the Oise/Hauts-de-Seine departments'); (e) territorial ('in the city area'); (f) directional ('returning to, entering'); (g) territorial ('in the Paris area').

6   (b): a novel written by Zola; (d): a 'body part' is not a possession, (e): one does not 'own' one's birthday.

7   (a) 'leaving at midday', not 'for midday'; (b) **en** goes with **fourni** in a phrase meaning 'supplied with'; (c) a market is a place, not a person; (d) there are several whole numbers between ten and fifteen.

8   (g) autour de; (h) sur; (i) dès; ( j) en face de; (k) à part (cela).

## 6.1   Topic structures and *reprise*

1   (a) Elle tourne autour du soleil, la terre/La terre, elle tourne autour du soleil; (b) Je crois qu'elle tourne autour du soleil, notre planète/Notre planète, je crois qu'elle tourne autour du soleil; (c) La troisième planète du système solaire, elle tourne autour du soleil une fois par an/Elle tourne autour du soleil une fois par an, la troisième planète du système solaire; (d) Il y a des milliards d'années qu'elle tourne autour du soleil, la patrie de l'espèce humaine/La patrie de l'espèce humaine, il y a des milliards d'années qu'elle tourne autour du soleil.

2   (a) Ces fleurs on va les mettre dans un pot/On va les mettre dans un pot, ces fleurs; (b) Il y en a des survivants/Des survivants, il y en a; (c) L'ordre du jour de ce matin, on le connaît/On le connaît, l'ordre du jour de ce matin; (d) Elle lui a présenté un bouquet de fleurs à la reine, Marie/Marie elle lui a présenté un bouquet de fleurs à la reine/(A) la reine, elle lui a présenté un bouquet de fleurs, Marie; (e) Bernard il l'a trompée, Sophie/Il l'a trompée Sophie, Bernard/Sophie, il l'a trompée, Bernard/Bernard, Sophie, il l'a trompée/Sophie, Bernard il l'a trompée; (f) Pierre, je crois qu'il a rencontré Chirac à une réception/Je crois qu'il a rencontré Chirac à une réception, Pierre; (g) Chirac, je crois que Pierre l'a rencontré à une réception/Je crois que Pierre l'a rencontré à une réception, Chirac; (h) Ils en ont eu de la chance/De la chance ils en ont eu; (i) La nièce des Dupont, elle a été reçue au bac/Elle a été reçue au bac la nièce des Dupont; ( j) Les Dupont, leur nièce a été reçue au bac; (k) La peine de mort, on est contre (ça); (l) Marianne en portait un ridicule, de chapeau.

3   (a) Je peux manifester pour le Tibet, cela ne changera rien; (b) Cela ne nous concerne pas; (c) On ne mange pas très bien en Suisse; (d) Je ne suis pas contre la propreté; (e) Il y a tout le temps des nouilles dans les caniveaux; (f) Il a mangé trois pommes; (g) Je ne suis pas allée à l'Odéon; (h) Les roses donnaient le rhume des foins à mon père; (i) La dent de ma soeur ne tenait pas bien.

4   (a), as the dog is part of the new information. If the question is about the animals, then (b), as **le chien de mon propriétaire** would be a related NP, and therefore given.

5   **camembert** and **corbeau** have already been mentioned: the new information is about what the crow did with the cheese.

7   (a) **les gars** is one of those 'solidarity' expressions which are typically detached; (b) the saddle belongs to the horse, and therefore counts as given information; (c) lines (**lignes**) are a kind of punishment (**punition**), so the nouns are related; (d) **les fourmis** has already occurred in the discourse; (e) in view of what happened, Etienne is very much present 'in the mind' of Renée.

10  (a) right (vehicle clearly present in the situation); (b) none (the father is part of the new information).

11  Henri is the **crétin** (right detachment of term of abuse).

13  (a) non-contrastive: 'I don't líke that noise'; (b) contrastive: 'Í'm leaving; yóu're staying'; (c) non-contrastive: 'we prómised to be good'; (d) contrastive: 'Í tried too'.

15  (Il) y a le téléphone qui sonne.

16  (a) certains avaient déjà commencé; (b) il m'en manque un; (c) les gens ne sont plus dehors; (d) une fois que quelque chose a été signé; (e) des policiers arrivent . . . certains regardent; (f) pour allumer le fourneau de ma soeur, il y a un dispositif spécial.

17  (a) C'est un kir royal que je voudrais/ce que je voudrais c'est un kir royal; (b) C'est le président qui a ouvert la séance/celui qui a ouvert la séance c'est le président; (c) C'est un fou qui a inventé ça/Celui qui a inventé ça, c'est un fou.

18  (a) Ce qu'il a décidé, c'est de s'absenter; (b) Ce qu'elles préfèrent, c'est de ne pas essayer; (c) Ce qu'il nous faut, c'est un nouveau gouvernement.

19  (a) Ce qui est incroyable, c'est qu'ils ne sont jamais chez eux; (b) Ce qui est étonnant, c'est qu'il ait pu commettre trois meurtres; (c) Ce qui m'agace, c'est d'avoir à faire trois kilomètres; (d) Ce qui nous inquiète, c'est qu'il a pu y avoir un accident; (e) Ce qui a provoqué la collision, c'est l'ivresse au volant; (f) Ce qui me frappe, c'est qu'il est presque toujours absent.

## 6.2  Extending the range of grammar: 'macro-syntax'

1  (a) j'y ai jamais été; (b) on a pas à s'en plaindre; (c) il y pleut tout le temps; (d) on pouvait pas s'y baigner; (e) j'aime pas tellement ça.

2  (a) j'ai fait le métier de chauffeur-livreur; (b) la dernière fois que j'ai eu une crise; (c) je suis angoissée par la moindre contrariété; (d) dans ce métier; (e) qui disent que l'histoire des camps est fausse.

4  (a) ce tableau est amusant; (b) il n'est pas question de vacances; (c) le lendemain, il y a eu une grande surprise; (d) parfois il y en a dans les maisons, parfois non; (e) finalement, étant donné l'importance de l'enjeu, le projet Patagonie est intéressant.

6  (a) Pour le moment ça a l'air d'aller; (b) Alors il a donc écrit ce livre, mais il a aussi relancé un petit peu l'idée du royaume de Patagonie; (c) Pendant la guerre j'avais créé une petite épicerie de campagne; (d) et on nous a obligés à nous mettre tout nus; (e) Il y a de très rares cas de malades qui n'ont dès la naissance aucune sensation de douleur.

## 7.2  Singular and plural (especially nouns)

1  (a) [lə pɛʀ, le pɛʀ]; (b) [la mɛʀ, le mɛʀ]; (c) [yn dam, de dam]; (d) [œ̃ tip, de tip]; (e) [sə bɔnɔm, se bɔnɔm]; (f) [sɔ̃ mɛk, se mɛk]; (g) [nɔt sœʀ, no sœʀ]; (h) [mɔ̃ nəvø, me nəvø].

2  (a) [se pətit taʃ fasil]: (i) 4, (ii) 1; (b) [ʒə ve o gʀɑ̃ magazɛ̃]: (i) 3, (ii) 0; (c) [se detɛstabl batimɑ̃ nwaʀ lɛ e ɑ̃fyme]: (i) 6, (ii) 1; (d) [lœʀ satelit skʀyt lə teʀitwaʀ]: (i) 3, (ii) 0.

4  (a) [se zɑ̃tʀəpʀiz]; (b) [le zo]; (c) [de zanimo]; (d) [se zelɛv]; (e) [me zuvʀaʒ].

5   (b) and (d) are ambiguous: unlike most determiners, **leur** has only one spoken form. But plurality is shown in (c) by the presence of [z]; its absence in (a) means that this has to be singular.

6   un oeuf [œ̃ nœf], des oeufs [de zø]; un boeuf [œ̃ bœf], des boeufs [de bø]. Final *f* not pronounced in plural. "Regularized" spoken pattern: [œ̃ nœf, de zœf], [œ̃ bœf, de bœf]

8   [vɛ̃ zapsɑ̃s]; *standard*: [vɛ̃ tapsɑ̃s].

9   (a) **les z'yeux**; (b) **les z'investisseurs z'institutionnels** (with *-z-* carried over into the singular). **Zinzin** is, in addition, a long-established synonym of **truc** or **machin** ('thingummyjig').

10  (a) animal, apôtre, histoire; (b) épaule, assiette, oreille, os.

## 7.3  Masculine and feminine (especially adjectives)

1   **doux**, *-x* to *-ce*; **tiers**, *-s* to *-ce*; **épais**, *-s* to *-sse*; **sot**, *-t* to *-tte*; **blanc**, *-c* to *-che*; **frais**, *-s* to *-che* (and also *-i-* to *-î-*); **actif**, *-f* to *-ve*; **culturel**, *-l* to *-lle*; **sec**, *-c* to *-che* (and *-e-* to *-è-*); **neuf**, *-f* to *-ve*; **bas**, *-s* to *-sse*; **muet**, *-t* to *-tte*; **gentil**, *-l* to *-lle*; **nul**, *-l* to *-lle*.

2   Written only: none. Spoken only: **social, rationnel, aigu, fini, compliqué, vrai, supérieur**. Both: **fragile, intense, possible, rapide, magique**.

3   [difeRɑ̃, difeRɑ̃t], [ymɛ̃, ymɛn], [fRɑ̃sɛ, fRɑ̃sɛz], [sɛ̃, sɛ̃t], [syksɛsif, syksɛsiv], [pResi, pResiz], [ɑ̃fɑ̃tɛ̃, ɑ̃fɑ̃tin], [Rəliʒjø, Rəliʒjøz], [kɔmœ̃, kɔmyn], [səgɔ̃, səgɔ̃d], [kɔ̃tɑ̃, kɔ̃tɑ̃t].

4   **protestant**: (a) II, (b) II; **musulman**: (a) II, (b) II; **catholique**: (a) I, (b) I; **hindou**: (a) II, (b) I; **juif**: (a) III, (b) III; **allemand**: (a) II, (b) II; **corse** (a) I, (b) I; **espagnol**: (a) II, (b) I; **andalou** (a) IV (**andalouse** in fem.), (b) II; **anglais**: (a) II, (b) II; **belge**: (a) I, (b) I.

5   I: [kɔRɛkt], [kRɥɛl], [nyl]. II: [dus (du)], [tjɛRs (tjɛR)], [epɛs (epɛ)], [sɔt (so)], [blɑ̃ʃ (blɑ̃)], [fRɛʃ (fRɛ)], [bas (ba)], [mɥɛt (mɥe)], [ʒɑ̃tij (ʒɑ̃ti)], [lɔ̃g (lɔ̃)]. III: [nœv], [sɛʃ], [aktiv].

7   I: **tendre**; II: **doux, tiers, épais, sot, blanc, frais, bas, muet, gentil, long**; III: **actif, sec, neuf**; IV: **cruel, nul, correct, public**.

## 7.4   Conjugating verbs

| 1 | ʒdɔn | ʒɑ̃vwa | ʒəʒu | ʃtʀavaj |
|---|---|---|---|---|
|   | tydɔn | tɑ̃vwa | tyʒu | tytʀavaj |
|   | idɔn | ilɑ̃vwa | iʒu | itʀavaj |
|   | ɔ̃dɔn | ɔ̃nɑ̃vwa | ɔ̃ʒu | ɔ̃tʀavaj |
|   | vudɔne | vuzɑ̃vwaje | vuʒwe | vutʀavaje |
|   | idɔn | izɑ̃vwa | iʒu | itʀavaj |

2   (a) je (ne) sais pas; (b) je sais bien; (c) je suis fatigué.

3   (a) je vois; (b) je (ne) crois pas; (c) tu appelles; (d) il veut; (e) tu attends; (f) je (ne) peux pas; (g) il (ne) sait pas.

4   (a)   ɛl + paʀl + ɛ          **elle parlait**
    (b)   ʒə + mɑ̃ʒ + Ø          **je mange**
    (c)   t'+ avɑ̃s + ɛ          **t'avançais**
    (d)   i + pus + ʀɛ          **i'pousserait**
    (e)   kə + ʒ + ʀgaʀd + Ø   **que j'regarde**
    (f)   ɔ̃ + din + Ø           **on dîne**
    (g)   ʒ + apɛl + ʀɛ        **j'appellerais**
    (h)   ty + fym + ɛ          **tu fumais**
    (i)   iz + ɛm + ɛ           **ils aimaient**
    (j)   ɔ̃ + etydj + ɛ        **on étudiait**

5   (a)   ʃpɑ̃sɛ            ʃ + pɑ̃s + ɛ
    (b)   tytʀavajʀɛ       ty + tʀavaj + ʀɛ
    (c)   ɔ̃deʒœn           ɔ̃ + deʒœn + Ø
    (d)   ivwajaʒɛ         i + vwajaʒ + ɛ
    (e)   tyetydi          ty + etydi + Ø
    (f)   ʒaʀɛt            ʒ + aʀɛt + Ø
    (g)   ɛltusɛ           ɛl + tus + ɛ
    (h)   itɔ̃bʀɛ           i + tɔ̃b + ʀɛ

7   [ekʀi, ekʀiv]; [mɛ, mɛt]; [mɔʀ, mɔʀd]; [nɥi, nɥiz]; [sɥi, sɥiv]; [vɛ̃, vɛ̃k]. Consonant retained in **mettre, mordre, nuire**. In **vaincre**, *c* changes to *qu* (**vaincs, vainquons**).

9   [ba, bat], [kɔ̃dɥi, kɔ̃dɥiz], [di, diz], [ʀɔ̃, ʀɔ̃p], [syfi, syfiz]. (a) long stem; (b) and (c) long stem for **battre** and **rompre**, otherwise short stem.

10   [dɔʀ, dɔʀm], [mɑ̃, mɑ̃t], [paʀ, paʀt], [sɛʀ, sɛʀv], [sɔʀ, sɔʀt], [vɛ, vɛt]. They differ in that the infinitive, future and conditional are formed on a further stem [dɔʀmi], etc., which (**vêtir** apart) is the same as the past participle.

11 Single stems: [kʀwa], [kœj], [ɛkstʀɛ], [fɥi], [ʀi], but infinitive in [ʀ] not [e], and glide [j] inserted before vowel endings: [kʀwajɛ], [fɥijɛ].

12 [ty + mã + Ø], [sa + syfi + ʀa], [ɛl + kõdɥiz + ɛ], [ɔ̃ + sɔʀ + Ø], [i + mɔʀd + ʀɛ], [ɛl + sɥiv + Ø].

13 Group B in matching order: **bouger, se procurer, détester, forcer, avoir peur de, pousser, donner l'absolution, faire semblant de, diminuer**.

## 8.1 Interconnections: verb structure and other areas of grammar

1 (a) je pars; (b) il part; (c) ils partent; (d) tu attends; (e) ils entraient; (f) (ne) t'énerve pas; (g) il(s) se porte(nt) bien; (h) elle me dit bonjour; (i) je le veux; (j) il(s) me la donne(nt); (k) tu lui donnes ça; (l) ça (ne) me plaît pas; (m) on (ne) se parle jamais; (n) (il) faut que tu te sauves; (o) je lui en ai donné; (p) il me le prête; (q) je (ne) lui parle pas; (r) elle me la passe; (s) il me les rend; (t) je la fais venir; (u) je veux que tu arrêtes; (v) je les aime.

2 (a) [ʒãtã]; (b) [ʒəʃɛʀʃ]; (c) [ʃtʀavaj]; (d) [ʒdeziʀ]; (e) [ʃpʀefɛʀ]; (f) [ʒəlvø]; (g) [ʒlezevy]; (h) [ʒɥidipa mɛʀsi]; (i) [tivapa]; (j) [tymlaãpʀœ̃te]; (k) [izãnɔ̃ase]; (l) [imlapʀɔmi]; (m) [illəlœʀapʀezãte]; (n) [ʃo kõstiʀ]; (o) [ɔ̃tpaʀdɔn]; (p) [ɔ̃təlmɔ̃tʀ]; (q) [ɔ̃vatlapʀezãte]; (r) [kõslədiz].

3 (b), (c), (a), (d); (g), (h), (f), (e).

4 (a) noun: œ̃ + (n)ivɛʀ (**un hiver**); (b) verb: ɔ̃ + (n)i + va (**on y va**); (c) verb: i + diz + Ø (**i'disent**); (d) noun: de + zil (**des îles**).

5 (a) sa joue, ça joue; (b) tes bêtes, t'es bête; (c) c'est Jean, ses gens; (d) Jean sait, j'en sais.

6 **ne** between clitic and verb in (a), (f), (i), preventing reduction to **qu'est** in (i); inversion in (c), (h) and (j); verb with person/number suffix (**-ons**) in (f); non-topic nouns at beginning of sentence in (b) and (e); no subject clitic (**il**) before second verb (**chante**) in (g); **nous qui sommes** rather than **nous qu'on est** in (d).

7 Possibilities: (a) c'est moi que je l' veux; (b) tu jettes ces papiers; (c) i' chante et i' danse; (d) y'a Jean, i' s'amuse; (e) t'arrêtes pas d'essayer; (f) j'bois et j'fume; (g) voilà Marie qu'elle arrive; (h) i' court après le bus qu'ça va partir.

# Appendix 2: Explanations of Grammatical Terms

These explanations are merely brief, informal reminders and only terms actually used in this book are included. More extensive coverage can be found in, for example, Hawkins and Towell (1996), Judge and Healey (1983), Morton (1997), Nott (1998) or Price (1993).

ACTIVE/PASSIVE   Variant forms of a sentence which provide different perspectives on an event or state of affairs: **Marie trompe Pierre** (active) as against **Pierre est trompé par Marie** (passive). The direct object of the active sentence (**Pierre**) is the subject of the passive; the subject of the active (**Marie**) is, in the passive, located after the verb in an agent phrase introduced by **par** (**par Marie**). The verb takes a special passive form consisting of the auxiliary verb **être** and the past participle (**est trompé**).

ADJECTIVE   A word which ascribes a quality to the referent of an accompanying noun (**bon, mauvais, intéressant**). *Attributive adjectives* are adjoined directly to the noun (**le ciel bleu**); *predicative adjectives* are introduced by **être** or an equivalent verb (**le ciel est bleu**). Some adjectives specify nouns rather than describing them: thus *demonstrative adjectives* (**ce, cette, ces**) and *possessive adjectives* (**mon, ma, mes**) single out a particular individual or individuals. These two categories are sometimes called *demonstrative* or *possessive determiners*: see DETERMINER.

ADVERB   A rather varied class of words which add to the information provided by verbs (**je marche <u>lentement</u>, il arrive <u>bientôt</u>**), adjectives (**c'est <u>presque</u> parfait**) or prepositional phrases (**<u>juste</u> après le départ**). *Interrogative adverbs* (**pourquoi?, comment?, où?**) introduce certain WH-QUESTIONS.

AFFIRMATIVE/NEGATIVE   Alternative forms of a sentence used respectively for asserting or denying an event or state of affairs: **je comprends** (affirmative); **je ne comprends pas** (negative).

AGREEMENT   The conventions that require verbs to have the same person and number as their subject, or adjectives and determiners to have the same gender and number as the noun which they modify.

ANIMATE/INANIMATE   Animate nouns refer to living beings (people, animals), inanimate nouns to objects or abstractions.

ANTECEDENT   The noun phrase to which a pronoun refers back. **Jean** is the antecedent of the personal pronoun **lui** in: **quand j'ai vu Jean, je lui ai dit bonjour**; **les enfants** is the antecedent of the relative pronoun **qui** in: **les enfants qui jouaient**.

ARTICLE   The *definite article* indicates that a noun refers to a particular individual (person or thing): **le (garçon), la (fille), (les) garçons**. The *indefinite article* indicates that a noun refers to an unspecified person or thing: **un (garçon), une (fille), des (filles)**.

ATTRIBUTIVE   See ADJECTIVE.

AUXILIARY (VERB)   A 'helping' verb involved in forming certain tenses: **avoir** in **j'ai vu, aller** in **tu vas voir, être** in **il est arrivé**. See TENSE.

CLAUSE   A sentence containing a single verb (or auxiliary plus verb) and forming part of a larger, more complex sentence. **Je sais bien que Marie est arrivée** contains two verbs and consequently two clauses: **je sais bien** and **Marie est arrivée** (linked by the conjunction **que**). Similarly, **Marie est partie mais elle est vite revenue** consists of **Marie est partie** and **elle est vite revenue** (linked by the conjunction **mais**).

CLEFT   See 6.1.8.

CLITIC   See 7.4.2.

COMMENT   See 6.1.3.

COMPARATIVE   Form of an adjective indicating a greater (or lesser) degree of a quality: **plus grand, moins aimable**. Other comparative structures are used in reference to items which have a quality in equal degree: **aussi grand que lui**.

COMPOUND (TENSE)   A tense formed with an auxiliary verb, for example the perfect, the pluperfect, the compound future with **aller** + infinitive. See also CONJUGATION, SIMPLE (TENSE) and TENSE.

CONJUGATE    To enumerate systematically the forms of a verb ( **je suis, tu es, il est . . .** ; **j'avais, tu avais, il avait . . .** ).

CONJUGATION    A group of verbs which are 'conjugated' in the same way, i.e. which follow the same patterns (the regular **-er** group, for instance).

CONJUNCTION    A word used to join clauses together in order to build up more complex sentences. If the clauses are simply juxtaposed, the conjunction is a *co-ordinating conjunction* (**et, mais, ou**). If one clause slots into another, the conjunction is a *subordinating conjunction* (**quand, afin que, parce que**). See also SUBORDINATE and CLAUSE.

CO-ORDINATING (CONJUNCTION)    See CONJUNCTION.

CO-ORDINATION    Linking of two clauses by means of **et, mais** or **ou**. See CONJUNCTION.

DECLARATIVE/INTERROGATIVE    Alternative forms of a sentence used for making statements and questions, respectively: **il est arrivé** (declarative); **est-il arrivé?/est-ce qu'il est arrivé?** (interrogative).

DEFECTIVE (RELATIVE CLAUSE)    See 2.3.4.

DEMONSTRATIVE (ADJECTIVE)    See ADJECTIVE.

DEMONSTRATIVE (PRONOUN)    Singles out the referent of a noun when the latter has been mentioned already and therefore need not be specified again: **celui-ci, celle-là** (instead of **ce garçon, cette fille**).

DETACHED (NOUN PHRASE)    See 6.1.2.

DETERMINER    General term for various categories of word which can occupy the first position in a noun phrase, preceding the noun and any adjectives and/or numerals. Determiners include articles, demonstrative adjectives and possessive adjectives (the latter are, in fact, often called demonstrative or possessive determiners).

DIRECT/INDIRECT (QUESTIONS)    An indirect question is introduced by a verb like **demander** and cannot form a complete sentence by itself. It retains the meaning but not the grammatical structure of the original question. An example is **si je partais** in **Jean m'a demandé si je partais**: his actual words would have been a direct question like: **'est-ce que vous partez?'**. Indirect questions are signalled by conjunctions such as **si, pourquoi, comment**. A

direct question, on the other hand, is a complete, independent sentence
(**est-ce que vous partez?**). If a speaker is being quoted, his/her exact words
are retained and, in writing, quotation marks are placed round the direct
question: '**Est-ce que vous partez?', m'a demandé Jean**.

DIRECT/INDIRECT (STATEMENTS)    An indirect statement is introduced by a
verb of saying (**assurer, déclarer, dire**) and reproduces the meaning but
not the grammatical structure of the utterance being reported. It cannot
form a complete sentence by itself. For example, **qu'il partait** in **Jean m'a
assuré qu'il partait**. The speaker would actually have used an equivalent
direct statement like: '**Je pars**'. Indirect statements are introduced by **que**.
Direct statements are, in writing, placed in quotation marks: '**Je pars**',
**annonça Jean**.

DISJUNCTIVE (PRONOUN)    A personal pronoun that can occur independently
of a verb: **moi, toi, eux**. Also known as an *emphatic* pronoun.

DISLOCATED (SENTENCE)    See 6.1.1.

ETHIC (USE OF PRONOUNS)    See 3.3.4.

EXPLETIVE    For expletive **ne** see 2.1.1; for expletive use of pronouns see
3.3.4.

GENDER    French has two grammatical genders: masculine (**le chat**) and
feminine (**la chatte**).

GENERIC    Noun phrase designating a general category (**les chats ont sept
vies**) as opposed to a particular group of individuals who belong to the
category (**les chats qui habitent cette maison**).

IMPERATIVE    Form of the verb used for expressing commands: **venez! (ne)
sors pas!**.

IMPERSONAL (USE)    The pronoun **il** (like *it* in English) is used impersonally
when, instead of referring to a noun, it is there simply because the verb
needs a subject of some sort: **il faut que, il pleut**. Verbs like **sembler** or
**valoir** also have impersonal uses: **il semble que, il vaut mieux attendre**, as
opposed to personal uses like **il semble fatigué, tu sembles triste, elle vaut
mieux que ça**.

IMPERSONAL (VERB)    One which occurs only in the third person, with impersonal **il** as subject: **falloir, s'agir, pleuvoir**.

INANIMATE   See ANIMATE/INANIMATE.

*INCISE*   A phrase signalling direct quotation of a speaker's words: **dit-il, demanda-t-elle**.

INDEFINITE   See PRONOUN.

INDICATIVE/SUBJUNCTIVE   Alternative sets of verb forms (known as *moods*), each occurring in various tenses. The indicative is the 'default' mood and has much the wider occurrence of the two; the subjunctive is restricted mainly to subordinate clauses expressing necessity, volition, doubt or uncertainty.

INDIRECT (OBJECT)   See OBJECT.

INDIRECT (QUESTION, STATEMENT)   See DIRECT/INDIRECT.

INFINITIVE   The form of the verb traditionally used for dictionary entries and serving as the basis for classification into conjugation types. The infinitive can follow a range of nouns and verbs, often with a linking preposition (**j'ai l'intention de partir, elle aime voyager**).

INTERROGATIVE   See DECLARATIVE/INTERROGATIVE.

INTERROGATIVE (ADVERB)   See ADVERB.

INTRANSITIVE   See TRANSITIVE/INTRANSITIVE.

INVERSION   Placing a noun or pronoun after the verb: **dit-il** as opposed to **il dit**.

MAIN CLAUSE   A clause into which a subordinate clause is 'slotted'. See CLAUSE and SUBORDINATE.

MODIFIER   A general term for words like numerals, adjectives or adverbs, which provide further information about the words that they accompany.

MOOD   See INDICATIVE/SUBJUNCTIVE.

NEGATIVE   See AFFIRMATIVE/NEGATIVE.

NOUN   A word referring to a person, place, thing or concept; in French, a noun is typically preceded by an article, can be modified by adjectives, and functions as subject or object of the sentence.

NOUN PHRASE   A noun (or pronoun) together with any accompanying determiners, numerals, adjectives or other modifiers: **Marie; elle; ce petit garçon; les trois mousquetaires d'Alexandre Dumas**.

NP   Abbreviation of NOUN PHRASE.

NUMBER   French has two grammatical numbers: singular and plural (relevant to nouns, verbs and adjectives).

OBJECT (DIRECT)   The noun phrase designating the party that undergoes the action referred to by a verb (**Pierre** in **Marie a visité Pierre**). In English and French the object typically follows the verb. As well as being the objects of verbs, noun phrases can be the object of prepositions: thus **la salle** is the object of **dans** in **dans la salle**.

OBJECT (INDIRECT)   The noun phrase designating the party that benefits from an action, or is otherwise indirectly affected by it. In French the indirect object is preceded by **à** if it is a noun; some pronouns have distinct indirect object forms (**lui, leur**). In **J'ai donné un cadeau à Pierre**, the indirect object is **Pierre**, while the direct object is **un cadeau**: it is the gift, and not Pierre, that is actually handed over (i.e. 'undergoes the action').

PARTICIPLE   Adjectival form of a verb, referring either to present time (*present participle*: **marchant, finissant**) or to past time (*past participle*: **marché, fini**). The past participle combines with an auxiliary verb to form the perfect, pluperfect and future perfect tenses (**j'ai fini, j'avais fini, j'aurai fini**).

PASSIVE   See ACTIVE/PASSIVE.

PERSON   Information conveyed by verbs and personal pronouns, indicating whether the reference is to the person speaking (first person: **je**), the person spoken to (second person: **tu**) or the person or thing spoken about (third person: **il/elle**). Similarly in the plural: **nous, vous, ils/elles**.

PERSONAL   See PRONOUN.

PREDICATIVE   See ADJECTIVE.

PREFIX   Element placed at the beginning of a word in order to modify its meaning or add further grammatical information: for example, **in-/im-** for forming negatives (**impossible**), [ʒ(ə)] to specify first person in spoken French verbs (see 7.4.2).

PREPOSITION   Word placed immediately before a noun phrase and giving information about location, direction, time or various more abstract relationships (**de, à, sur, après, avec, pour, sans**, etc.).

PREPOSITIONAL PHRASE   The unit formed by a preposition together with its accompanying noun phrase (**à Paris; dans un avion Air France**).

PRONOUN   A word used to avoid repeating or specifying a noun. Pronouns can be personal (**je, tu, il/elle, me, te** ... ), demonstrative (**celui-là** ... ), relative (**qui, dont**), interrogative (**qui?, quoi?**) or indefinite (**quelqu'un, quelque chose**). Like nouns, they can function as subjects, objects or indirect objects (but may be restricted to one or other of these roles: **me** cannot be a subject, for example).

PSEUDO-CLEFT   See 6.1.8.

REFERENT   Person, thing, etc. to which a noun refers on a particular occasion.

REFLEXIVE VERB   A verb with a pronoun object which refers back to the subject (**tu te baignes, il se lève**).

RELATIVE CLAUSE   A category of subordinate clause which, like an adjective, provides information about a noun: **qui sont arrivés** in **les enfants qui sont arrivés**, for instance. A relative clause is linked to its noun by means of a relative pronoun (**qui** in **les enfants qui sont arrivés; dont** in **les enfants dont je connais la mère; que** in **les enfants que j'ai rencontrés**). See also 2.3.1.

RELATIVE (PRONOUN)   See RELATIVE CLAUSE.

RESUMPTIVE (RELATIVE CLAUSE)   See 2.3.4.

SIMPLE (TENSE)   A tense formed by changing the form of the verb itself, not by using an auxiliary: **je partirai** as opposed to **je vais partir**. See also COMPOUND (TENSE) and TENSE.

STEM   Main part of a verb, to which prefixes and suffixes (endings) are added: **parl-** in **parler**, for example.

SUBJECT   The noun phrase designating the person or thing that performs the action or is in the state referred to by the verb (in an active sentence) or that undergoes the action (in a passive sentence). In English and French the subject is typically the NP preceding the verb, and the verb agrees with it in number and person (**Marie** in **Marie visite Pierre; nous** in **nous sommes fatigués; les petits garçons** in **les petits garçons ont été visités par Marie**).

SUBJUNCTIVE   See INDICATIVE/SUBJUNCTIVE.

SUBORDINATE   Term applied to a clause which is slotted into another clause and in that sense is subordinate to it. Thus in **j'ai dit que j'étais fatigué**, the clause **que j'étais fatigué** occupies the object position or slot, which could otherwise be filled by a noun phrase (**j'ai dit trois mots/quelque chose/ bonjour**). Similarly, **que j'ai lu** in **le livre que j'ai lu** occupies an adjective slot (compare **le livre rouge/précieux**).

SUFFIX   Ending added to a word in order to change its category or provide further grammatical information relating to tense, number, person, etc.: for example **-ment** for making adjectives into adverbs, **-ais** for forming the imperfect (in written French).

SUPERLATIVE   The form of an adjective indicating the highest or lowest degree of a particular quality: **le plus grand**, **le moins aimable**.

SYNONYM   A word which is identical or nearly identical in meaning to another word: **auto** and **voiture**, **craindre** and **redouter** are pairs of synonyms.

TAUTOLOGY   An expression in which the same information is repeated unnecessarily: for example, popular French **monter en haut**, which has the same meaning as **monter**.

TENSE   Form of the verb locating an action, event, etc. in time. The following tenses are referred to in this book: present (**je parle**), perfect (**j'ai parlé**), past historic (**je parlai**), pluperfect (**j'avais parlé**), past anterior (**j'eus parlé**), double compound past (**j'ai eu parlé**), imperfect (**je parlais**), simple future (**je parlerai**), compound future (**je vais parler**), future perfect (**j'aurai parlé**), present conditional (**je parlerais**), past conditional (**j'aurais parlé**).

TOPIC   See 6.1.3.

TRANSITIVE/INTRANSITIVE   A classification of verbs into: (a) *intransitive verbs*, which cannot take an object (**exister**, **marcher**, **mourir**); (b) *directly transitive verbs*, which must be followed by a direct object (**détruire**, **exprimer**, **visiter**); (c) *indirectly transitive verbs*, with an object introduced by **à** or **de** (**plaire**, **remédier**, **hériter**).

VERB   A word designating an action or state, and marked for person and tense.

VERB PHRASE   A verb together with any accompanying adverbs, auxiliaries, noun or pronoun objects, infinitives, etc: the underlined sections of **je**

<u>veux partir</u>, le président <u>voyage beaucoup</u>, tous les voyageurs <u>doivent changer d'avion</u>.

VP    Abbreviation of VERB PHRASE.

WH-QUESTION    A question to which **oui** or **non** would be unnatural answers because specific information is asked for: **quel âge avez-vous?**, **quelle heure est-il?**. WH-questions are introduced by *interrogative adverbs* (**pourquoi, comment, où**), *interrogative pronouns* (**qui?, quoi?, lequel?**) or *interrogative adjectives* (**quel** + noun). Almost all these words have English equivalents beginning with *wh-*, hence the term WH-question.

YES/NO QUESTION    A question which simply seeks confirmation or denial, not further information, and to which natural answers are **oui** or **non**: **est-ce que le film t'a plu?**, **vous cherchez quelque chose?**.

# Appendix 3: Using the International Phonetic Alphabet

### Why use a phonetic alphabet?

An agreed spelling system exists for standard French, but not for *français populaire* or for regional varieties. Without a uniform way of representing these in writing, it would be impossible to give an accurate idea of their pronunciation.

Even in standard French, spellings and sounds often do not correspond. Different though they may look, **sans**, **cent**, **sent** and **sang** are identical in pronunciation. On the other hand, the *b* in **absurde** is not the same as the *b* in **abri**, while *c* is sometimes pronounced [k] and sometimes [s].

### Terminology

The term *letter* refers only to spelling; the signs used in the IPA are called *symbols*. A *phonetic transcription* is an IPA version of a word, sentence or text (corresponding verb: *to transcribe*). Note that this Appendix introduces only the symbols relevant to standard French; many more are available for other varieties of French and, of course, for other languages.

### Two basic principles

(a)   A phonetic transcription represents pronunciation, not spelling. For example, 'silent' letters like *gt* in **doigt** or *ent* in **disent** are omitted: [dwa, diz].

(b)   One phonetic symbol is used for each individual vowel and consonant. The three-letter orthographic sequence **eau** corresponds to a single vowel, and the transcription is therefore [o]. Similarly with *qu*, which usually corresponds to a single consonant [k]. Conversely, the *x* in **exprès** is a sequence of two consonants in pronunciation, and is transcribed [ks]. When reading from a phonetic transcription, every symbol must be pronounced.

---

Exercise 1.  Transcribe: **piste, voix, voie, quitte, poids, pois, bateau, laxiste.**
(You can check your answers in any up-to-date French–English dictionary. They all use the IPA to indicate pronunciation.)

---

### *IPA transcriptions and symbols*

Individual phonetic symbols and phonetic transcriptions are usually placed between square brackets. Capital letters and apostrophes are not carried over into the transcription: **l'Albanie**, for example, would be [lalbani].

Certain special symbols represent aspects of pronunciation not indicated in the spelling:

[ʀ]  ('small capital r'). This indicates the 'back' or 'uvular' pronunciation of *r* typical of modern Parisian French: **rire** [ʀiʀ]. Lower-case [r] is used for accents where *r* is trilled with the tip of the tongue.

[ə]  ('schwa'). This inverted *e* represents the pronunciation of the *e* of **le, de, venir** (similar to the first vowel of English *about*): [lə, də, vəniʀ].

---

Exercise 2.  Transcribe: **Paris, Afrique, devoir, Canada, se leva.**

---

Special symbols alternate with more familiar ones in conveying differences between vowel sounds which the spelling shows haphazardly or not at all.

[e]  ('close e') for the *é* of **bébé** or the *-er* of **parler** [bebe, paʀle].

[ɛ]  ('open e') for the sound of *ê* in **bête** or *è* in **mère** [bɛt, mɛʀ].

---

Exercise 3.  Transcribe: **Québec, élève, élever, Grèce, pré, prêt.**

---

[o]  ('close o') for the *o* of **mot** or the *au* of **haut** [mo, o].

[ɔ]  ('open o') for the *o* found in **bonne** or **fort** [bɔn, fɔʀ].

> **Exercise 4.** Transcribe: **gauche, rose, Rome, homme, hexagone, côte, cote.**

[ø]   ('slashed o') for the *eu* of **peu** or **deux** [pø, dø].
[œ]   ('o-e digraph') for the *eu* of **peur** or the *oeu* of **soeur** [pœʀ, sœʀ].

> **Exercise 5.** Transcribe: **veut, veulent, peuvent, Europe, heureux.**

[ɑ]   ('back a') for the *â* of **mâle** or **pâte** in some pronunciations [mɑl, pɑt].
[a]   ('front a') is for the *a* of **mal** or **patte** [mal, pat]. A large (and ever-increasing) number of speakers use this vowel also in **mâle** or **pâte**, and therefore have no [ɑ] in their sound system.

Other special symbols are for sounds which are spelt with combinations of letters.

[ʃ]   ('long s' or 'esh') for the *ch* of **cher**, **achat**.
[ɲ]   ('n with left hook') for the *gn* of **agneau**, **Espagne**.

> **Exercise 6.** Transcribe these four words.

Occasionally, symbols that look familiar are used in an unfamiliar way:

[y]   represents the *u* of **sur** or **rue**: [syʀ, ʀy].

N.B. [u] is used for the *ou* of **tour** or **ouvert**: [tuʀ, uvɛʀ]. The *u* of **puis** is represented by [ɥ] ('inverted h'), a short version of the [y] of **sur**, used before *i* and, less often, before other vowels: [pɥi], [pɛʀsɥade].

> **Exercise 7.** Transcribe: **utile, musée, vouloir, outil, fourrure, Suisse, huit, nuage.**

> **Exercise 8.** There is a slight but significant pronunciation difference between **Louis** and **lui**. Insert a different symbol for each: [l . . . i] and [l . . . i].

[j]   is for the *y* of **Yougoslavie**, the *i* of **piano** or the *il* of **travail**: [jugɔslavi, pjano, tʀavaj]. Phoneticians call this symbol 'yod'.

N.B. The first consonant of **jour** is transcribed [ʒ] ('long z'). So is the last consonant of **garage**.

---

**Exercise 9.   Transcribe: yeux, pied, pareil, jour, garage, des gens, de Jean.**

---

Finally, note the tilde ˜ which is placed over a vowel to indicate nasalization. Standard French has four nasalized vowels:

[œ̃] as in **un**:   [œ̃]
[ɔ̃] as in **bon**:   [bɔ̃]
[ɛ̃] as in **vin**:   [vɛ̃]
[ɑ̃] as in **blanc**:   [blɑ̃]

Other vowels can also be nasalized, and there are many examples in regional varieties of French. In Paris and northern France most speakers nowadays use only three of the above vowels, replacing [œ̃] by [ɛ̃], so that **brin** and **brun** are both [bʀɛ̃].

N.B. In standard French there is no [n] or [m] after nasalized vowels in the pronunciation: it is wrong therefore to insert [n] or [m] in the transcription. This applies particularly to words like **bonté** [bɔ̃te] or **blancheur** [blɑ̃ʃœʀ] where another consonant – [t], [ʃ] – follows the vowel.

---

Exercise 10.   Identify the following place-names, which contain examples of all four standard French nasalized vowels:

[bəzɑ̃sɔ̃]   (birthplace of Victor Hugo)
[dœ̃kɛʀk]   (Channel port)
[kɑ̃]   (capital of Lower Normandy)
[amjɛ̃]   (cathedral city in Picardy)
[ʀwɑ̃]   (capital of Upper Normandy)
[ljɔ̃]   (third, or possibly second, city of France)
[məlœ̃]   (prefecture of Seine-et-Marne department)

---

Exercise 11. Transcribe the standard pronunciation of: **ton, tant, brun, saint, nation, enfin, content, canton, trente, parfum, incompétent**.

Exercise 12. Say what the names of the following *départements* are in ordinary spelling (the post codes are given so that you can check your answers in, for example, the *Petit Larousse Illustré*):

| | | | |
|---|---|---|---|
| [ɛ̃] | 01 | [eʀo] | 34 |
| [ɛn] | 02 | [møz] | 55 |
| [ob] | 10 | [ɔʀn] | 61 |
| [od] | 11 | [oʀɛ̃] | 68 |
| [œʀ] | 27 | [jɔn] | 89 |

Exercise 13. Reading practice.
[kɔm sɔ̃ nɔ̃ lɛ̃dik, lalfabɛ fɔnetik ɛtɛʀnasjɔnal saplik a tut le lɑ̃g də nɔtʀə planɛt – mɛm sil fo paʀfwa de siɲ syplemɑ̃tɛʀ. ɛ̃si le fɔnetisjɛ̃ pœv til ɛ̃dike, sɑ̃ zɑ̃biɡɥite e dyn fasɔ̃ ynifɔʀm, tu le zaksɑ̃ e vaʀjɑ̃t ki ɛɡzist o mɔ̃d. se dɑ̃ sə byt kə lalfabɛ a ete kɔ̃sy vɛʀ la fɛ̃ dy diznœvjɛm sjɛkl. il a ete œ̃ pø ʀevize dəpɥi, mɛ se pʀɛ̃sip de bɑz nɔ̃ ʒamɛ ʃɑ̃ʒe.]

# References

## 1 Publications relating to the French language

Ager, D. 1990: *Sociolinguistics and Contemporary French*. Cambridge: Cambridge University Press.

Arnold, M. 1968: *Petites conversations*. London: Hulton Educational.

Ball, R. 1997: *The French-speaking World: A Practical Introduction to Sociolinguistic Issues*. London: Routledge.

Barnes, B. 1985: *The Pragmatics of Left-detachment in Standard Spoken French*. Amsterdam: Benjamins.

Batchelor, R.E. and Offord, M. 1982: *A Guide to Contemporary French Usage*. Cambridge: Cambridge University Press.

Bauche, H. 1951: *Le Langage populaire* (new edition). Paris: Payot.

Bauer, C. et al. 1984: *Aspects du discours radiophonique*. Paris: Didier.

Behnstedt, P. 1973: *Viens-tu? Est-ce que tu viens? Tu viens? Formen und Strukturen des direkten Fragesatzes im Französischen*. Tübingen: Narr.

Blain, M., Hallier, P. and Loufrani, C. 1979: Enquête pédagogique sur les relatifs. *Recherches sur le français parlé*, 2, 209–22.

Blanche-Benveniste, C. 1990: *Le Français parlé: études grammaticales*. Paris: CNRS.

Blanche-Benveniste, C. 1997: *Approches de la langue parlée en français*. Gap/Paris: Ophrys.

Blasco, M. 1995: Dislocation et thématisation en français parlé. *Recherches sur le français parlé*, 13, 45–65.

Boudard, A. and Etienne, L. 1970: *La Méthode à Mimile: l'argot sans peine*. Paris: La Jeune Parque.

Burdin, C. 1981: *Le Français moderne tel qu'on le parle*. Paris: De Vecchi.

Cadiot, P. 1988: De quoi ça parle? A propos de la référence de *ça*, pronom-sujet. *Le Français moderne*, 56, 174–92.

Capelovici, J. 1990: *Le Français sans fautes: répertoire des erreurs les plus fréquentes de la langue écrite et parlée*. Paris: Acropole.

Carlier, A. 1996: 'Les Gosses, ça se lève tôt le matin': l'interprétation générique du syntagme nominal disloqué au moyen de *ce* ou *ça*. *Journal of French Language Studies*, 6, 133–62.

Coveney, A. 1990: Variation in interrogatives in spoken French: a preliminary report. In J.N. Green and W. Ayres-Bennett (eds), *Variation and Change in French*. London/New York: Routledge, 116–33.

CREDIF 1968: *Enquête sur le langage de l'enfant français, Document 2*. Saint-Cloud: Centre de recherche et d'étude pour la diffusion du français.

Culioli, A. 1983: Pourquoi le français parlé est-il si peu étudié? *Recherches sur le français parlé*, 5, 291–300.

Décugis, J.-M. and Zemouri, A. 1995: *Paroles de banlieue*. Paris: Plon.

Désirat, C. and Hordé, T. 1976: *La Langue française au 20ᵉ siècle*. Paris: Bordas.

Deulofeu, J. 1977: La Syntaxe et les constructions binaires. *Recherches sur le français parlé*, 1, 30–60.

Deulofeu, J. 1979: Les Enoncés à constituant lexical détaché. *Recherches sur le français parlé*, 2, 75–110.

Dubois, J. 1967: *Grammaire structurale du français: le verbe*. Paris: Larousse.

Duneton, C. 1998: *Le Guide du français familier*. Paris: Seuil.

Duneton, C. and Pagliano, J.-P. 1978. *Anti-manuel de français*. Paris: Seuil.

Dupré, P. 1972: *Encyclopédie du bon français*. Paris: Editions de Trévise.

Eschmann, J. 1984: *Texte aus dem 'français parlé'*. Tübingen: Narr.

Fischer, M. 1987: *Sprachbewußtsein in Paris*. Vienna/Cologne/Graz: Böhlau.

François, D. 1974: *Français parlé*. Paris: SELAF.

Frei, H. 1929: *La Grammaire des fautes*. Paris: Geuthner.

Gadet, F. 1992: *Le Français populaire*. Paris: Presses Universitaires de France.

Gadet, F. 1997: *Le Français ordinaire*. Paris: Armand Colin.

George, K. 1996: 'De la belle ouvrage': cross-gendering in unconventional French. *Journal of French Language Studies*, 6, 163–75.

Georgin, R. 1951: *Pour un meilleur français*. Paris: A. Bonne.

Georgin, R. 1952: *Difficultés et finesses de notre langue*. Paris: A. Bonne.

Georgin, R. 1959: *Le Code du bon langage*. Paris: Editions Sociales.

Goudaillier, J.-P. 1997: *Comment tu tchatches! Dictionnaire du français contemporain des cités*. Paris: Maisonneuve et Larose.

Grevisse, M. 1964: *Le Bon Usage: grammaire française*. Gembloux: Duculot/Paris: Hatier.

Guénette, L., Lépine, F. and Roy, R.L. 1995: *Le Français tout compris*. St.-Laurent: Editions du Renouveau Pédagogique.

Guiraud, P. 1965: *Le Français populaire*. Paris: Presses Universitaires de France.

Hawkins, R. and Towell, R. 1996: *French Grammar and Usage*. London: Arnold.

Hermant, A. 1936: *Chroniques de Lancelot du Temps*. Paris: Larousse.

Judge, A. and Healey, F. 1983: *A Reference Grammar of Modern French*. London: Arnold.

Lambrecht, K. 1981: *Topic, Antitopic and Verb Agreement in Non-standard French*. Amsterdam: Benjamins.

Larjavaara, M. 1999: Primarily transitive verbs without objects in modern French. *Journal of French Language Studies*, 9, 105–11.

Leeman-Bouix, D. 1994: *Les Fautes de français existent-elles?* Paris: Seuil.

Lodge, R.A. 1993: *French, From Dialect to Standard*. London: Routledge.

Ludwig, R. 1988: *Korpus: Texte des gesprochenen Französisch. Materialen I*. Tübingen: Narr.

Mansion, J. 1952: *A Grammar of Present-day French*. London: Harrap.

Martinet, A. 1969: *Le Français sans fard*. Paris: Presses Universitaires de France.

Matthews, S. 1989: French in flux: typological shift and sociolinguistic variation. In *Georgetown University Round Table on Languages and Linguistics (1988)*. Washington, DC: Georgetown University Press, 188–203.

Moreau, M.-L. 1986: Les Séquences préformées: entre les combinaisons libres et les idiomatismes. Le cas de la négation avec ou sans *ne*. *Le Français moderne*, 54, 137–60.

Morin, Y.-Ch. and Kaye, J. 1982: The syntactic bases for French liaison. *Journal of Linguistics*, 18, 291–330.

Morton, J. 1997: *English Grammar for Students of French*. London: Arnold.

Moufflet, A. 1935: *Encore le massacre de la langue française*. Toulouse: Privat/Paris: Didier.

Mourlet, M. 1996: *Les Maux de la langue*. Clichy: Valmonde-Bartillat.

Muller, B. 1985: *Le Français d'aujourd'hui*. Paris: Klincksieck.

Nott, D. 1998: *French Grammar Explained*. London: Hodder and Stoughton.

Offord, M. 1990: *Varieties of Contemporary French*. Basingstoke: Macmillan.

Pastre, G. 1986: *Le Français télé . . . visé*. Paris: Belfond.

Pazery, N. 1988: Les Enfants de l'école primaire et le passé simple. *Recherches sur le français parlé*, 8, 137–48.

Pierre-Adolphe, P., Mamoud, M. and Tzanos, G. 1998: *Tchatche de banlieue*. Paris: Mille et Une Nuits.

Pohl, J. 1965: Observations sur les formes d'interrogation dans la langue parlée et dans la langue écrite non littéraire. In *Actes du X^e congrès international de linguistique et de philologie romanes*. Paris: Klincksieck, 501–16.

Price, G. 1993: *L.S.R. Byrne and E.L. Churchill's A Comprehensive French Grammar* (4th edition). Oxford: Blackwell Publishers.

Rat, M. 1978: *Je connais mieux le français*. Verviers: Marabout.

Rigault, A. (ed.) 1971: *La Grammaire du français parlé*. Paris: Hachette.

Sand, J. 1983: Le Subjonctif en français oral. In *Actes du huitième congrès des romanistes scandinaves (1981)*. Odense: Odense University Press, 303–13.

Sanders, C. 1993: *French Today: Language in its Social Context*. Cambridge: Cambridge University Press.

Sauvageot, A. 1962: *Français écrit, français parlé*. Paris: Larousse.

Sauvageot, A. 1972: *Analyse du français parlé*. Paris: Hachette.

Söll, L. 1974: *Gesprochenes und geschriebenes Französisch*. Berlin: Erich Schmidt Verlag.

Spence, N.C.W. 1996: *The Structure(s) of French*. Egham: Runnymede Books.

Tesnière, L. 1959: *Eléments de syntaxe structurale*. Paris: Klincksieck.

Thévenot, J. 1976: *Hé! la France, ton français fout le camp!* Gembloux: Duculot.

Thomas, A.-V. 1956: *Dictionnaire des difficultés de la langue française*. Paris: Larousse.

Tuaillon, G. 1988: Le Français régional: formes de rencontre. In G. Vermès (ed.), *Vingt-cinq communautés linguistiques de la France*, vol. 1. Paris: L'Harmattan, 291–301.

Walter, H. 1988: *Le Français dans tous les sens*. Paris: Laffont.

Yaguello, M. 1991: *En écoutant parler la langue*. Paris: Seuil.

Yaguello, M. 1998: *Petits Faits de langue*. Paris: Seuil.

## 2  Other publications

Adler, P. 1984: *Bonjour la galère*. Paris: Balland.

Belloc, D. 1990: *Les Aiguilles à tricoter*. Paris: Julliard.

Bouvier, P. 1977: *Métro-polis*. Paris: Tigres en papier.

Cavanna 1978: *Les Ritals*. Paris: Belfond.

Cavanna 1979: *Les Russkoffs*. Paris: Belfond.

Céline, L.-F. 1952: *Voyage au bout de la nuit*. Paris: Gallimard.

Céline, L.-F. 1967: *Mort à crédit*. Paris: Gallimard.

Cordelier, J. 1976: *La Dérobade*. Paris: Hachette.

Exbrayat, C. 1975: *Jules Matrat*. Paris: Albin Michel.

Fallet, R. 1956: *La Grande Ceinture*. Paris: Denoël.

Fallet, R. 1975: *Le Beaujolais nouveau est arrivé*. Paris: Denoël.

Goscinny-Uderzo 1977: *Astérix le Gaulois*. Paris: Hachette.

Hanska, E. 1981: *J'arrête pas de t'aimer*. Paris: Balland.

Hanska, E. 1986: *Fascination*. Paris: Mercure de France.

Izzo, J.-C. 1995: *Total Khéops*. Paris: Gallimard.

Lassaygues, F. 1985: *Vache noire, hannetons et autres insectes*. Paris: Barrault.

Leymergie, W. 1995: *Fréquence mômes*. Paris: Belfond.

Queneau, R. 1959: *Zazie dans le métro*. Paris: Gallimard.

Rochefort, C. 1961: *Les Petits Enfants du siècle*. Paris: Grasset.

Sabatier, R. 1956: *Boulevard*. Paris: Albin Michel.

San-Antonio 1967: *Béru et ces dames*. Paris: Fleuve Noir.

San-Antonio 1974: *Un os dans la noce*. Paris: Fleuve Noir.

Sempé-Goscinny 1960: *Le Petit Nicolas*. Paris: Denoël.

Simonin, A. 1960: *Du mouron pour les petits oiseaux*. Paris: Gallimard.

Smaïl, P. 1997: *Vivre me tue*. Paris: Balland.

Tramber and Jano 1981: *Fait comme un rat*. Paris: Les Humanoïdes associés.

## 3  Sources of examples

Code letters refer to newspapers, magazines, media channels, compilers or authors (relevant details above), code numbers to pages when applicable.

| | |
|---|---|
| AC | Culioli |
| ACT | *Actuel* |
| AM | Moufflet |
| ASA | Sauvageot 1972 |
| ASM | Simonin |
| BBA | Blanche-Benveniste 1997 |
| BBE | Blanche-Benveniste 1990 |
| BKB | Barnes |
| BM | Muller |
| BT | Behnstedt |
| CB | Bauer |

| CE | Exbrayat |
|------|----------|
| CR | CREDIF |
| CRE | Rochefort |
| DB | Belloc |
| DF | François |
| DH | Désirat/Hordé |
| DLF | *Défense de la langue française* |
| DP | Duneton/Pagliano |
| DU | Duneton |
| DZ | Décugis/Zemouri |
| EDJ | *L'Evénement du jeudi* |
| EHA | Hanska 1981 |
| EHF | Hanska 1986 |
| EXP | *L'Express* |
| FCR | Cavanna 1979 |
| FCT | Cavanna 1978 |
| FH | Le Havre corpus |
| FI | France-Inter |
| FR3 | (television channel) |
| GD | Goudaillier |
| GFO | Gadet 1997 |
| GFP | Gadet 1992 |
| GU | Goscinny-Uderzo |
| HB | Bauche |
| HF | Frei |
| IVR | Ivry corpus |
| IZ | Izzo |
| JC | Cordelier |
| JDB | Deulofeu 1977 |
| JDE | Deulofeu 1979 |
| JE | Eschmann |
| JS | Sand |
| KL | Lambrecht |
| LA | Lassaygues |
| LB | Leeman-Bouix |
| LBN | *Libération* |
| LFCM | Céline 1967 |
| LFCV | Céline 1952 |
| LFM | Leymergie |
| LG | Guénette |
| LJ | Larjavaara |
| LT | Tesnière |
| MB | Blain |
| MBD | Blasco |
| MM | Boudard/Etienne |
| NO | *Le Nouvel Observateur* |

PA      Adler
PB      Bouvier
PPA     Pierre-Adolphe
PG      Guiraud
PS      Smaïl
RB      Author's corpus
RL      Ludwig
RFB     Fallet 1975
RFC     Fallet 1956
RQ      Queneau
RS      Sabatier
SAB     San-Antonio 1967
SAO     San-Antonio 1974
SGN     Sempé-Goscinny 1960
SM      Matthews
TF1     (television channel)
TJ      Tramber/Jano

# Index